Professional Conduct
and
Legal Concerns
in
Mental Health
Practice

Professional Conduct
and
Legal Concerns
in
Mental Health
Practice

Joan Rinas, Ph.D., C. Psych.
Psychologist in Private Practice
Chatham, Kingsville, and Windsor, Ontario, Canada

Sheila Clyne-Jackson, Ph.D., C. Psych.
Psychologist
Psychology Department
Windsor Board of Education
Windsor, Ontario, Canada

APPLETON & LANGE
Norwalk, Connecticut/San Mateo, California

0-8385-7960-4

Copyright © 1988 by Appleton & Lange
A Publishing Division of Prentice Hall

88 89 90 91 92 / 10 9 8 7 6 5 4 3 2 1

Prentice-Hall of Australia, Pty. Ltd., Sydney
Prentice-Hall Canada, Inc.
Prentice-Hall Hispanoamericana, S.A., Mexico
Prentice-Hall of India Private Limited, New Delhi
Prentice-Hall International (UK) Limited, London
Prentice-Hall of Japan, Inc., Tokyo
Prentice-Hall of Southeast Asia (Pte.) Ltd., Singapore
Whitehall Books Ltd., Wellington, New Zealand
Editora Prentice-Hall do Brasil Ltda., Rio de Janeiro

Library of Congress Cataloging-in-Publication Data
Rinas, Joan.
   Professional conduct and legal concerns in mental
health practice.
   Includes index.
   1. Mental health personnel—Professional ethics.
2. Mental health personnel—Legal status, laws, etc.
I. Clyne-Jackson, Sheila. II. Title. [DNLM:
1. Mental Health Services—standards—United States.
2. Mental Health Services—United States—legislation.
WM 30 R578p]
RC455.2.E8R56   1988   174′.9362   87-37413
ISBN 0-8385-7960-4

Production Editor: Eileen Lagoss
Designer: Steven M. Byrum

PRINTED IN THE UNITED STATES OF AMERICA

To our families for their patience through all of this

Contents

Preface

In the last several years, the ethical and legal challenges facing the mental health professional have become ever-increasing concerns. To fulfill their obligations to their clients as well as to society, such professionals need to keep abreast of all the latest ethical and legal developments in their field of practice. The difficulty in maintaining these professional obligations arises because of the wide variety of sources from which to solicit this information. Relevant background in ethics is likely to be published in anything from law reviews and professional journals to government publications. To complicate the situation further, much of the information regarding professional practice may vary in specificity and extensiveness from profession to profession and from one location to another. In attempting to locate necessary information, the practicing professional is likely to experience difficulty, not only in simply locating the relevant material, but also in discovering what material is available.

The purpose of the present text is to pull together basic ethical concerns that affect the many different mental health disciplines, for example, nursing, occupational therapy, psychiatry, psychology, and social work. It attempts to cover such areas as ethical obligations toward individual clients, to society, and to themselves, as well as specific intervention issues involving procedures such as problem analysis, therapy, and research.

Such a book poses advantages for the professional and the layperson. First, it would ensure that basic information regarding the ethical and legal practice of the mental health practitioner is readily available in an organized and relatively comprehensive format. Second, it would sensitize the public regarding the obligations that professionals have toward them as well as educate them about ethical and legal issues in the mental health field.

In addition to being of use within the applied field, such a resource book could be an invaluable tool within the academic setting. Such a text would make it easier for students in various areas of the "helping" professions to be introduced to professional ethics and legal regulations regarding client intervention. It would also simplify the onerous task facing course instructors lecturing on this topic. A frequent complaint of the mental health field is that upcoming professionals are not cognizant of ethical or legal issues affecting mental health practice and are forced to learn by trial and error. The availability of such a training book would help alleviate this problem and help protect the public in the process.

I

Basic Principles

Responsibility

1

Within the mental health field, responsibility is a concept that pervades all areas of professional practice. This chapter therefore serves as an introduction to issues that are covered in greater detail throughout the rest of the book. Although responsibility is a complicated issue, it primarily entails an obligation to promote and safeguard the dignity, well-being, and growth of clients, colleagues, the mental health profession itself, and society as a whole. This goal is not always easy to achieve because of conflicting loyalties, lack of knowledge, and minimal resources.

Prior to the 1960s the mental health profession was concerned almost exclusively with techniques of practice. In the practitioner's search for a cure that fits his or her theory of practice, clients were treated according to the whim of the therapist and their personal goals and preferences ignored or dismissed as unimportant. Client abuse was a natural consequence of this type of attitude as exemplified by long-term involuntary hospitalization, intrusive treatment techniques, exorbitant treatment costs, and so on. Despite professional intervention, most clients showed little progress as a result of treatment and a percentage actually deteriorated.

Issues such as these were seized on by the social reform movement of the 1960s with the result that a demand for accountability within most factions of society was made. Since professionals could not rise to the challenge and substantiate the worthiness of their approaches they lost respect among the general public. Criticism of established practices increased and created concern with regard to human rights issues.

In response to public pressure laws were enacted to clarify and limit the powers of professionals. In the mental health field, for example, the power to commit a person to a hospital involuntarily was increasingly curtailed until at present only a few extreme conditions are considered sufficient to justify such an action. Laws limiting the use of "captive" groups such as prisoners and mental patients for research also have been passed.

In a similar manner, the promotion of responsible behavior has become a primary concern among the various professions composing the mental health field. The development of increasingly stringent and detailed codes and guidelines reflects a major change in orientation within the mental health profession. Boards and licensing bodies that govern the behavior and practices of their members have developed codes to describe a variety of professional standards, including obligations to the consumer, competency requirements, correct billing procedures, and so on. To ensure the development of appropriate expertise, certain professional groups will not grant a license to practice unless the prospective professional has been trained in an accredited program. Even after getting a license, professionals who do not conform to approved standards may be censured by the licensing body, and potentially lose their right to practice. Such strong controls reflect the importance with which the professions now view the conduct of their members and serve as a protection to the consumer. It is therefore to the advantage of the professional to become as knowledgeable as possible about ethical and legal issues that apply to his or her area of practice. Despite the availability of professional standards and an increased sensitivity to ethical issues, many educational facilities provide minimum, if any, training in this area. As a result, graduates are produced who are not aware of their various responsibilities or fail to take them seriously.

As described previously the issue of responsibility is a complicated one and can be viewed from many angles. Looking at this issue through the eyes of the practitioner, there are many competing factors that need to be considered. At times, the responsible course of action is clear. Situations frequently arise, however, in which the needs of the client, the laws of society, professional codes of ethics, and personal standards clash. Such situations become increasingly confusing when a quick decision is required and when loyalties conflict. Guidelines such as those described within various codes of ethics may be too general to be of help in specific instances and are often subject to interpretation. As a preparatory step for dealing with potential ethical dilemmas, the practicing professional therefore needs to become sensitive to the various issues that are involved and ways of dealing with them.

The rest of the chapter presents an overview of different areas of responsibility confronting the practitioner and is organized under the following headings: Public Behavior, Service Provision, Business Practices, Protection, and Advancement of Knowledge. Each of these areas is covered in greater detail in the chapters that follow.

PUBLIC BEHAVIOR

Practitioners need to be constantly aware of the potential impact they have on the general public and the need to keep their behavior within the range of acceptability. Any behavior that would reflect negatively on the layperson's opinion of the professional should be avoided. Public drunkenness, displays of temper, and similar excesses reveal a lack of control and could potentially reduce trust and respect not only for the individual involved but also for the professional body as a whole. Ideally, professionals should serve as role models to the rest of the community, revealing a "healthy" approach to life and other people. This type of professional demeanor is particularly important in the mental health field if the practitioner is to be taken seriously when trying to assist others in leading a healthy life.

SERVICE PROVISION

Within the area of service provision, many responsibilities fall on the professional. Some of these responsibilities include respect for clients' rights and the need to provide a quality service.

Quality Service
A major duty for most mental health professionals is to help clients attain their goals and lead a happier existence. In order to accomplish this goal, professionals must first have the necessary competence to provide a service, and second, sufficient time and resources to provide the service adequately. If not, clients should be referred to alternative programs or professionals.

Competence. Professionals should provide services only in those areas in which they are trained and fully qualified. Should professionals wish to expand to a different area of expertise (e.g., medicine to psychiatry, marriage counseling to individual therapy), they must obtain the training necessary to receive a degree in that area. Simply reading a book or receiving supervision for a period of time does not satisfy the requirement for expertise in new areas.

Since clients are likely to make assumptions, sometimes faulty ones, about a professional's qualifications, they should be informed of the therapist's credentials and the strengths and shortcomings of whatever approach the therapist plans to use. The therapist must also let the client know if he or she is receiving supervision and what implications this has for the client.

Therapeutic Atmosphere. Assuming that the client understands the professional's expertise and is willing to proceed with therapy, the professional must then take steps to provide a good therapeutic atmosphere. This step is necessary to facilitate awareness and change in the client. The relationship which the practitioner fosters has to provide the basis for needed improvements. The practitioner must also be fair and respectful in his or her manner of treating the client. One important example is respect for the client's time. Despite the financial advantage to professionals who are paid on a fee-for-service basis, clients should not be overbooked and made to wait in line so that the practitioner does not have to deal with "empty" time. In addition, clients should be seen for their allotted time and not rushed through a session because of other commitments. They also should be aware of the cost, if any, of different services, and the fees should be in line with professional standards. In other words, clients need to be treated fairly and professionals need to remember that this is part of their obligation as a service provider.

Development of Resources. The policy of most professional bodies, in the past and today, has been to produce limited numbers of professionals. The motivation behind this policy is to prevent flooding the market and to ensure that the status and earning potential of graduates remains high. This course of action appears rather selfish in nature and contains serious consequences for the consumer. Long waiting lists exist for most specialized services offered within the mental health field. As a result, professionals' time is at a premium and there is strong pressure for staff to carry such heavy caseloads that the quality of service delivered to clients is seriously compromised. This problem is usually worse in community agencies or any "free" service settings. Individuals who cannot afford "private" services are therefore forced to wait for longer periods of time before getting help and risk getting a poorer quality of service because of the many demands on staff time.

One way to minimize this problem is to increase the number of professionals available for service. This change can only be accomplished if professionals allow more people to be trained in their respective fields, thereby opening their educational doors wider.

When appropriate staff are available, the problem may be one of limited budgeting within specific fields. Mental health workers have an obligation to lobby with their employers for increased staff and should not compromise the services available by providing quantity service rather than quality. Professionals should also keep apprised of grant money that may be available for different projects and programs so that external resources are tapped as well. In other words, the mental health worker has an obligation to be more than a service provider in circumstances where the service that is provided is less than adequate because of monetary or professional shortages.

Service Abuse. Mental health professionals must also try to ensure that their services are not misused. Service abuse is more likely to occur in third-party situations, that is, when the professional's loyalties are split between two or more clients and the professional does not have complete control of the information at his or her disposal. A psychological assessment of a student, for example, should be used to assist the individual in increasing scholastic proficiency. If such assessments were, in fact, being used to channel students of lesser abilities into dead-end or poor-quality programs, the mental health professional should first of all try to educate the facility with regard to his or her ethical concerns and the recommended way to use test results. If the mental health worker is unsuccessful in changing how the information is used, however, he or she should consider discontinuing the service despite the personal risk this entails.

Alternative Services. When the treatment needed for the client falls outside of the therapist's realm of expertise, referral to an appropriate professional or agency must be facilitated by the counselor. For this purpose, the mental health worker must first of all, be aware of what services are available in the community, and second, how they would relate to the client's area of concern. Substance abuse programs, crisis clinics, family therapy settings, and bereavement groups are just a few of the possible services available. Prior to making a referral to other services in the community, the professional should become knowledgeable about the range of services that are available, what criteria must be met for admission to a particular program, and most importantly the quality of the services offered. Without such information, it would be inadvisable to make a referral as the client may mistakenly believe that a referral by the therapist necessitates endorsement of the program.

Referrals are made for two major reasons; first of all, because the client requests an alternative service, and second, because the professional feels the client would be better helped elsewhere. If the mental health worker feels the client is involved with too many services or counselors, however, the professional has an obligation to communicate that opinion to the client rather than automatically make a new referral. Overtreatment could easily lead to confusion on the client's part and unnecessarily complicate the therapeutic process.

Clients' Rights

Clients, for their part, must be able to place their trust in the therapist in order to communicate their most intimate thoughts and feelings. Therapists in return owe clients respect and protection of their rights. This protection, and its limitations and constraints, should be fully understood by the mental health worker prior to starting a practice and should be communicated to all clients so that they are aware of the shortcomings of the relationship. The following sections highlight the professional's major obligations to the client.

Informed Consent. The criteria for making an informed consent are described in detail in Chapter 3 but the major components will be reviewed in this section. In general, a client must be properly informed not only about what procedures (assessment or treatment) are being recommended but also about the parameters of such procedures; that is, what physical risks exist, the likelihood of success, and so on. The therapist must be realistic with the client regarding the chances of making significant improvement. It is unethical to guarantee or to imply to the client that a particular treatment approach will produce a "sure cure." As no treatment procedure works with every client, this involves misrepresentation. The client needs to be wary of such promises, as they may be an attempt to increase business and lure him or her into an expensive form of therapy.

Consent by the client is necessary at all stages of the assessment or treatment process. It is the duty of the mental health worker to ensure that the client has sufficient and accurate comprehension of any proposed procedures and is able to give consent voluntarily. In addition, the consent is only considered valid if the client fits the criteria for competency; otherwise, consent must be obtained by the client's guardian.

Blanket consent forms, giving permission for whatever evaluative or treatment procedures are "deemed necessary," are not acceptable by modern standards. A form that gives permission to release information, for example, should provide restrictions about the type of information (e.g., occupational therapy report, social work history) that is being released. The party or parties receiving the information should also be delineated as well as the expiry date of the consent form. This consent procedure should be followed for "internal" referrals as well, that is, from one department to another within the same facility (e.g., nursing to recreational therapy).

Informed consent is even more critical if the procedures being recommended are experimental in nature and the client is asked to be a subject in a research study. This particular type of consent may be difficult to obtain if the professional needs to have naive subjects due to the nature of the research project. Failure to provide the individual with sufficient information on which to base a decision is unethical and immoral. Many guidelines have been set out to protect the client from overly zealous researchers who may lose sight of the client's needs and rights because of their own ulterior motives. Without adherence to such standards, clients are likely to be deceived or "seduced" into an experimental procedure.

Feedback. Clients also have the right to know the results of their efforts, including assessment findings and what progress, if any, they are making in therapy. The reporting of such information contains a number of hazards.

Since the majority of assessments is requested to determine the basis for problems it is expected that at least some of the findings will be of a negative nature. It is important that clients be given information in such a way that they can understand and appreciate the implications.

The attitude and communicative style of the practitioner is extremely important to the listener. An air of concern, empathy, and supportiveness can be of great comfort to the listener, especially when the information is not that desirable. This type of attitude encourages the listener to ask questions and to clarify misunderstandings. It reduces the risk that clients will only attend to negative comments and helps clients to deal with their feelings about the information divulged or about the practitioner per se so that these feelings can be worked through.

Although the professional should not be so blunt as to cause defensiveness or unnecessary distress in the client, the practitioner should also be careful not to err in the opposite direction, that is, to be overly obscure and selective regarding the information provided. In an effort to protect the client from potential discomfort or even to protect the therapist from the client's anger, some mental health workers attempt to withhold sensitive information from their clients or report it to them in such ambiguous terms that there is little chance of comprehension. Clients have the right to understand the range and seriousness of their problems in order to make a choice regarding what, if anything, to do next.

When there is little hope for improvement (e.g., mental retardation, brain damage, terminal illness), some professionals argue that the individual should be protected from such knowledge under the assumption that this would affect their ability to enjoy life to the maximum and possibly inhibit their actions. Others would argue the opposite, that is, that it is necessary for the individual to know that he or she has a problem in order to deal effectively with it.

In addition to providing feedback to the client, it sometimes becomes necessary to report the results to other parties. This requirement is common when the practitioner has been hired by another party. The amount and type of information delivered should vary according to the purpose of the referral and the nature of the receiving party. For example, an employer would be interested in a different type of information than would an insurance company or a court of law. It is therefore important for the professional to determine the nature and extent of the information that should be provided to the referring party and limit it accordingly. In addition, the client should be informed before consenting to the procedure that information will be released.

Professionals have a responsibility to encourage feedback to other individuals whenever they believe that such feedback will ultimately be of benefit to the client. Within the educational system, for example, students often risk labels such as "unmotivated" and "retarded," because of lack of knowledge on the part of appropriate authorities. Once the student and relevant staff (i.e., teachers, principals) learn the nature of any specific disability that may exist, their expectations can be realigned and the student provided with the type of support and direction that is needed. An understanding of strengths and limitations also assists the student to make realistic decisions regarding career and educational aspirations and helps to reduce inappropriate pressures that may exist from other people.

Privacy. Privacy differs somewhat from confidentiality and involves the right of the individual to withhold information. While it may be necessary to gain personal information about a client in order to evaluate problems or to develop an appropriate treatment program, a professional should never consider that it is his or her right to know. Nor should the client be pressured to divulge information that he or she may not wish to impart.

Confidentiality. Clients need to appreciate the therapist's responsibility with regard to information that is divulged to him or her. First of all, they have a right to expect that information given to the therapist will only be shared with those individuals or agencies designated by the client. The professional needs to recognize that confidentiality is the right of the client, not the counselor's. In other words, it is the client who must decide to whom the professional should, and should not, disclose information. Unless the client has been declared incompetent to make such a decision, for example, because of intellectual limitations or age, the client's instructions regarding confidentiality must be honored. When the client is not considered competent (e.g., as a result of mental illness, intellectual limitations, or age), the individual's guardian should act as the decision maker in this area, not the professional.

There are a few limiting circumstances in which the client's right to confidentiality can be breached. One such instance occurs with children. With the exception of emancipated children (i.e., children who are living on their own), parents have the legal right to information about their offspring under most circumstances. Another instance in which private information must be divulged is in court, assuming privileged communication does not exist for that particular profession. When the therapist is ordered to testify against a particular client in court, the therapist must risk a contempt charge if he or she refuses to divulge the content of counseling sessions because of ethical beliefs. Privileged communication, as practiced in some parts of the United States and Canada, protects some professional groups (e.g., lawyers, physicians, and psychologists) from discussing clients in a legal proceeding. Where privileged communication does not exist, not only personal testimony but also all material pertaining to the client (e.g., records, test data) can be subpoenaed and form part of the evidence. Since privileged communication does vary from one location to another, it is the responsibility of professionals to become aware of their status with regard to court appearances and notify each client accordingly.

Confidentiality is also difficult to safeguard when the professional has more than one client to serve. While most mental health workers are devoted to their clients' needs, they may frequently have to juggle the demands of employing institutions, insurance agencies, the legal system, family pressures, and so on. Consider, for example, what happens when a psychiatrist is hired by a court of law to assess a suspect. In this case the court, who needs the information for a proper determination, and the suspect, whose cooperation is necessary to obtain the required information, are clients. A similar situation involves a professional whose employer has hired the individual to work with clients and to provide assessment and progress reports on a regular basis. Because of the centralized filing system that usually exists in such facilities, reports are generally accessible to many individuals and the professional has only limited control of the client's file. Situations such as these split the loyalties of the professional, are difficult to resolve, and require special consideration and treatment.

A similar conflict can arise when two professionals are working with the same client. Undoubtedly, both are receiving the confidences of the client in some way. Although these two individuals do not have the right to discuss the client without the client's permission, it is common practice for one professional to contact the other to discuss the case. Such occurrences are more prevalent in clinical settings that utilize a team approach to treatment.

Another situation in which confidentiality should be breached is when the professional suspects child abuse or when the client is acting in a manner which is potentially dangerous to self or others. This topic is covered in greater detail in the section entitled Protection.

BUSINESS PRACTICES

In addition to the standard ethical and legal responsibilities facing all mental health practitioners, individuals who work within the private sector have many practical business concerns. In order to survive financially, the independent practitioner must develop a keen business mind while at the same time adhering to ethical standards with regard to advertising, record keeping, fee setting, debt collection, and so on.

Advertising

In order to establish a new business or to promote a service, practitioners are often obliged to advertise. Unlike a commercial business, professionals are required to adhere to certain standards when letting the consumer know what services are available. Aside from the advantages to the business owner, the purpose of the promotional activity should be to assist the recipient in obtaining a general understanding of the practice. More specific information, for example, about fees and hours, can be obtained through direct inquiry. Price advertising is usually discouraged because it can lead to competitive warfare through the lure of bargain prices. Other professionals argue that it is unfair to withhold such information from referral sources because of their right to know what the services cost. This latter information is always available to an individual on request.

In first setting up a practice, professionals are prohibited from soliciting clients directly. They are entitled to send out announcement cards to potential referral sources but, even in doing this, restrictions are imposed. In general, the private practitioner must limit the information on the card to such items as name, address and phone number, highest level of education achieved in the field of practice, office hours, type of clientele serviced (e.g., adolescents), and a brief description of the services available (e.g., family therapy, diagnostic assessments). If the business consists of more than one professional, it is usually necessary to limit the firm's name to the surname of each of the partners rather than contriving special titles, for example, mental health clinic. With specific reference to psychological practice, for example, it has been asserted that "names other than those of the practising psychologists are misleading and confusing to the public; and also tend to obscure the fact that it is an individual psychologist who is responsible for the conduct of a practice."[1]

In addition to sending out announcement cards, the new practitioner is also allowed to be *appropriately* listed in the telephone directory, although limits may exist with regard to the number of directories in which the individual can be listed. Announcements similar to that appearing on the announcement cards also can be placed in a local newspaper on occasion. Regulations exist regarding the kind of sign or "shingle" that can be used in front of the office, with restrictions about such matters as the content of the sign, the size of the letters, and the use of lighting. The general recommendation is to present information in a way that is modest and in good taste.

If, in the course of the practice, the practitioner wishes to announce the introduction of a nonclinical service (e.g., an educational group on weight control), a description of the service (e.g., through the use of pamphlets) can be sent out to appropriate agencies and other potential referral sources. In doing this, however, the professional must guard against making false claims for success, should not include evaluative testimonials from former clients, and should not imply that the techniques being used in the program are unique unless this has been empirically established. The important point is that the consumer not be deceived through the use of inaccurate or incomplete information.

A more subtle form of advertising occurs when the practitioner takes part in a radio or television show, agrees to give a talk to a local group, or arranges informal luncheon meetings with referral sources. When involved with the general public, the professional must guard against promoting his or her services and should respond to questions about mental health practice on a general rather than personal level. The professional can certainly respond to questions about services offered if such questions are asked privately, assuming the professional does not make false claims. The professional should also avoid promoting his or her services by undermining other professionals in the field. The temptation to ignore or circumvent such rules may be higher if the business is at risk because of a limited cash flow.

Office Management

The practitioner who is maintaining a private business has similar responsibilities to the professional working within an institutional setting with regard to such issues as record keeping, confidentiality, clients' rights, conflicts of interest, and so on. Since the professional has the responsibility of managing an office, he or she also must be sensitive to a number of other issues, for example, staff training and supervision, appointment bookings, restrictions with regard to incorporating, fee collecting, and emergency procedures.

Staff Training and Supervision. Unlike an institutional setting, the practitioner has the responsibility to train staff to behave in an ethically appropriate manner toward clients. For example, most laypersons are not as sensitive to issues of confidentiality as they should be and, without proper training, may be more likely to gossip to friends or family about events that take place in the office. Counselors who work for an employer do not usually concern themselves about such matters because staff indoctrination is usually the responsibility of the administration. It is also the practitioner's responsibility to ensure that the clients are treated with respect and that the staff have the expertise to deal with emergency situations or other problems that may arise, for example, an angry family member who demands to know how a client is doing.

Appointment Bookings. The independent practitioner also has to establish rules with regard to bookings. Because of the need to cover the high cost of overhead, the temptation may exist to see as many clients as possible in the course of 1 day. Some professional groups have developed the habit of overbooking to avoid being idle in the case of cancellations. This type of business practice sets up lengthy waiting times and shows little respect for the client's time. At the most, clients should not have to wait more than 10 or 15 minutes, assuming an emergency situation has not arisen.

Another disadvantage to overbooking is the risk of burnout. Professionals who go from one client to another, day after day, begin to feel that they are on an assembly line and are more likely to suffer attentional difficulties and fatigue. Burnout, in turn, can lead to poor judgment and constitutes a disservice to the client who expects and pays for quality help.

Incorporating. Professionals also are often tempted to have their practices incorporated because of the business advantages that result. Such a practice is usually discouraged by professional governing bodies so that the practitioner does not try to avoid accepting responsibility for the business practices used and the quality of care given to clients. At the most, incorporation may be allowed "only insofar as it applies to the 'housekeeping' details of the firm."[2]

Emergency Procedures. An additional responsibility that faces business owners is providing appropriate service coverage when they are away because of sickness, vacation time, and so on. Many practitioners rely on a 24-hour answering service to advise them of emergencies that arise outside of office hours. In this way, home telephone numbers are not available to clients who may abuse that privilege. In addition, clients should be apprised of emergency facilities that are available in the community so that they have an alternative source of help if their counselor is inaccessible to them at a critical time. During vacation periods, clients can also be provided with the name of another professional that they can call for help if necessary.

Payment Policies. Before making a commitment to become a client, the individual has the right to know what fees will be charged and whatever office policies may exist with regard to payment. In establishing a fee, professionals should take into consideration the client's ability to pay as well as the standard fee charged by comparable professionals. Recommended rates are often established within different states or provinces and serve as a guideline to the professional with regard to hourly rates for different types of service. Although professionals are usually advised to follow the standard rate, many use a sliding-fee scale to accommodate clients with low incomes. Many practitioners are also advised not to charge for certain types of services, for example, telephone calls. In addition, they should not make referrals to other colleagues to collect a fee (i.e., fee splitting).

In addition to advising clients with regard to costs, the mental health professional should also inform clients of collection policies, for example, whether they are expected to pay at the time of their appointment or monthly, or whether they will be charged for missed appointments. Clients should also be advised of the professional's policy with regard to delinquent accounts, for example, whether there is a monthly interest rate, or whether the professional uses a collection agency or relies on small claims court to resolve payment problems. In situations when the practitioner uses an external agency to collect a bill, Faustman[3] urges caution because of the risk of being sued for breaching confidentiality. Collection agencies have a reputation of being rather aggressive in their attempts to obtain payment and it is also possible that the client will complain of psychological harm as a result of their involvement. Faustman suggests that this risk would be minimized if the professional were to discuss this office practice with the client beforehand and have a consent form signed so that the client's name can be released to a collection agency if payment becomes a problem.

PROTECTION

Mental health professionals are sometimes faced with situations in which some segment of society may need protection. The need to maintain confidentiality versus the need to provide protection to vulnerable members of the public can create a serious conflict. Few universal rules are available for resolving this dilemma and frequent confusion occurs over where responsibility to the client ends and that to society begins.

Philosophical positions regarding this issue vary greatly. At one extreme are those professionals who believe they should be solely responsible to their clients. The confidences of the client are therefore considered absolute and never to be compromised. Supporters of this viewpoint believe that the long-term benefits of the therapeutic relationship to society as well as to the individual should take precedence over all other considerations. In addition, failure to protect client information is believed by many to interfere with the free flow of information required in the therapy situation.

Risk to a Third Party

Most professionals would agree that where there is clear and imminent danger to the health or life of others, action must be taken to protect the endangered party. The Tarasoff decision reached in the California courts has impressed on the professional the need to warn the intended victim or victims of threatened harm.[4] The establishment of clear danger, however, is frequently difficult to determine. Since mental health professionals work with emotionally troubled individuals clients often express antisocial and exaggerated feelings toward others without the actual intent or ability to carry out the threat. If the professional mistakes angry fantasy for serious intentions the individual may cause serious disturbance to the client and the intended victim. In addition, the working relationship with the client may be destroyed, thereby ending the possibility of providing further assistance. On the other hand, should the therapist fail to take an intended threat seriously, loss of life or well-being of the intended victim may result. This decision is therefore not to be taken lightly. Where the professional judges the danger to be clear and substantial, the individual is constrained to act in a preventative manner. Alternatively, if the danger is not considered to be acute, the therapist should take measures to ensure that the client is followed in therapy, and the therapist should continue to evaluate the danger.

Once the determination of danger has been made, the direction in which the professional must move is reasonably clear, that is, warning the intended victim or appropriate authorities if the victim cannot be found. There may be other circumstances, however, in which the professional's course of action is neither direct nor simple, for example, situations in which the intended victim is not clearly identified. In this case the mental health worker would be unable to warn a specific person. Would contact with the police be considered an acceptable breach of confidentiality at this point? A worker who does inform police regarding risk to an unknown victim may receive a less than enthusiastic response.

Risk to the Client

Another dilemma for the therapist is dealing with the client who is not acutely violent but has the potential for violence at the slightest provocation. Even when the worker believes that the client's "fuse" has run out, legal assistance may be difficult to obtain. The need to protect a client from harm is a most important responsibility. Within the context of therapy, the therapist works constantly to help clients become aware of how they hurt themselves emotionally, socially, or otherwise so that they can live a happier and fuller existence. Complications arise, however, when the client is at risk of hurting himself or herself economically or physically. In the case of a manic client who suddenly starts to mismanage money and other financial dealings, the practitioner must determine if the client is still capable of managing business affairs without risk of significant loss. If not, the therapist must take steps to secure a guardian for the client and therefore risk depriving the client of the right to privacy and independent decision making.

Interference with the client's rights is more extreme if there is risk of death or serious injury. Since the criteria for involuntary admission are stringent hospitalization for such an individual may not be readily available. In such cases, what should the professional do? Must the therapist abandon all other duties and "babysit" the client until the crisis has passed? Even if this alternative were possible, and it rarely is, it is unlikely that the client in question would be obliging.

In situations such as these there is no ready formula to follow. A common safeguard to take in difficult situations is consultation with colleagues and supervisors. These individuals may be able to assist the professional directly involved with the client to gain some perspective and to enlist the assistance of relevant services and agencies.

In the area of client protection, a dilemma that is more likely to confront medical professionals (e.g., doctors and nurses) than anyone else arises because of the mixed views regarding euthanasia or "mercy" killing. This is more of an issue when dealing with clients who are suffering from an interminable medical condition and have no hope of improvement. Society is not as likely to be sympathetic to an emotionally disturbed client's desire to die even though that person may be plagued by an intractable mental disorder or is able to get little pleasure out of life because of situational factors beyond control.

When an individual's physical well-being is the issue and the client is either in a chronic vegetative state or the victim of unbearable pain, the issue of euthanasia often surfaces and becomes a problem for anyone counseling such individuals or their families. Differing attitudes about euthanasia can create pressure for those staff who have face-to-face contact with the client or with the client's family and have to deal with their mental state regarding the illness. Although most practitioners would not be tempted to take an active part in actually ending a client's life (i.e., active euthanasia), they may be tempted to let the client die if they see a problem developing rather than intercede on the client's behalf (i.e., passive euthanasia). Alternatively, they may have to deal with family members who are suffering emotionally because of the client's condition and who may be torn between wanting the client to die and not wanting to feel responsible for that person's death. Since nurses are often the frontline workers with chronic-care clients, they have to bear the brunt of this pressure and must balance their sensitivity for the client's suffering with their own need to respect the law.

Children in Need of Protection

Recent changes in child protection laws have placed professionals under the obligation of reporting to authorities even suspected cases of child abuse. Physical and sexual abuse can often be detected by a physician if visibly evident or by other professionals, assuming the child is willing and able to talk about what happened. It is much more difficult to establish the presence of emotional abuse or neglect. Once a professional becomes suspicious that child abuse or neglect may be occurring, such suspicions must be reported to the appropriate authorities. The mental health worker cannot be prosecuted for making a false report unless there was an ulterior motive involved, for example, to punish or harass the parents in some way.

The need to be sensitive to potential abuse situations is a serious responsibility for the professional. Failure to report may lead to a ruined life for a child and the potential for continued abuse in future generations. To motivate the professional to notify the appropriate authorities of suspected abuse, negative sanctions have been established including the risk of prosecution and fines of up to one thousand dollars.

Beyond the need to report suspected abuse, the mental health professional has obligations to the client. If the client is the child, the therapist must assist the child in dealing with his or her feelings regarding the abuse, family relationships, and so on. If the client is the parent, the topic of the abuse should be addressed and assistance offered to remediate the problem. In assisting the parent, the therapist must guard against attitudes of blame and condemnation as these may damage the working relationship and possibly deprive the client of the assistance the individual needs to become a more effective parent.

The need to balance these various responsibilities is a common problem for the public health nurse who frequently visits clients within the confines of their home and therefore has access to information that is not available in an office setting. Although many clients undoubtedly value this type of home service, others may perceive the nurse as an intruder or spy who invades their personal space, approves or disapproves of the way in which they run their household, and tells them how to do things differently. Being able to view the client in a natural setting is a valuable resource for the nurse and not only provides information on the home environment itself but also on social dynamics within the family. Even though the client may initially try to be on the best behavior, it is usually only a matter of time before the nurse gets to see what problems do exist. Neglect or abuse of children is more readily evaluated in the natural environment. The observation of this type of behavior places the nurse in a position of having to report on the client and possibly reducing whatever trust has already been established.

The public health nurse is also exposed to a variety of cultural and economic differences. When working with different cultural groups, for example, the nurse must be fully aware of different norms that may affect the way an individual lives or raises children and take these into account when deciding whether to report on the home environment to another agency. Significant differences in values and living standards may also make it difficult for the nurse to relate with the family in question and to evaluate its needs. Frontline workers such as these have an obligation to consult with their colleagues on a systematic basis to ensure that they can maintain their objectivity in such situations.

Professional Monitoring

Society not only needs protection from the "dangerous" client but also from malpracticing professionals. One of the most difficult situations with which a mental health professional may be faced is dealing with a colleague who is displaying irresponsible or inappropriate professional behavior, for example, seeing clients socially. When a mental health practitioner becomes aware that unethical practices are occurring, the professional is constrained to approach the individual involved to ensure that the person is aware of the problem and to encourage a change in practice. If the individual refuses to make the necessary adjustments the mental health professional has an obligation to notify the appropriate licensing body so that formal steps can be taken to investigate the complaint. Issuing a formal complaint against a colleague is typically a difficult step to take and may be inappropriately avoided by some professionals because of the bad feelings that may result.

In areas where peer reviews are the norm, similar problems exist. It remains difficult and awkward to criticize colleagues (and possibly friends) regarding their professional practices. Avoidance becomes an easy avenue to take under such circumstances but is obviously a disservice to the client.

ADVANCEMENT OF KNOWLEDGE

One major goal of the mental health field is to increase society's understanding of human behavior and to improve the way in which we approach different facets of life. Although the general public primarily associates the mental health field with the treatment of mental disorders, there is much more that mental health professionals can offer.

Research is constantly being conducted to advance knowledge not only in the prevention and treatment of psychopathology but also in other areas of human endeavor. The need to promote knowledge is a critical responsibility within the mental health field.

Because of their background in research methodology as well as human behavior, psychologists fall within the category of social scientists. Their training prepares them to study all aspects of human behavior, including such areas as child development, learning theory, memory, and sensation and perception. The relevance of such research is to provide useful improvements within such fields as education, industry, and crime control.

Although research findings are available to the public through journal publications, there is usually a serious communication gap between the discovery of new facts and their application within relevant fields. This problem arises for a number of reasons. First, journal articles are often difficult for the layperson to understand, partly because of the technical writing style and also because of professional jargon. Second, there is such a wealth of knowledge within the social science field that information relevant to a particular subject may be difficult to access. With the advent of computers, this latter problem should significantly decrease. Even if the information is fully accessed and understood, however, it requires an organized effort to change the status quo and to integrate new information into old. Practitioners should therefore take steps to keep abreast of new findings in their field and to assist the system in translating this knowledge into practice. Professional organizations should also play a role in advancing knowledge. An organized approach to disseminating research findings should be an ongoing educational goal for each professional group if it is to accept its responsibility to the public.

REFERENCES

1. Ontario Board of Examiners in Psychology (1980). *Bulletin, 6*(1), 2.
2. Ontario Board of Examiners in Psychology (1976). *Bulletin, 2*(1), 1.
3. Faustman, W. (1982). Legal and ethical issues in the debt collection strategies of professional psychologists. *Professional Psychology, 13,*(2), 208.
4. *Tarasoff v. Regents of the University of California,* Supp. 131 *California Reporter* 14 (1976).

Competence

2

In order to practice in a particular field the professional has to reach a minimal level of competence. On a general level, four major categories of information must be acquired: (1) comprehensive knowledge in the field of endeavor, (2) knowledge of ethics, (3) awareness of where the professional's limits lie, and (4) awareness of relevant legislation affecting professional practice. On a specific level, the professional should be aware of alternative services available in the community so that appropriate referrals can be made. If the professional is planning to work in a nontraditional setting (e.g., industry, education) or in specialty areas (e.g., sex therapy, psychoanalysis), relevant knowledge should be acquired in such fields before taking on that role.

To accomplish these goals, it is not sufficient to simply acquire a core of knowledge in a particular area. The professional who wishes to practice in anything other than a strictly academic setting has to be able to use such knowledge to affect change. Disservice to a client can often be blamed on inadequate work which, in turn, is often a direct function of the qualifications of the person doing the work. An example from personal experience was that of a mental health worker who was employed by a self-help organization and had allowed herself to get deeply involved with an extremely disturbed woman. This woman had been sexually abusing her son for years and, after this boy made a successful suicide attempt, began abusing the next oldest boy. Although this woman required intensive psychotherapy because of the seriousness of her problems, she was receiving supportive counseling. Although the mental health worker obviously meant well, she had allowed the relationship to develop on a more personal level, which may have led to unreasonable expectations on the part of the client. The worker found it extremely difficult to extricate herself from this role and attempts to do so generally led to suicidal threats on the part of the client. Despite the worker's good intentions, she did not have the expertise to deal with this type of personality disorder and the woman should have been referred to an appropriate professional shortly after she was assessed by their agency. Regrettably, when the worker eventually attempted to do this, she found it difficult to find anyone who was willing to accept this woman as a client because of the severity and chronicity of her problems.

To accomplish these goals, it is not sufficient simply to acquire a core to be addressed and are covered in the following sections: Definition, Developmental Issues, Maintenance Issues, Limitations, and Methods of Control.

DEFINITION

Within the mental health field, "competence" is a very difficult concept to define on anything but an abstract level. This difficulty is understandable because of the variability among and within different disciplines regarding human behavior. By virtue of having to develop educational curricula, each profession has had to make decisions about what knowledge to impart and which skills to teach under the assumption that such instruction will produce a competent professional. This assumption is not always a valid one and has resulted in the need for external and self-regulation as described in the section entitled Methods of Control.

In an attempt to provide a better understanding of what constitutes competent practice, many disciplines have developed standards for providers in the field. Within the social work field, for example, the following standards were recommended regarding individuals working within a hospital setting.[1] First of all, the task force that developed such standards recommended that competency in this type of setting necessitated knowledge in a number of core areas, including the health care system itself (i.e., federal, provincial, local), normal versus pathologic behavior, interdisciplinary differences, legal and ethical standards, and community awareness. In addition to basic knowledge in such areas, the social worker also needs to acquire such practical abilities as interviewing and communication skills, counseling techniques, program evaluation skills, and administration skills, as well as consultative and advocacy expertise. Although other disciplines may place different emphasis on which skills and areas of knowledge are most critical, there are probably many similarities between the different fields in how they attempt to define competence.

DEVELOPMENTAL ISSUES

Competence can be achieved in a number of different ways although the techniques by which this goal is achieved have varied over the years and across disciplines. For example, within the nursing profession, acquisition of a diploma was initially considered sufficient to practice in this field. Dating back to 1923, however, "nursing leaders were calling for the baccalaureate degree to be the standard; and since 1960, the American Nurses' Association (ANA) has publicly supported this position."[2] Similar changes have occurred in other professions in an attempt to obtain qualified practitioners.

Historically, professionals were those individuals who engaged in scholarly activity and were involved in such fields as teaching, law, religion, and medicine.[3] According to Young:

> Professional training as we know it today was virtually nonexistent. Except for those who entered the priesthood, the young gentleman was expected to "practice" his profession by associating himself with someone more skilled and knowledgeable than himself. Although questions of ethics were taken quite seriously, those practicing were not accountable to anyone, and the individual client had no recourse if dissatisfied with the service. There was no tradition of quality control or minimum standards for acceptable service.[4]

Since that time a number of quality control techniques has evolved because of the need to maintain standards of appropriate practice and to reduce client abuses. Under the assumption that professionals would be better able to practice their trade if they were given appropriate training, educational curricula and criteria were established. To ensure adherence to acceptable standards, the accreditation process in which an official review board gives its stamp of approval to organizations that meet certain criteria has developed gradually.

At the present time, most health care professions require a minimum of 3 years of college- or university-level training consisting of a combination of theoretical instruction as well as supervised practical experiences. Other professions require a much longer time frame in order to acquire mastery of their field (e.g., psychiatry, psychology), although evidence is lacking to show that "the level of degree has any relationship to measures of client outcome."[5]

In addition to being formally evaluated regarding their acquired level of expertise, advanced trainees and interns must also demonstrate competence by writing a major dissertation on an approved subject or conducting a research study that contributes significantly to their field of endeavor. The choice of doing a paper versus a piece of research is not given to trainees who must be skilled in experimental design and statistical evaluation because of the nature of their discipline (e.g., psychology graduates). Professionals who get actively involved in this training process have an obligation to ensure that trainees in their field acquire the necessary skills and use them appropriately. They therefore have a responsibility to structure course content and placement experiences appropriately and to provide for sufficient supervision in the field.

Prior to even entering the training arena, the interested candidate has to meet certain entry criteria. The stringency of such admission standards varies according to the level of expertise needed to achieve mastery in a particular discipline, as well as the popularity of the field itself. Obviously a profession that attracts many applicants can afford to be more selective. Entry into a program is also affected by the anticipated dropout rate and society's need for more professionals of this nature.

Many disciplines have learned to rely on entry examinations as a major source of information regarding an applicant's suitability. These examinations have been strongly criticized over the years and accused of either being discriminatory toward certain minority groups because of examination content or of being poor predictive measures.[6,7] Since the material included in such selection devices is usually derived from experienced professionals in the field, such individuals have a responsibility to demonstrate empirically that the tests validly and reliably measure what they purport to measure. If this ideal is impossible to reach, the tests should be given the proper weight in the decision-making process and only taken into consideration within the context of other information on the applicant.

In the sections that follow, difficulties that have arisen over the years in developing and evaluating an individual's level of competence are covered in greater depth.

Academic Training

Academic study is a necessary part of professional development and is included to ensure that members in the field possess at least basic knowl-

edge. The critical question becomes one of what to teach and how to do
so.

Qualifications of Instructors. The responsibility to make individuals
proficient in a particular field is a weighty one and has serious implications for society because the graduating professionals can only be as good
as their acquired skills. Although many health care providers may be "natural" at working with people, others need to acquire their skills in a more
formal manner. The responsibility to produce new graduates primarily
falls on people within the same field. Regrettably, many instructors are
solely academic in orientation. Strupp[8] has pointed out that faculty members may be poor role models for their students and place too heavy an
emphasis on theoretical background because many of them lack practical
experience of their own. Although some might analogize that "you don't
have to be a chicken to know how to lay an egg," the academic professional may lack the nuances of the face-to-face experience with a client
and not be as sensitive to all of the ethical or clinical complexities that
arise.

Course Content

Interdisciplinary Differences. Within the mental health area, the content of such instruction will certainly vary according to the importance
placed on certain factors by the different disciplines. For example, nurses
and medical interns who intend to specialize in psychiatry will be more
exposed to physical theories of mental disorder and chemical methods of
treatment than will students in other fields (e.g., social work or psychology). These latter disciplines tend to devote more of their academic time
learning about interpersonal dynamics and methods of counseling.
Another type of interdisciplinary difference arises because disciplines
that do not require graduate-level training may be more concerned about
the acquisition of practical than of research-oriented skills and therefore
course content is adjusted accordingly.

Training programs that lead students to believe that they are, or
should be, competent to handle "anything that walks through the door"
are misleading. All professionals have limitations. The most basic limitations relate to the field of training. A registered nurse, for example, may
be competent in nursing skills but not in performing surgery. A psychologist may be competent to provide psychotherapy but not to prescribe
medication. Therefore it is necessary to teach students to recognize and
respect the limitations of their fields of endeavor.

Intradisciplinary Content. Over the years, many theories have evolved
regarding the methods by which students should be taught in order to
maximize professional development. The two major approaches include

1. The "scientist-professional" model, in which students are primarily trained to be critical thinkers and social scientists rather than memorizers of fact[9,10]
2. The "explicitly professional" model, in which trainees are expected to have broad-based competence in their field as well as technical skills[11]

The need to train a professional *how* to think is the primary focus of the "scientist-professional" method. As far back as the 1920s, Flexner[12] and Whitehead[13] proposed that professional education focus on scientific thinking rather than on the acquisition of specific knowledge or techniques. They condemned programs in which the emphasis was on an encyclopedic memorization of material. Training in scientific thinking by itself, however, has not been sufficient to prepare a professional to practice in a certain field. The result of this narrow-based teaching method has been to produce an individual who knows how to study human behavior but not necessarily how to deal with it.

Training in scientific methodology may also be redundant for disciplines in which professionals primarily work as service providers and are not expected to act as investigators in their field. Critics of this approach have therefore argued "that it was inefficient, and even unethical, to train future clinicians in research skills they would probably never employ while failing to provide a truly comprehensive preparation for professional practice."[14]

At the present time, most training programs take into consideration the need to have a broad knowledge base and to utilize relevant skills. Under this approach, a minimum number of years of course work is mandatory. Students work toward comprehensive mastery in all areas composing their discipline, with little opportunity for specialization until later stages of professional development. Specialization that arises too early in the training process has a tendency to limit the student's progress because that person becomes too narrowly focused. Professionals who act in a teaching role with such students have to explore their own values with regard to training so their methods are in line with recommended orientations.

In addition to helping students acquire a core of knowledge, instructors also have an obligation to teach students how to apply their knowledge appropriately. Not only does this entail experiential training but also exposure to the ethical principles of working in the field. Lack of knowledge in ethics has led to an abuse of clients in the areas of research and direct clinical practice. Community concern about the violation of human rights has increased the number of legal actions directed against mental health providers over the last several years. Although professionals within the academic arena may not be affected by these regulations because they often lack direct contact with clients, they certainly have a responsibility to sensitize their students regarding legally and ethically appropriate conduct. Many of these legal actions have resulted in new laws to protect the vulnerable client and rightfully limit the freedom of the mental health professional to practice. This latter topic is covered in detail in Chapter 3 and therefore will not be repeated in this chapter.

The effect that ethical knowledge has upon decision making was demonstrated by Tymchuk et al.[15] In an effort to determine what kinds of ethical decisions posed the greatest and least problems for mental health providers, Tymchuk presented psychologists with a series of vignettes containing moral dilemmas. The findings indicated that the professionals were better able to deal with ethical problems that are currently popular (e.g., issues of confidentiality, client dangerousness, morality). The weakest consensus concerned matters such as test security and interpretation, research activities, advertising, and fees. These results suggest two important requirements of ethics training. The first involves the need to become more aware of existing ethical codes as such knowledge should improve the quality of decision making in complicated situations. Ethics training also provides some motivation to keep informed about current issues. As in other fields, ethical concerns are likely to come to the surface as a result of societal pressures that, in turn, are likely to arise because of existing abuse in the mental health system. The rapid rise of public interest in ethical areas indicates a growing awareness on both fronts regarding the need to reevaluate previously accepted attitudes about practice to avoid unwarranted complacency in areas as yet unchallenged.

Practical Training
Professionals who take on the responsibility of training students on an academic level should also accept the need for experiential training and include it as part of the student's graduating requirements. Otherwise students not only lack exposure to actual clinical problems but may be poorly prepared to deal with the realities of practice in the working world. Jacobs[16] has pointed out that graduates are often expected to fit other roles besides that of frontline workers. Such roles include consultation, paraprofessional training, supervision, program development, evaluation, and so on. Being in a natural setting allows students to recognize the diversity of functions they may be expected to perform and provides "food for discussion" during meetings with supervisors. At present, practical experience in the form of internships and practica comprises an integral part of most professional training.

Supervised experience in a natural setting fulfills several important functions for the student. First of all, the student has an opportunity to learn from role models in the field. Many course instructors tend to be overly academic in orientation and may lack ongoing experience with clinical populations. The opportunity to work with a trained professional who is actively practicing his or her trade should be richly informative to the student. It also allows the intern to observe and discuss the supervisor's nonclinical functions and to discover what the day-to-day life of a professional really entails.

Second, students begin to obtain broad-based experience because they are typically obliged to work in a variety of settings, for example, psychiatric hospitals, crisis intervention clinics, and chronic care units. This diversity of placements allows the student to experience a multiplicity of problems, clients, techniques, and settings. Alcoholics, autistic children, schizophrenics, and psychogeriatric populations are just a few of the client groups to which the intern may be exposed. Through such exposure students should be better able to adopt a more realistic attitude toward mental health work and to decide whether specialization or generalized clinical practice appeals to them the most.

In addition to getting exposure to real clinical populations and problems, internship placements also allow the student to gain experience working with other disciplines. The opportunity for team work can be an enriching experience, not only by expanding knowledge but also in learning how to work effectively with different areas. It also helps the student to develop an appreciation for other areas of expertise and how to interface with them despite whatever differences may exist. The student's supervisor has an ethical responsibility to assist the trainee in appreciating and respecting other areas while, at the same time, recognizing the uniqueness and contributions to be made by his or her own discipline.

In the course of their practical experience, students also become aware of the underlying "politics" of different organizations. At this state of development, interns are generally discouraged from getting actively involved in such maneuverings. The practical placement forces the students to recognize that their professional role comprises more than just clinical work. Regrettably, the "political" role of the professional is rarely covered in either textbooks or lectures and therefore the only avenue open to the student is to learn about it through the placement experience.

Another important aspect of practicum training is exposure to day-to-day ethical issues and dilemmas. While such basics may be learned in lectures, the application of these standards may require guidance from a practicing professional. The matter of informed consent, for example, may seem fairly straightforward in a lecture hall. When faced with an abusive alcoholic, a battered spouse, or a molested child, however, previously clear lines of duty may become muddied by emotion and conflicting responsibilities. The availability of an experienced supervisor should help the trainee to sort through such issues in order to act appropriately under the circumstances.

Supervision

General Principles. The quality of the practical experience is directly affected by the quality of the supervisory experience. Supervision is available at many different levels including administrative and clinical. Administrative supervision extends to trainees and the fully qualified practitioner by virtue of being employed by a particular organization. Administrative matters cover such issues as dress codes, work hours, attendance at meetings, delegation of responsibility, services offered, lines of command, and so on.

Clinical supervision is the method of overseeing the manner in which clients are treated and is only a requirement for those individuals who have not reached the final level of their training. Supervision is one way of ensuring that mental health trainees are providing services in an ethical, professional, and competent manner. It is also a way of assisting paraprofessionals in doing as good a job as possible without the advantage of formal training. Since supervisors can be held legally responsible for the work they supervise, it is not a responsibility to be taken lightly.

In addition to providing protection for the client, supervision also serves a training function in that it teaches the intern how to practice his or her trade. In order to accomplish this goal, it seems logical that supervision should be provided by members of the same trade. Professionals from one discipline do not ordinarily provide clinical supervision for those of a different discipline even though administrative lines often cross professional boundaries.

In a psychiatric unit, conflicts have sometimes arisen regarding the right of one discipline to supervise another. Since psychiatrists often bear much of the legal responsibility for inpatients because of admission and discharge policies, they may feel that other disciplines should report to them about their clinical work and follow suggestions that are given. This problem is further complicated in that psychiatrists are often the administrative heads and therefore feel justified in controlling what and how services are offered. Many battles can ensue between psychiatry and other department heads because of the fine line that sometimes exists between clinical and administrative rights. Although the ultimate goal should be to work out such difficulties in a constructive fashion, mutual agreement regarding levels of responsibility may be difficult to obtain because of rivalry between the disciplines and whatever pecking order may exist on an administrative level. Added to this problem is the requirement of many health insurance plans that mental health benefits can only be paid to nonmedical staff (e.g., nurses, psychologists) if their work is supervised by a physician.[17,18] Because of the similarities between medical and nursing practice, the nurse who wishes to practice as an independent health provider may be at a higher risk of being charged with going beyond areas of competence. A question that may have to be resolved at a legal level is "under what conditions a particular nurse has actually exceeded his or her scope of authority and thereby violated the state's medical practice act."[19]

Differences also exist between the disciplines regarding the level at which supervision is needed and how informally it can be provided. In some settings, supervision may be equated with peer review and be done within the context of case conferences. In other words, the staff who is working with a particular client is expected to provide a progress report and to discuss with the health team what steps to take next.

Although supervision can sometimes be done within a group meeting, other disciplines may require staff who are not fully qualified (e.g., nursing students, students with BSWs or MAs) to meet on an individual basis with someone who is in order to discuss cases. In psychology, for example, formal supervisory meetings are a requirement until full registration has been attained. Even after obtaining their PhD, graduates who wish to practice as psychologists must meet with an approved supervisor over a minimum period of 1 year. Although rather unwieldy, some professional boards have recommended that supervisors spend an equal amount of time with the supervisee as the supervisee spends with the client. Although this approach serves a valuable training function for the trainee, it is obviously highly demanding on the supervisor's time and may not be viewed as particularly cost-efficient by administrative staff. Registration and the right to practice without supervision can only be obtained after graduates have passed a written and oral examination and have demonstrated to their supervisors their ability to practice in a competent and ethical manner. In a treatment facility, complaints have sometimes been directed against the psychology profession because too much time is devoted to supervisory work, thereby taking away from the time available for direct service. Professionals who fail to fulfill their supervisory role, however, risk being investigated and possibly disciplined for improper practice.

Other disciplines do not require a doctorate or registration in order to practice their trade. Although doctorates are available in the social work field, social workers are able to practice independently with a master's degree. Within psychology, much debate has been generated in the last several years by individuals who believe that those with an MA degree should also be allowed to practice independently, assuming their field of practice would be restricted in accordance with their level of training and experience.

For many disciplines, the level of supervision is also likely to vary in accordance with the degree of sophistication and training of the supervisee. At early stages, the client requires more protection and the trainee more guidance to ensure that he or she does not get involved in matters that are too difficult to handle. Novices should therefore be exposed to fairly simple and straightforward problems at first and, as they demonstrate their competence, gradually be introduced to more complicated matters.

Clients' rights must also be considered when training students. Clients should never feel pressured into accepting an inexperienced therapist. Issues related to informed consent are discussed in greater detail in Chapter 3. Within the supervisory context, however, it entails telling the client at the earliest possible moment of the student's status, the student's supervisory requirements, the client's right to have a fully qualified therapist, and so on.

Supervisor's Role. The first requirement for supervisors is that they have the necessary expertise to provide training in line with their students' needs. In the course of regularly scheduled meetings, supervisors must ascertain the trainee's present level of functioning in different clinical areas and only assign work that is commensurate with the supervisee's abilities. Since supervisors are obliged to act as role models, they should not permit the student to engage in practices that they themselves cannot perform. In addition to regular discussions with their protégé, professionals are well-advised to watch the student in action to avoid being misled about what is really transpiring with the client. Audio- and videotapes are also useful in monitoring the student–client interaction although this can sometimes create concerns about confidentiality. The client should be reassured that such tapes will only serve a supervisory function and will be erased once they have been examined by the supervisor.

In addition to being cautious about the quality of student–client interactions, supervisors also should be cautious about documenting their role with the student. For their own protection, supervisors would be well-advised to maintain an ongoing record of contacts describing the activities in which the supervisee is engaged, the clinical and ethical issues that are covered in the course of the supervisory sessions, and so on. In addition, all formal communications (e.g., reports, letters) sent out by the trainee should be countersigned by the supervisor to demonstrate awareness and approval of the student's activities.

For obvious reasons, supervisors are also discouraged from providing supervision at a distance. In other words, it would be inappropriate for the supervisory contact to be limited to telephone conversations or written correspondence. Since the supervisor needs to be physically available to the student and sensitive to the administrative and political climate that is likely to affect the student's performance, it is essential that the supervisor work in the same setting. Despite their own caseload, professionals who take on the supervisory role must ensure that they are easily reached if an emergency arises so that students are not left to fend for themselves.

Under ideal circumstances, the supervisor should also have some face-to-face contact with the supervised clients. This latter recommendation has obvious logistical problems. While direct contact with the supervisee's clients may be feasible in a smaller, well-contained practice, in larger institutions (e.g., children's aid societies, crisis intervention units)

where the caseload is large and where contacts may be short-term or occur away from central office buildings, the time required to meet each
client individually and to plan a treatment method would be prohibitive.
Such stringent requirements for supervision would negate any advantage
of having students in the setting because of the time commitment that
would be involved on the part of professional staff.

Finally, supervisors have a responsibility to treat their students with
respect despite their junior position. Students should not be manipulated
into taking on too heavy a caseload or other functions that should be
the responsibility of the supervisor. Supervisors should also refrain from
assuming both an administrative and clinical role with the same individual to avoid conflicts of interest. The individual responsible for the student's administrative evaluation should judge on the basis of work habits
(e.g., punctuality at meetings, absenteeism) and not on the student's clinical work. The opposite can be said about the clinical supervisor who
should only take work habits into consideration if they directly affect
client welfare, for example, being late for a therapy session.

Supervisee's Role. The supervisee also has a number of responsibilities
that should not be ignored. In the past, the duties and responsibilities
of the supervisee have been given almost no consideration. It would be
misleading and misguiding to consider that a supervisee is without responsibility to the supervisor. In reality, supervisors may actually sue
their supervisees under certain conditions.[20]

First, supervisees have the responsibility to represent their training,
experience, and skills accurately and completely. Failure to indicate weaknesses in certain areas of practice may trick the supervisor into assuming
a higher level of skill than really exists and may lead to inappropriate
case assignments. Disservice to the client under such a circumstance is
probable. The student may also resist getting involved in clinical activities without the supervisor's approval. All interventions must be planned
in consultation with the supervisor and never done independently.

The supervisee also has a responsibility to represent properly his or
her clinical status and limitations with clients and others. More specifically, the title or designation used by the student should not be misleading and should appropriately define his or her role. The trainee has the
additional responsibility of representing his or her relationship with the
supervisor accurately. The supervisee must not use the supervisor's name
or reputation to meet personal needs without the prior agreement of the
supervisor.

Specialization

In the course of training, many professionals develop some areas of specialization. These are the areas within which they tend to be most knowledgeable and competent. Because of the vast subject matter within each

discipline, it would be difficult if not impossible for mental health providers to remain current with all of the literature in the field. Areas of specialization generally develop because of this and are usually those areas in which the students have the greatest interest.

In most training programs, specialization occurs during the later stages of professional development so it does not interfere with the acquisition of general knowledge. For example, a clinician-in-training may want to practice primarily with autistic children, with the elderly, as a sex therapist, and so on. Before doing this, it is critical that the student has already acquired traditional knowledge and skills that can be brought to the specialty area. Building on this core of knowledge, the individual must then acquire the information and techniques specific to the new area. For some specialties such as sex therapy, accredited training programs already exist and certification may be required before graduating students can consider themselves to be qualified sex therapists.

Individuals who do have the motivation to expand their expertise to specialty areas at a postgraduate level are encouraged to do so but should proceed toward this goal in an appropriate rather than expedient fashion. It is not sufficient just to accumulate knowledge in a particular field (i.e., through journals, workshops, coursework). Attempts should also be made to learn through practice, under the guidance of someone who is already trained in that area.

In the United States, certain disciplines (e.g., psychiatry, psychology) have actually developed formal guidelines that must be followed in order to obtain specialty licensing. These guidelines include many stringent requirements and, in addition to formal examinations, necessitate several years of supervision in the specialty area even though the individual is already fully licensed as a general practitioner in a field. Specialty certificates are available for such areas as hypnosis and forensic work. Similar types of licensing are also suggested for other approaches in which special skills are critical; for example, marriage counselor, sex therapist, and industrial consultant.

Program Evaluation
One criticism that may be directed at all training programs is their failure to obtain a thorough evaluation of their level of effectiveness. While most programs utilize some kind of evaluation procedures, they are generally informal and loosely derived rather than the formal, objective measures favored by researchers. Often the effectiveness of the program is inferred from the test results of the graduating students although, on occasion, the students may be asked to rate the quality of their training. Although professionals have an ethical responsibility to evaluate the quality of their training methods, this is often difficult to do because training goals are often vague and difficult to measure. Research conducted by Norcross and Stevenson[21] discovered that few programs have concrete objectives

and training goals. Instead, most program goals consist of a few paragraphs describing general orientations. Other programs have no written structure at all. Without a knowledge of program objectives, it is almost impossible to develop appropriate evaluative instruments. Professionals have an obligation to put more effort into this task in order to fulfill their responsibilities to themselves as well as to society.

Koocher[22] has proposed a multimethod approach to program evaluation, including periodic examinations (written and oral) as well as samples of the student's behavior in which performance skills are assessed in standardized situations. Since the client is the final recipient of the clinician's skill, Newbrough[23] further recommended that a client-satisfaction measure be taken although it may be difficult for a client to be entirely honest if he or she has any anxiety about upsetting the counselor-in-training. Norcross and Stevenson[24] further propose that formal evaluation standards be developed for programs as well as students, and that a coordinated national program of clinical training and evaluation be established to oversee programs and uphold standards.

MAINTENANCE ISSUES

Once training is completed and the professional is practicing in the community, it becomes the individual's personal responsibility to ensure that the services offered continue to meet acceptable standards. To do so, the professional must keep up with current developments and expansion of knowledge in the field.

Rationale

As a result of ongoing research or the manifestation of new problems in society, clients' needs are often changing and new methods are being developed to deal with these changes. One contemporary example has resulted from the dramatic increase in acquired immune deficiency syndrome (AIDS) and the need for professionals to assist victims as well as their families to deal with the emotional concomitants of the disease. The incidence of anorexia nervosa and bulimia has also increased drastically over the last several years. Such problems have not responded as well as they should to traditional forms of therapy and therefore the professional has to expand his or her knowledge in order to deal effectively with such difficulties. Keeping up on different treatment techniques is also critical for the psychiatrist who relies on psychotropic forms of treatment. New drugs are constantly being developed and without ongoing professional development, the psychiatrist may be at a disadvantage in discovering a better treatment method, learning about new side effects, and so on. Although the psychiatrist may depend on the pharmaceutical salesperson to keep him or her apprised of these changes, the salesperson obviously has a vested interest in promoting particular products and therefore may not be the most objective source of information. Therapists also need to be aware of new techniques that arise, particularly if they have been well researched and seem to work particularly well with certain clients. In this way, the clinician can be in a position to improve the quality of the services offered through additional training or, alternatively, to refer the client to a service that does offer the best approach.

Keeping abreast of current developments does not imply that professionals should alter their methods of practice with every new development reported in the literature. Professionals who give in to the temptation to be "trendy" inevitably employ techniques without the expertise to do so.

Despite the need to maintain competence in the field, it is too easy for professionals to become settled in their ways and to resist new approaches. Professional development can be a time-consuming process despite the long-term advantages it may offer to the client and professional alike. Many attempts have been made to keep professionals informed about new developments and in some disciplines (e.g., medicine), practitioners are even obliged to accumulate continuing education credits through conventions, workshops, and so on, to maintain their status. In an attempt to attract people to ongoing training sessions, conventions are commonly held in fairly exotic places. In this way, they provide an opportunity for the busy professional to combine training with vacation time and therefore save on travel costs. Unfortunately, for those who prefer to earn such credits dishonestly, many loopholes exist. For example, it is not uncommon for practitioners to register for workshops but to show up only after the workshop is over to pick up their credit certificates. Such behavior is certainly unethical and helps to defeat a system that was designed for the benefit of practitioner and client alike.

Alternative Methods

For the ethical professional who sincerely wants to keep up in the field, a number of options are open. Professional journals and books are one of the more obvious resources for new information. The governing boards for many disciplines as well as professional organizations generally circulate newsletters keeping their members aware of important changes that occur. In situations where a practitioner is unsure as to the proper thing to do, it is also possible to contact such boards or organizations for advice. Peer consultation is another way of expanding knowledge. In this respect, professionals who work within a public facility often have more options available to them because of inservice training. It is also relatively easy for members of the same department to arrange formal meeting times to discuss relevant issues in the field, to arrange talks from other specialists in the community, and so on. The independent practitioner tends to be more isolated from such educational outlets because they are not as readily available and therefore require more planning on the practitioner's part.

As mentioned earlier, conventions and workshops are another educational resource for the serious professional. Workshops generally provide more intensive training on a particular topic than do conventions and often act as a stimulant to the attendant by providing new ideas and by allowing professionals to share their thoughts on different matters. Professionals who take on the role of a workshop presenter should only do so if they have the appropriate expertise and something worthwhile to offer. The workshop should be advertised in an ethically appropriate fashion so that registrants are aware what topics are to be covered, what level of expertise is necessary to benefit from the workshop, and so on. At the completion of the training sessions, presenters have a responsibility to solicit feedback from attendants regarding the manner in which the material was covered and the subject matter so that improvements can be made if further workshops are planned. Evaluative techniques can also be used to determine how much was learned from the workshop, although a good measure may be difficult to obtain because of the variability in the attendants themselves; for example, entry level knowledge, motivation to learn new material, or fatigue. Although fatigue may seem like a facetious issue, it is an important variable for many individuals at workshops in that partying and socializing is a common outlet. Wine-and-cheese parties and other social gatherings are commonly listed in the attendant's schedule and may even be included in the costs. Professionals are not necessarily moderate at such events and their ability to concentrate the next day may be affected.

Complications

In terms of professional development, the major limitations to workshops is the time factor. Since they are confined to a few days, attendants do not have an opportunity to solidify their newly-acquired knowledge through practice. As long as the registrant is aware of these limitations, problems are not likely to arise. Problems are also unlikely for individuals who have a reasonable knowledge of the topic prior to the workshop. There is the danger that individuals without much expertise will mistakenly believe that attendance at the workshop has made them experts and that they are now competent to apply whatever skills may have been taught. Attendants at hypnosis workshops may be deluded in this way. Although many individuals have a layperson's knowledge of hypnosis and are attracted to the workshop because they want to learn how to use it, one workshop is certainly not sufficient for most individuals to use these techniques appropriately. Another popular workshop is on the topic of marriage or family counseling. As most people realize, a little knowledge can indeed be a dangerous thing. The practitioner runs the risk of seriously injuring a family unit if, on the basis of one workshop, the individual starts working in this area.

Having attended a workshop, participants must additionally guard against misrepresenting their professional qualifications as a result of such training. Although it is appropriate to include ongoing professional training in a curriculum vitae, such training should be properly designated; that is, as a workshop, university course, supervised internship, or whatever. An example from personal experience was that of another professional who improperly represented himself on a curriculum vitae by listing three universities to his training credit, including Harvard. This vita was used as an exhibit when this man was called as a witness at court. When the cross-examining lawyer questioned him about his excellent qualifications and asked when he had attended these various educational institutions, the man was forced to admit that he had only attended one of the universities as a student. The other two universities, including Harvard, were the sites for 1-day workshops that he had attended. Although it was unclear if this individual was purposefully trying to mislead others regarding his credentials, this was probably the impression that was created.

LIMITATIONS

When to Say "No"

Lack of Skill. Professionals should guard against the attitude that they are the only ones who can provide a good service. In adopting this stance, they may delude themselves into denying the presence of serious limits and accept all cases assigned to them regardless of the problem. Professionals who practice in isolation are more likely to fall victim to this kind of attitude because they lack contact with their peers. Private practitioners who are not on salary and therefore depend on the income brought in by their clientele may also rationalize their ability to service everyone. Community networking and self-awareness is critical in order to keep in touch with the parameters of the practice and external alternatives.

Unresolved Personal Issues. For professionals who have been able to resolve past difficulties in their personal life, such insights may serve as strengths in working with certain clients. For example, a social worker who was raised in an alcoholic home may have been able to gain vast amounts of insight into the workings of the alcoholic family. These insights may be an advantage when treating clients from a similar background. For many individuals, past issues of this nature are often unresolved and therefore still cause discomfort and emotional turmoil to the professional when faced with similar problems in a client. Emotional turmoil of this nature may cause significant blind spots in the course of treatment because the counselor cannot deal with the problems objectively. For example, a registered nurse may have difficulty working on a cancer ward or with dying children because he or she has not resolved feelings surrounding the death of a loved one. Another example is the individual who was raised in an abusive home environment and has developed a negative attitude toward men because she frequently observed her father beating her mother. Working as a marriage counselor would seem foolish for this individual and would be a disservice to the couple as long as this type of attitude remains.

A professional who is in doubt about whether to take on a particular client would be wise to seek the advice of another professional. Alternatively, personal therapy should be considered if the mental health provider's attitudes about certain areas are likely to interfere with his or her effectiveness, especially if the worker does not have the luxury of refusing certain types of clients.

History of Failure with Certain Clients. If a professional has had little success in working with a particular client population (e.g., substance abusers) over a reasonable period of time and has developed a defeatist attitude from this experience, it would be inadvisable to take on more clients of this type or even to act as a supervisor in this area. In most communities, alternative services and therapists are usually available to the client and may have a more positive attitude about working with this type of individual.

Lack of Interest. Professionals certainly vary with regard to their interest areas and the kinds of problems they best like to treat. If a counselor is completely disinterested in certain topics (e.g., mental retardation, rape counseling), accepting work in that area is contraindicated.

Physical Limits. Another limiting factor relates to the physical well-being of the professional. Working with clients in a mental health setting requires a great deal of energy and concentration. Counselors who are physically unwell may be depriving clients in a number of different ways. First of all, individuals who feel stressed because of their own physical condition are more likely to become irritable and impatient towards those around them. Harsh or critical comments could seriously damage a working relationship and possibly destroy the therapeutic process. Concentration is also affected by physical stress and could potentially lead to poor judgment calls. To avoid such possibilities, professionals suffering this kind of problem may wish to consider a leave of absence and the need to refer clients to another professional for a period of time. If professionals are in doubt regarding the intrusiveness of their physical functioning on the practice, temporary supervision should be considered so that they can get feedback from someone else about the appropriateness of their work. The feasibility of taking any of the above steps must be evaluated by each professional individually. Most importantly, professionals must be willing to be honest with themselves about the extent to which clients are being affected and be willing to take precautionary steps.

Burnout. A worker may become overly stressed at work because of the nature of the job, for example, too many meetings, administrative pressures, or a large client load. Too many demands on the professional's time often lead to symptoms of burnout and, as a result, the professional is less able to function effectively at work. For example, the mental health worker may overreact to comments made in the course of therapy and admit a client to hospital prematurely or unnecessarily. More seriously, the worker may underestimate the gravity of the client's complaints and fail to take seriously the presence of suicidal ideation. Although many professionals must work within conditions that promote burnout because of understaffing and economic restraints, they should seek ways to insulate themselves against such pressures as much as possible. This may include such alternatives as establishing a client waiting list and learning to say "no" to extra commitments. Delegating nonclinical responsibility to others is another method of reducing the work load and of reenergizing in those areas that matter the most, that is, client service.

How to Deal with Limits

When mental health professionals are faced with a situation that would require them to practice outside their sphere of practice, they have a number of alternative courses of action from which to choose. Possibilities that have already been discussed include skill expansion through ongoing professional development and external monitoring through supervision.

Referral to a professional competent in areas relevant for that client is another route to follow and is often the simplest and most efficient solution. In pursuing this route, the referring agent is responsible for arranging a smooth and positive transfer of the client. As part of this responsibility, the referring professional must be confident that the other individual does indeed have the necessary expertise and is receptive to taking on the client in question. The decision to refer the client elsewhere must be discussed within the context of the therapy session so that the client has an opportunity to deal with his or her feelings about this change and to decide whether to allow the referral to take place.

Dealing with limits may be more of a problem in small communities because of a shortage of alternatives. Since there may be a lack of professionals or specialty services in confined areas, professionals may be faced with a difficult ethical dilemma. While needing to stay within their limits, they also have a responsibility to provide service to a community with a multiplicity of problems. Peer consultation and ongoing professional development is critical under such circumstances so that clients can be treated in the best way possible. Discussions with colleagues should help to maintain some objectivity and to explore alternative ways of dealing with difficult cases. Even when sufficient resources are lacking in the community, professionals are advised not to experiment with new ways of doing things but to rely on the skills they already know they have. Without supervision from an expert in a "new" field, it is too easy for individuals to rationalize that they are doing something properly even though serious mistakes are being made.

METHODS OF CONTROL

In an attempt to ensure good quality service, a number of different regulatory mechanisms have developed over time. Methods of control have been implemented at different stages of practice. First, certain criteria must be passed before an individual can even use a professional title or practice independently in that field. Second, procedures have been developed to control the quality of the work once professional status has been granted. Methods of control are also in place to prevent individuals outside the profession from misrepresenting themselves as members of a particular discipline. Although there are difficulties inherent in all of these approaches, they have developed in an attempt to protect the client and professional alike.

Many different methods have evolved over the years. Methods that have already been covered in the chapter include formal training standards, clinical supervision, continuing education requirements, and the establishment of ethical codes and professional standards. In order for these methods to work, the individual has to exercise a reasonable amount of self-control over his or her actions. As a way of remaining accountable, professionals need (1) to reexamine and reevaluate their methods and manner of relating with clientele on a regular basis, (2) be open to and available for feedback from others, and (3) be willing to make adjustments in their actions when appropriate. Responsible professionals also have an obligation to keep a detailed record of their transactions rather than avoiding the scrutiny of others by refusing to document their actions.

Despite the emphasis on self-regulation and adherence to ethical practice, abuses still occur and have necessitated the development of external controls. One level of control is on a judicial level, with civil and criminal codes serving as "legitimate legal mechanisms to assure quality by holding practitioners liable for malpractice, negligence, or criminal practices, such as fraud.''[25] Other forms of quality control depend on self-regulation in the form of peer review, licensing boards, and so on.

Legal Control
In the mental health field, criminal charges are rarely brought although a practitioner can be charged with criminal negligence if it can be proven that his or her actions (or lack of action) resulted in the death of a client. Civil charges are much more frequent and can potentially lead to heavy fines and the revocation of a professional's license to practice. Actions at this level attempt to determine, first, whether a reasonable standard of care was utilized with a client, and second, whether the client suffered harm as a result of the services provided (e.g., loss of a job, marital breakup, exacerbation of symptoms). A major difficulty of such malpractice suits is establishing what a "reasonable" health care provider would have done under similar circumstances. In other words, negative treatment outcomes are not automatic evidence of malpractice if it can be demonstrated that the practitioner utilized reasonable care in attending to the client.

As of 1979, about 300 cases alleging negligence on the part of a therapist had been heard in the United States. These cases involved such matters as sexual abuse, wrongful commitment, physical assault, poor supervision, and premature release.[26] Most of the psychotherapists named in these cases were working in hospital settings.

There are many other potential risk areas for the practitioner and many of these are covered in detail in Chapter 3 (e.g., issues of confidentiality, informed consent, invasion of privacy, and going beyond one's competence). Within the therapeutic arena, practitioners need to exercise a lot of caution when using intrusive forms of treatment (e.g., electroconvulsive therapy, drugs). Risk is also high when dealing with suicidal or homicidal clients. In the past, abuses have also been frequent when dealing with the institutionalized or incompetent client and have led to numerous lawsuits as described in Chapter 3.

The professional also needs to be wary when he or she is not the direct service provider. Paraprofessionals or students who are supervised by licensed professionals are viewed as extensions of the professional and the supervisor can therefore be held liable for their actions. By virtue of being affiliated in business with other professionals, a partner in a group practice also risks being named as a codefendant in any legal actions against his or her partners.

Licensure and Certification
Like licensure, certification ensures that certain qualifications are met before practitioners can identify themselves with a restricted title. Unlike licensing, however, it does not prevent uncertified practitioners from offering services in competition with those who are fully certified to prac-

tice in an area. Although this method of accreditation is widely used as an alternative to licensure in the United States as well as in Canada, its inability to limit who can and cannot perform certain functions increases consumer risk.

In contrast, licensing acts are clear about areas of practice that *belong* to that professional group. Governing boards have also defined credentials necessary to secure such a license, and generally provide a national registry of those individuals who have the right to use a particular professional title. Regulations are also circulated to members outlining their various responsibilities, areas constituting unprofessional conduct, disciplinary methods, and so on.

Occupational licensing is one of the most restrictive regulatory methods in effect. Besides determining who is qualified to practice in a certain field, such organizations are given a lot of responsibility for disciplining errant members. In addition, they have the right to investigate individuals who attempt to practice in the field without the proper license, to order them to desist, or to arrange legal prosecution. Through the threat of sanctions, professional boards therefore make it costly for unlicensed people to make false claims and thus, hopefully, reduce the incidence of abuse.

As already mentioned, licensing boards also have the right to affect the quality of practice within its own discipline although their ability to do this is passive in nature rather than active. In other words, they do not actively seek out information on the practitioner to evaluate professional acceptability. Instead, they depend on information from external sources (e.g., consumers or professional colleagues) to sensitize them to possible abuse on the part of their members. For the consumer, this process provides a vehicle for obtaining retribution for improper practice without incurring the expense of a lengthy legal suit.

When the complaint comes from another member of the profession, the board may recommend that the complaining individual first address concerns to the professional in question. Approaching a colleague with a professional or ethical concern is not an easy matter and is probably avoided by many practitioners because of the bad feelings that may result. This step, however, is important for a number of reasons: first, to obtain more information about the professional's behavior to see if there really is cause for concern about the services provided; second, to determine if the professional is aware that he or she may be behaving inappropriately; and finally, to see if such awareness causes the professional to adjust the manner of practicing. If concerns still exist after approaching the professional, the appropriate step to take at this point is to advise the licensing board in writing of the concerns so that they can investigate the matter more thoroughly and take whatever steps are necessary to correct the problem. On the basis of their investigation, the complaint may be dismissed. Alternatively, the professional risks being dealt with in a number of punitive ways, depending on the seriousness of the infraction, for example, a verbal or written reprimand, a fine, or temporary suspension of the right to practice. For punitive as well as educational purposes, some boards also publish the name of the offending member and details of the complaint in their regular newsletter.

Not only do licensing boards provide advantages to the consumer because of internal and external monitoring, they also help to protect the reputation of the profession by excluding incompetents. Rules about advertising also protect the members from the stresses of marketplace competition and professionals are advised to adhere to whatever local standards have been developed regarding fees. The right to advertise, however, is in a state of revision as a result of rulings from the Federal Trade Commission.

On a more negative note, a number of complaints have been directed against licensing or certification bodies. Derbyshire[27] argues that within the medical field, for example, licensing does not really pose a serious risk for charlatans and that they have operated for long periods of time without detection. Their exposure is frequently a matter of accident and most do not even bother to forge a license. Similar difficulties exist in controlling the practice of psychology.[28] In a survey of 56 Illinois communities in 1981, Beach and Goebel compared 1300 advertisements under the heading "psychologist" with state records of psychologists. Beach and Goebel stated: "Results showed that almost 40% of the advertisements surveyed were illegal. Twenty percent of individual practice advertisements and 80% of the group practice advertisements were illegal."

Hogan[29] adds that licensing may actually exacerbate, rather than control, the problem of quackery. Historical data have indicated that quackery has traditionally flourished when the supply of practitioners is restricted. Young[30] reported that fraudulent practitioners made as much as $2 billion from innocent clients in 1967.

Criticisms have also been directed against professional boards because of the criteria they have established for licensure. Hogan[31] has argued that evaluation techniques used by licensing boards bear only accidental relationships to competent practice and do not satisfy validity requirements. In addition, Rayack[32] reported that licensing boards vary their registration criteria in accordance with factors that are irrelevant to competence. More specifically, Rayack indicated that licensing boards fail more applicants, despite their qualifications, when labor market conditions worsen in order to reduce the number of professionals entering the market and thereby strengthen the competitive position of those already licensed. Licensing can also cause problems by becoming overly inclusive regarding the types of services that fall within the professional monopoly. Despite the self-serving advantages of establishing such monopolies, the public may be denied appropriate services from paraprofessionals who have sufficient expertise to function in clearly defined areas.

Another criticism of professional boards is their failure to take appropriate action against incompetent members. Existing evidence regarding this "failure" has been gathered mainly in the fields of medicine and law. Derbyshire[33] indicated that in some areas of the United States, no disciplinary procedures exist at all. At the time of his study, Derbyshire estimated that 5 percent of all physicians (i.e., 22,500) were incompetent due to such factors as drug addiction, alcoholism, senescence, or reliance on obsolete techniques, even though less than 1 percent were actually disciplined.

There is a number of reasons for minimal disciplinary action on the part of professional boards. Practical reasons include lack of funding and insufficient professional staff to carry out thorough investigations. In addition, inadequate definition of proper practice and lack of agreement across geographical boundaries or within a professional group itself serve to hamper procedures.

The composition of a professional board also has a strong effect on its effectiveness. Hogan[34] reports that boards that are dominated by same-professional members (e.g., nurses dominating nursing discipline boards) are less effective than boards that include individuals from other disciplines. Dolan and Urban[35] found that a mixture of professionals makes it difficult for committee members to reach a consensus regarding what actions should be taken which, in itself, may be a deterrent to disciplinary action.

Concerns regarding professional self-regulation have also been established within the legal profession. Despite its distinction from the mental health field, these concerns have relevance for the clinical practitioner because similar problems can obviously arise in any self-regulated discipline. More specifically, Carlin[36] found that a number of different factors were taken into consideration by disciplinary boards in deciding how to respond to an errant member. Carlin concluded that their reaction to complaints depended on such things as the amount of money that was involved in the case, the number of times a particular offense was committed by that individual, and the amount of public exposure that the case received. Carlin concluded that the bar appeared less concerned with the moral integrity of the individual professional than with preserving its public image and reputation.

In addition to resistance on the part of a professional board to sanction a member, colleagues of incompetent professionals may "cover up" episodes of misconduct and honor with what Derbyshire[37] refers to as the "curtain of silence." Professionals strongly resist testifying against each other even when personally convinced that their colleague is incompetent to the point of engaging in dangerous practices.

Work settings such as hospitals may prefer to "export" their problems rather than involve themselves in potentially costly termination procedures and lawsuits. In order to accomplish this goal, incompetent practitioners may be guaranteed excellent references to assist them in procuring work elsewhere and thus rid the employer of any administrative hassle.

Peer Review

Peer review has evolved as a professional auditing method to ensure that services provided to the public are satisfactory. Within the medical field, auditing was proposed as far back as 1914 in an attempt to evaluate the basis for surgical failure.[38] In an attempt to improve the environment in which they had to work (i.e., hospitals), surgeons were also instrumental in developing hospital standards.[39] Implementation of such standards eventually fell under the responsibility of the Joint Commission on Accreditation of Hospitals (JCAH) although this commission was initially more concerned about defining structural requirements than quality care. The JCAH has also been challenged for limiting its membership to physicians and excluding other health care staff who are fully qualified in their respective fields (e.g., nurses, psychologists).

Since practitioners insisted that their work only be evaluated by individuals in the same field, the term "peer review" was coined. Unlike other forms of quality control, peer review was designed to evaluate a provider's performance and not just the ability to demonstrate knowledge on a formal examination. In the mental health field, the need for this type of quality became evident in the 1970s because of professional abuses of prepaid health care plans, "primarily in the residential treatment centers for the emotionally disturbed."[40]

As a way of controlling this problem, Professional Standards Review Organizations (PSROs) were established throughout the country to review the appropriateness of services delivered under Medicare and similar health care programs. Because of abuses of another important health care plan (Civilian Health and Medical Plan of the Uniformed Services [CHAMPUS]), the Department of Defense "entered into contracts with the American Psychological Association and the American Psychiatric Association to design and implement independent national systems of peer review for mental health services."[41] Interest has also been expressed "in having the Department of Defense seriously consider negotiating a similar peer review contract with the American Nurses' Association."[42] In 1977, another accreditation program was established (the Council on Accreditation of Services for Families and Children [CASFC]). The standards established by the CASFC were "based on a social work, rather than on a medical, model."[43] The council also recommended that peer reviews be "conducted by volunteers who are senior staff members of social service agencies."

On the basis of work done by these various organizations, recommendations regarding peer review and how it should be conducted have been established. For example, the CHAMPUS regulations indicated that reviews should be primarily retrospective in nature, that is, focused on work that had already been done. Reviewers, however, may be asked to provide an opinion about the necessity for ongoing care in order to determine whether benefits should continue. Specific review points were also defined so that "if mental health outpatient care reached a specified number of sessions (8, 24, 40, and 60), the cases would be subject to review screening."[44] Manuals have been developed for reviewers as well as reviewees so that they would have some guidelines with regard to the review procedure and what was expected of them.

Although some practitioners may view such a procedure as threatening and possibly unnecessary, it has become an acceptable method for evaluating direct service, especially when health care insurance plans are involved. Since they were not developed for use as a training technique (i.e., for individuals not yet qualified), peer reviews are generally not implemented until the individual is already practicing in the field.

In order to make judgments about the manner in which a professional is practicing, a number of assumptions have to be made. The development of appropriate peer review standards hinges on the ability to identify and objectively measure factors that are essential to good quality service, a goal that is difficult to achieve because of problems of definition as well as measurement.

Such measures often include an evaluation of the practitioner's behavior in comparison with the norm for that professional group. Another possibility is taking outcome measures in which the professional's competence is assumed from the effect he or she has on the client. Outcome as well as process measures are difficult in the mental health field because the practitioner is not always dealing with overt, and therefore observable, behavior. Even when the behavior in question is observable, qualitative judgments often have to be made as to whether the client's actions are mentally "healthy" or inappropriate. The context in which the behavior occurs may also have to be taken into account, further adding to the complication of getting fair measures and establishing the normative standard of care.

As described by Theaman,[45] the primary function of peer reviews "is not to set standards for the profession but to monitor adherence to standards the profession sets for itself." In order to accomplish this goal, reviewers obviously have to take into account professional codes that have already been established for that field. More specifically, the insurance plans expect the reviewers not only to give an opinion regarding the appropriateness of the services provided but also to comment on whether they are really necessary. One obvious problem that arises for reviewers is whether to focus on the terms "appropriate" and "necessary" or to base their opinions on the utilization of usual and customary procedures. For PSRO reviewers, they are specifically asked to determine whether a practice is using "usual, customary or reasonable" methods. "*Usual* is defined as a practice in keeping with the (professional's) general modus operandi. *Customary* refers to the range of usual practices within a given geographic area. *Reasonable* is defined as a practice that is usual and customary or, in the opinion of the PSRO, is justifiable in the special circumstances of the specific case in question."[46]

Added to the problem of establishing reasonable criteria for making fair judgments, peer reviews have been criticized because of confidentiality issues although attempts have been made to minimize this problem by protecting the client's name, by informing the client of this requirement before services begin, and by exercising strict control over the client's peer review file.

Other criticisms relate to the mechanics of implementing such reviews, for example, how to assign cases to reviewers, how to pick reviewers, and how to decide when a review is necessary. Even when reviews have been done, they have been criticized for being overly lax. Although reviewers may recommend against coverage of future care, they tend to be extremely "reluctant to limit or deny benefits for past care."[47] Despite these various problems, however, peer review at least makes an attempt to look at direct service and does take a more *active* role in trying to ensure competence in its professional body than do other methods of control. In addition, it has probably been instrumental in improving record keeping on the part of the professional. Health providers in many hospital settings, for example, have had to adapt to standardized record-keeping systems (e.g., the problem-oriented medical record). Through this approach, an ongoing problem list is available for every client with individualized plans set out for dealing with each of the current problems on the list. In itself, this type of recording helps to keep practitioners more accountable for their actions and makes client files much easier to review.

REFERENCES

1. Ontario Association of Professional Social Workers (1975). OAPSW practice standards for social work practice in the health field. *Ontario Association of Professional Social Workers, 3*, 18.
2. DeLeon, P. H., Kjervik, D. K., Kraut, A. G., & VandenBos, G. R. (1985). Psychology and nursing: A natural alliance. *American Psychologist, 40*(11), 1154.
3. Young, H. H. (1982). A brief history of quality assurance and peer review. *Professional Psychology, 13*(1), 9.
4. Ibid.
5. Herbsleb, J. D., Sales, B. D., & Overcast, T. D. (1985). Challenging licensure and certification. *American Psychologist, 40*(11), 1166.
6. Messick, S. (1967). Personality measurement and college performance. In D. N. Jackson & S. Messick (Eds.), *Problems in human assessment* (p. 834). New York: McGraw-Hill.

7. Ingram, R. E. (1983). The GRE in the graduate admissions process: Is how it is used justified by the evidence of its validity? *Professional Psychology, 14*(6), 711.

8. Strupp, H. H. (1976). Clinical psychology, irrationalism, and the erosion of excellence. *American Psychologist, 31*(8), 561.

9. Flexner, A. (1925). *Medical education: A comparative study* (p. 113). New York: Macmillan.

10. Whitehead, A. N. (1929). *The aims of education* (p. 46). New York: Macmillan.

11. Peterson, D. R. (1968). The Doctor of Psychology program at the University of Illinois. *American Psychologist, 23,* 511.

12. Flexner, *Medical education.*

13. Whitehead, *The aims of education.*

14. Stern, S. (1984). Professional training and professional competence: A critique of current thinking. *Professional Psychology: Research and Practice, 15*(2), 232.

15. Tymchuk, A. J., Drapkin, R., Major-Kingsley, S., et al. (1982). Ethical decision making and psychologists' attitudes toward training in ethics. *Professional Psychology, 13*(3), 412.

16. Jacobs, D. F. (1974). The agony and ecstasy of professional role change. In A. I. Rabin (Ed.), *Clinical psychology: Issues of the seventies* (p. 75). East Lansing: Michigan State University Press.

17. Lassen, C. L. (1982). The Colorado Medicare study: Perspective of the peer review committee. *Professional Psychology 13*(1), 105.

18. DeLeon, Psychology and nursing, 1157.

19. Ibid., 1158.

20. Cohen, R. J. (1979). *Malpractice: A guide for mental health professionals.* New York: Macmillan.

21. Norcross, J. C., & Stevenson, J. F. (1984). How shall we judge ourselves? Training evaluation in clinical psychology programs. *Professional Psychology: Research and Practice, 15*(4), 497.

22. Koocher, G. P. (1979). Credentialing in psychology: Close encounters with competence. *American Psychologist, 34,* 696.

23. Newbrough, J. R. (1980). Community psychology and the public interest. *American Journal of Community Psychology, 8,* 1.

24. Norcross & Stevenson, How shall we judge ourselves?

25. Zaro, J. S., & Kilburg, R. R. (1982). The role of APA in the development of quality assurance in psychological practice. *Professional Psychology, 13*(1), 113.

26. Trebilcock, M. J., & Shaul, J. (1983). Regulating the quality of psychotherapeutic services: A Canadian perspective. *Law and Human Behavior, 7*(2/3), 265.

27. Derbyshire, R. C. (1983). How effective is medical self-regulation? *Law and Human Behavior, 7*(2/3), 193.

28. Beach, D. A., & Goebel, J. B. (1983). Who is a psychologist? A survey of Illinois Yellow Page directories. *Professional Psychology: Research and Practice, 14*(6), 797.

29. Hogan, D. B. (1983). The effectiveness of licensing: History, evidence and recommendations. *Law and Human Behavior, 7*(2/3), 117.

30. Young, J. H. (1967). *The medical messiahs: A social history of health quack-*

ery in 20th century America (p. vii). Princeton, NJ: Princeton University Press.

31. Hogan, The effectiveness of licensing.

32. Rayack, E. (1967). *Power and American medicine: The economics of the American Medical Association* (p. 147). Cleveland: World Publishing Co.

33. Derbyshire, R. C. (1969). *Medical licensure in the United States.* Baltimore: Johns Hopkins University Press.

34. Hogan, The effectiveness of licensing.

35. Dolan, A. K., & Urban, N. D. (1983). The determinants of the effectiveness of medical disciplinary boards: 1960-1977. *Law and Human Behavior, 7*(2/3), 203.

36. Carlin, J. E. (1966). *Lawyers' ethics: A survey of the New York City bar.* New York: Russell Sage Foundation.

37. Derbyshire, Medical self-regulation.

38. Young, History of quality assurance, 10.

39. Crosby, K. G. (1982). Accreditation and associated quality assurance efforts. *Professional Psychology, 13*(1), 132.

40. Willens, J., & DeLeon, P. H. (1982). Political aspects of peer review. *Professional Psychology, 13*(1), 24.

41. Young, History of quality assurance, 12.

42. Willens, Political aspects, 24.

43. Crosby, Accreditation, 138.

44. Clairborn, W. L., Biskin, B. H., & Friedman, L. S. (1982). CHAMPUS and quality assurance. *Professional Psychology, 13*(1), 42.

45. Theaman, M. (1984). The impact of peer review on professional practice. *American Psychologist, 39*(4), 412.

46. Rosenberg, A. M., & Theaman, M. (1982). The Professional Standards Review Committee: Form and function. *Professional Psychology, 13*(1), 121.

47. Clairborn, CHAMPUS, 46.

Clients' Rights

3

Up to this point, the focus of the book has been on the obligations of the professional to society, his or her own professional body, and the client. In this chapter, the focus changes to that of clients' rights. Clients have the same basic rights as other citizens in a democratic society, although these rights frequently are not respected by the professional or exercised by the client. Except under clearly defined circumstances, a client does not lose civil or political rights simply by being admitted to a health care center for treatment. Although the right to freedom of movement may be restricted temporarily if admitted for treatment involuntarily, the client still has the right to adequate treatment, informed consent, private communication, and other basic human and civil rights. If a client believes rights are being violated unjustly, the client has the right to due process of law in order to appeal and possibly revoke any restrictions placed upon him or her.

Cobb[1] refers to three principles underlying human rights in a democratic society. In accordance with the "principle of positive presumption," each citizen is presumed to have certain inalienable rights. "The inalienability of rights means that rights of citizens are presumed to obtain in the absence of sufficient cause for their denial."[2] These rights cannot be removed without due process of law, which Cobb refers to as the second principle underlying human and civil rights. As Cobb states:

> Sufficient cause for abridgement of any right must be determined by legally defined and established procedures involving the elements of notice, right to counsel, fair hearing and right of appeal. . . . A corollary to the principle of due process is that the denial or abridgement of rights must be specific and separable; and if the denial embraces a range of rights, then this must be specified in the judgment and sufficient cause must be given for the range of application.[3]

In other words, an individual should not automatically lose other rights by virtue of losing one, unless there is justification for doing this. Cobb also refers to a third principle, that of "instrumental protection." This latter principle encompasses the laws and institutions established by society to protect and regulate their citizens' rights in various areas.[4]

The need to acknowledge a client's rights is upheld by all professionals involved in health care and is typically addressed in most ethical codes on professional behavior. Some health care facilities have developed mental health information services to inform clients of their rights and of a professional's obligations toward them. As another way of accomplishing this goal, other agencies have hired an ombudsman (or client advocate), whose function is to inform clients of their rights and to intercede for them if their rights are being violated. Other facilities have chosen to post information on client rights on bulletin boards for examination by their clients.

In spite of these attempts, a number of studies conducted on clients' rights continue to reinforce the view that professionals are relatively ignorant of this area or, at best, are confused between rights, duties, and obligations.[5] It is also fairly common for professionals and the public to confuse human or moral rights (e.g., the right to freedom from discrimination) with civil rights (e.g., the right to adequate health care, the right to refuse treatment). In many localities, specific human rights may evolve into civil rights by passing legislation to that effect, further adding to the confusion in this area. In general, professionals tend to underestimate the civil rights available to a client and frequently communicate such a false impression to their clients. A study by Swoboda et al. demonstrated "that a significant proportion of psychologists, psychiatrists, and social workers were unaware of two of the most basic laws that apply to their profession, one providing for the right of privileged communications and another requiring the reporting of child abuse."[6] In a study by Tancredi and Clark,[7] psychiatrists, psychiatric residents, nurses, and social workers were questioned regarding a client's rights under the following categories: voluntary admission to hospital, emergency involuntary admission, and nonemergency involuntary admission. Across all professionals sampled, there were many gaps of knowledge in each of these areas.

In an attempt to reduce the occurrence of violations in the area of client rights, a number of different associations have proposed a bill of rights for mental health clients. One of the earliest of these was a set of mental health standards proposed by Ralph Nader's Center for the Study of Responsive Law. The Center's recommendations were as follows:

Any person in a mental institution shall have the right

(1) to refuse drugs.
(2) to refuse electric shock.
(3) to refuse insulin shock.
(4) to refuse lobotomy.
(5) to remain silent.
(6) to remain fully clothed.
(7) to be allowed access to toilet facilities upon request.
(8) to refuse to participate in any research projects.
(9) to be given a copy of the statute under which he is being held upon request.
(10) to apply for habeas corpus and to be given detailed written instructions on how to apply for it.
(11) to refuse to be photographed or fingerprinted.
(12) to vote.
(13) to hold a driver's license.
(14) to refuse to work for the institution. If the person works voluntarily, he must be paid the minimum legal hourly wage.

(15) to send and receive uncensored and unopened mail, and to be given adequate writing paper, pencils, envelopes, and stamps.
(16) to have access to a telephone between the hours of 9 a.m. and 9 p.m. Local calls shall be allowed without charge, and the person shall be allowed long distance calls if he can pay the institution for them or can charge them to another number.
(17) to receive any visitors between the hours of 9 a.m. and 9 p.m.
(18) to be allowed to have unlimited access to his own money unless a conservator has been appointed, and to keep as much money in his personal possession as he deems necessary.
(19) to wear his own clothes and keep his own toilet articles.
(20) to have adequate private storage space for his personal effects.
(21) to be allowed to purchase personal articles such as variety store items.
(22) to be allowed at least two hours of physical exercise each day outside of his ward and, if the weather permits, outside of a building.[8]

The center also developed standards that specified how to keep clients informed of their rights, what they can do if their rights are violated, regulations on the use of seclusion or mechanical restraints, transfers to other institutions, confidentiality, informed consent, and so on.

Despite the availability of such standards, however, many professionals still remain unaware of clients' rights. Clients also remain basically ignorant regarding their rights and, as such, do not frequently exercise them. In addition to lacking knowledge about their legal and moral rights, they may "lack the capacity to exercise these rights. Clients are unorganized or are usually in health institutions for a relatively short time and are in an extremely vulnerable position, having to rely totally on the care provided by the institution against which they might wish to exercise rights."[9] In addition, "in learning the patients' role or as some would have it 'the sick role,' patients take their cues from health care personnel. Health workers are viewed as experienced and in control; if they ignore patients' rights in their everyday work, patients will tend to feel their own rights are not 'legitimate.'"[10] Clients having a grievance may also be reluctant to complain because they may not know where to direct their complaint.

This chapter is therefore included to familiarize professionals working within the health care system of clients' rights, under the assumption that the professional has a legal and ethical obligation to respect these rights. The chapter covers the following clients' rights: right to confidentiality, informed consent, and adequate treatment, in addition to the common civil rights granted the average citizen.

RIGHT TO CONFIDENTIALITY

Following some historical background on the confidentiality issue, this section goes on to contrast two frequently confused principles (confidentiality and privileged communication), to describe exceptions to the confidentiality rule, potential risk areas for the professional and client, and consequences for improper disclosure of confidential information.

The belief in a client's right to privacy has evolved over time for a number of reasons. In some cases, the revelation that a particular individual requires professional assistance for emotional problems can potentially lead to prejudicial attitudes and differential treatment on the part of friends and family. The stigma often attached to mental illness can significantly interfere with employment and educational opportunities as well. According to Westin

> the outward flow of medical data has enormous impact on people's lives. It affects decisions on whether they are hired or fired; whether they can secure business licenses and life insurance; whether they are permitted to drive cars; whether they are placed under police surveillance or labelled a security risk; or even whether they can get nominated for and elected to political office.[11]

For these reasons, professions that provide mental health care have developed a set of ethical standards in support of a client's right to confidentiality. Such standards usually include rules regarding storage of confidential material and conditions under which such information can be disseminated. In most circumstances, reports on clients should only be released after an appropriate consent is given by the client or if the client poses an immediate risk to self or others. In the latter situation, restrictions also exist regarding the appropriate recipients of such information; for example, public authorities or mental health providers. In cases where clinical data are used in research or as a teacher aid, the client's identity should be adequately disguised.

Regrettably, a number of practical difficulties have not been addressed in many of the professional standards that have been developed. For example, no mention is made as to *when* confidentiality becomes an issue for the practitioner. Does this issue become active only after the first face-to-face contact with the client or as early as the first phone call? This concern arises, for example, if a member of a client's family calls prior to the professional's first official contact with the client to determine if the individual has made an appointment.

Another problem is that many of the legal statutes regarding confidentiality only apply to individual contacts with a client. In most states, protective guidelines have not been developed for clients seen in either group or family therapy. As a result, any information given to the therapist by one individual in the presence of a third party is not legally confidential. There is also some dispute over what type of client–therapist information needs to be kept confidential. According to the New Zealand courts, for example, a physician is obligated to keep confidential "only what the patient communicated to the physician by means of writing, words or signs, and not to what the doctor himself saw when examining the patient, nor what he communicated to the patient, including his diagnosis."[12]

Confusion may also arise regarding the types of external controls exercised over health care providers in the area of confidentiality. Typically more controls exist if the professional is working in a health care facility rather than independently. In Ontario, for example, professionals working within a psychiatric facility are legally bound by the Mental Health Act[13] to respect a client's right to confidentiality in order to avoid legal sanctions. This act is not considered to apply when they are working independently. Instead, independent practitioners are bound primarily by their professional code of ethics and the threat of professional sanctions for improper conduct.

There are also many acceptable exclusions to the confidentiality rule that are bound to be confusing and unclear to the client and professional alike, particularly as these exclusions may vary across jurisdictions.

Confidentiality and Privileged Communication

Confidentiality is "a general standard of conduct that obliges a professional not to divulge information about a client to anyone."[14] Privileged communication, on the other hand, refers to a "rule in evidence law that provides a litigant with the right to withhold evidence in a legal proceeding that was originally communicated in confidence."[15] In other words, standards on confidentiality have evolved to protect the client's private communications outside the courtroom whereas privilege protects the client from having private information divulged within the courtroom.

The underlying rationale for testimonial privilege has evolved from the assumption that "the benefit to justice in allowing the testimony is outweighed by the injury to the relationship where the parties, fearing later disclosure, do not make full and adequate disclosure to one another. The argument for a psychotherapist–patient privilege essentially rests on the claim that it is the quality of the relationship between patient and therapist which is the catalyst for psychotherapeutic change"[16] and the assumption that the relationship could deteriorate if disclosures are made.

In many states, privileged communication was extended to therapist–client contacts in the mid–1970s in accordance with Rule 504 of the Federal Rules of Evidence. With regard to client–therapist privilege, Rule 504 states:

> a patient has a privilege to refuse to disclose and to prevent any other person from disclosing confidential communications, made for the purposes of diagnosis or treatment of his mental or emotional condition, including drug addiction; among himself, his psychotherapist, or per-

sons who are participating in the diagnosis or treatment under the direction of the psychotherapist including members of the patient's family.[17]

In some localities, privilege regarding client–therapist contacts is only allowed if the therapist is a medical doctor, thereby excluding such professions as psychology, nursing, and social work. In initiating therapeutic or diagnostic contact with a client, the nonmedical professional must inform clients whether or not their contacts are classified as privileged. In contrast with the United States, privileged communication in Canada only exists in the area of lawyer–client communications. With the exception of civil proceedings in the province of Quebec, there is no law that allows a mental health practitioner the right to withhold confidential information about a client in a court proceeding. The only exception to this legislation is in the case of court-appointed marriage conciliators in which a counselor is trying to assist the parties in reconciling their differences. Professionals who take on this role are not generally put in a position where they have to divulge information in court; otherwise, it would be extremely difficult for them to function as mediators. The therapist is granted absolute privilege in these cases in that he or she can refuse to divulge communications that have been made, even if both clients give consent to do so.

In locations that grant client–therapist privilege, the right to have information revealed in court is the client's choice and not the professional's. For example, if the client gives consent to having his or her interactions with a particular professional revealed in court, the professional has no legal recourse to refuse and may be punished for doing so; that is:

> clients, not therapists, are protected under privilege statutes. Once a client waives his/her privilege, a therapist is legally obligated to testify (unless the therapist is willing to assume the possible penalty for violation of the law by refusing on ethical grounds to break confidentiality).[18]

Privilege may also be claimed by the client's guardian or, if the client is deceased, by a personal representative.

The client's privilege may be waived by the court in a situation wherein the client wishes to use his or her psychological status as part of a legal defense (e.g., insanity plea). The client should also be aware that confidentiality can be broken and privilege waived in cases of child abuse, dangerousness to others, involuntary commitment, and court-ordered examinations.

Practitioners not granted privilege are advised to protect their clients' rights as best as they can by divulging only that information that is specifically relevant to the problem being presented in court. Only formal notes need be entered as evidence and the professional is not expected to reveal personal notes on the client, even if the client requests that this be done. To avoid the possibility of misunderstanding, notes on clients should be written in a clear and concise manner, placing proper emphasis on different problem areas and taking care not to include opinions and diagnostic impressions that cannot be substantiated. The report should also differentiate between that information provided by the client and the interpretations made by the therapist. If, during a court proceeding, the professional believes he or she has reasonable justification for withholding personal information about a client, the professional can typically ask to communicate that information to the judge in private so that the judge can decide whether or not it is critical to have the information made public before the court. The Illinois Code (Section 10) specifically includes

> a provision for an *in camera* examination of the requested evidence—that is, a preliminary review by the courts to decide whether the material subpoenaed must be produced for admission into evidence. Thus, the court has the opportunity to review the material sought and make a finding as to the relevance, probative value, prejudicial or inflammatory quality, availability of other avenues of proof, and the balancing of the interest of enhancing justice as opposed to injury to the therapeutic relationship.[19]

Exceptions to the Confidentiality Rule

There are many occasions under which confidential information about a client can be communicated to a secondary source, with or without explicit consent. The client should be informed whenever this occurs of the exact nature of what is disclosed, for what purpose, and to whom. Clients should also be informed whenever there is the risk that a decision about themselves may be based on a review of information in their files by such an external source, for example, as an insurance company. To provide some protection to the client in this area, as well as to provide guidelines to health care providers, Gilmore has cited ten principles developed by the Canadian Health Record Association that should be followed when dealing with a client's health records:

(1) All individuals, institutions and organizations maintaining, handling or processing health information shall:
    a) have written policies regulating access to, release of, transmittal of and destruction of health information;
    b) educate all their employees with regard to maintaining confidentiality of information, and have them sign a pledge of confidentiality. This procedure shall apply also to researchers, volunteers, contracted individuals and employees of firms and corporations performing contract work.

(2) Health information shall be accessed or released only for:
   a) direct care use—when requested by a physician or health care facility responsible for the direct care of the individual;
   b) individual use—when authorized by the individual or his legally authorized representative;
   c) secondary use—when requested by properly authorized persons or agencies;
   d) legal use—when required by law.
(3) Requests for confidential information should be in writing; however, policies governing verbal requests shall be outlined by the individual institution.
(4) Any authorization for release of information shall be an original and specific as to source, content, recipient, purpose and time limitations. Reproductions of original signatures shall not be accepted.
(5) Information released to authorized persons shall not be made available to any other party without further authorization.
(6) Health information and records shall be kept in a secured area and not left unattended in areas accessible to unauthorized individuals.
(7) In research, individual confidentiality shall be maintained in the handling of information and any reporting or publication of findings.
(8) When health information is sent to any service organization for processing, the contract shall include an undertaking by the recipient that confidentiality will be maintained.
(9) The authorized destruction of health information shall be by effective shredding, burning or erasure.
(10) Any misuse of health information shall be reported to the responsible authority.[20]

Client disclosures can usually be made in cases of public safety, legitimate societal interest, governmental and agency administration, involuntary commitment proceedings, research studies, court proceedings, and direct care intervention.

Public Safety. In accordance with statutory mandate, the appropriate government agency must be notified whenever there is evidence of such diverse problems as child abuse, a communicable disease, gunshot wounds, and so on. In the case of child abuse, "reasonable" suspicion of abuse is usually sufficient to justify a violation of confidentiality. A number of states also insist that proper authorities be notified whenever an individual is considered sexually dangerous, uses certain drugs, has an abortion, has a specific congenital deformity, and so on. Reporting in these instances typically does not require consent. Such compulsory reporting is considered justified in that it serves to protect the public by controlling certain inappropriate behaviors as well as certain disease entities. Compulsory reporting requirements should be communicated to prospective clients from the outset so they know what limits exist before making a commitment to the service.

A practitioner also is obligated to violate confidentiality if he or she has reason to believe that a client poses a danger to self or others so that the proper authorities can have the client apprehended and placed in protective custody. The obligation to break confidentiality only applies when there is the risk of physical harm to a person, however, and not simply the risk of financial loss or property damage.

In addition, when there is "reasonable cause" to believe that a crime has been committed, either by a professional or one of the professional's clients, a search warrant can be issued allowing enforcement officers full access to all client records. In these circumstances, there is no legal obligation to notify any of the clients of the search and subsequent violation of their privacy.

Legitimate Societal Interest. It also has been generally accepted that society has the legitimate right to personal information regarding a public figure. For example, in 1972, the American public felt it had the right to know that one of its vice-presidential candidates had been treated for psychiatric problems. Failure to inform the public of this information prior to nomination caused him to withdraw from the Democratic ticket when his psychiatric history was eventually disclosed.

Involuntary Commitment Proceedings. In the case of involuntary commitment, confidential information about a client can be released without consent in order to protect the client from himself or herself or other individuals that appear to be at risk because of the client. In this instance, the professional can disclose whatever information is necessary to support the contention that the client is potentially dangerous, that the client is in need of mental health services, and that such services are not being accepted voluntarily.

Research Studies. It also is common practice for confidential data from a client's record to be released for the purpose of research if certain conditions have been met. The American Hospital Association has listed a number of determinants that should be considered before releasing such information to a third party for research purposes.

(1) The importance of the project's purpose outweighs any nominal risk to individual privacy rights.
(2) The proposed methodology does not violate any limitations under which the medical record information was collected.
(3) The safeguards are adequate to protect the confidentiality and integrity of the medical record and information therein.
(4) The further use or redisclosure of any medical record information in patient-identifiable, physician-identifiable, or hospital-identifiable form requires the written consent of the chief executive officer of the hospital, who shall exercise due regard for the rights of others affected.

(5) The medical records of the hospital are a suitable source of information for the purpose for which they are to be used.

(6) The third party makes appropriate commitments for safeguarding the patient's privacy, including, in some instances, an agreement to refrain from contacting the patient or others.[21]

The primary concern is, by necessity, the client's right to privacy. To assure that this right is not violated in the process of doing the research study, precautions must be taken to ensure that the client is not identified throughout or after the study unless the client gives an informed consent, authorizing the release of specific information about himself or herself.

Third-Party Disclosures. Many government and health-related agencies have ready access to client information for purposes of administration, program planning, and program evaluation. Legal precedents have supported the right of such agencies to client files under the rationale that such access is necessary to ensure the quality of client care. In the state of Illinois, for example, no consent is required to look at records for such purposes as "funding, accreditation, audit, licensure, statistical compilation, research, or evaluation," assuming that "personally identifiable data are removed."[22]

One of the most frequent requests for client information comes from insurance companies that are paying for a portion of the psychiatric service. Problems have arisen when private practitioners have objected to their files being examined by health insurance companies for auditing purposes.[23] Although it has been generally accepted that such companies have the right to audit a professional's records to prevent the abuse of health insurance plans, mental health providers are recommending that some attempt be made to withhold the *content* of their client contacts while at the same time allowing the auditor to examine the *frequency* of such contacts. Professionals would also be wise to obtain informed consent from their clients before allowing the release of private information to the health insurance companies.

With the increasing emphasis on quality control, audits are also increasing in frequency as a way of ensuring that professionals are behaving appropriately with clients. Many government institutions that employ mental health providers are insisting on regular audits of their staff as part of their accountability requirements. As part of the audit, professionals are usually required to submit such information as frequency and length of sessions with a particular client, conditions justifying treatment, and a description of treatment approaches used. Practitioners who work under this type of accountability system are required to advise all clients that their files might have to be audited in the future. At the time of the audit, the client should have the opportunity to review the material that is to be shown to the audit committee to ensure that the professional is presenting an accurate picture. For the sake of confidentiality, all attempts should be made to protect the client's privacy in the course of the audit by withholding the client's name and by impressing on the committee the need to keep the information to themselves.

In addition to health insurance companies, other businesses with a legitimate interest in the client's record can have access as well. For example, practitioners who are involved in the medical treatment of a client making a claim for workers' compensation benefits are required to provide diagnostic and treatment reports on that client so that the board has sufficient information to adjudicate the client's claim. The health care provider does not necessarily need a consent from the client giving permission to disclose this information.

Most "third parties" are only able to obtain specific information about clients on their informed consent to the release of such information. On receipt of a duly signed release, a professional or an agency may be asked to release information to the client's lawyer, another agency, or a nonstaff physician or mental health professional. For an individual declared incompetent, information can be freely released to that individual's guardian. The guardian has the right to release private information regarding the client to third parties by way of an informed consent.

In the case of minors, rules vary widely from one jurisdiction to another regarding the release of information to third parties, including parents or guardians. In Illinois, for example, minors have the right to confidential communications from the age of 12. More specifically, the Illinois law states that the following individuals can have access to a client's file[24]:

1. Parents or guardians of a recipient under the age of 12
2. Recipients 12 or older
3. Persons authorized in writing by a recipient aged 12 or older
4. Parents and guardians of recipients between the ages of 12 and 13 if the recipient or the therapist does not object

A parent of a child between the ages of 12 and 18 has the right to petition the court for access if the child or therapist refuses access. The court must then decide between the rights of the child and the rights of the parent, keeping in mind the best interests of the child in question.

As a general rule, regulations regarding minors vary according to age and the degree of "emancipation" from parents. Emancipation is often defined in terms of the adolescent's economic and psychological independence from parental figures. A minor's right to privacy has also been recommended when he or she has initiated the therapeutic relationship independently of parents. Even within the context of family therapy, a therapist is discouraged from disclosing information to other family members if that information was given to him or her by the adolescent or child in private.

Court Proceedings. As described in earlier sections, confidential information must be released to the court upon request if privileged communication does not exist between the client and therapist. In addition, communications between a client and a professional is not privileged in situations where a professional's involvement with the client is at the request of a third party such as the court, an employer, or a protection agency. For example, a child protection agency may refer a parent for therapy as a necessary requirement for keeping the children in the family. In such situations, the agency has the right to information on the client's progress and mental state throughout the various contacts with the professional. The client has no right to expect this information to be kept confidential because of the circumstances under which he or she was referred. The client does have the right to be informed prior to giving any information that such communications may be revealed to the referring agency and can potentially have negative implications for the individual. For the client's protection, however, the information in the report should be discussed with him or her beforehand so that inaccurate statements can be challenged and changed if appropriate.

Intra-Agency Personnel. The records of either inpatients or outpatients may be seen by any member of a health team who is involved in that client's care, and no signed authorization is required. A problem regarding confidentiality may arise in large agencies in that clients' records are readily available to many other personnel besides direct health care providers; for example, secretarial staff, filing clerks, laboratory technicians, and students.

In many settings, the client is treated within a team context in that many individuals from a variety of professional groups have input into the diagnosis and treatment of a particular client. This team approach to therapy necessitates regular case conferences to keep updated on the client's assessment findings and treatment progress. At such conferences, information given by a client to a staff may be shared with other members of the health care team as well as students who may be attending the conferences as part of their training. Although conferences are standard practice and certainly necessary when several different professionals are involved in a client's care, the client may not be fully aware of the degree to which personal information will be shared with other people. Such "free" disclosure can create particular problems when a client has opened up about a sensitive or intimate problem with a trusted staff only to discover that everyone on the unit knows of the problem the next day.

In large institutions, auxiliary staff need to be specially trained in these ethical areas, not only in keeping information confidential but also in informing the client as to the limits of confidentiality. The independent practitioner also has the responsibility of training office staff so a situation does not arise, for example, when a secretary answers questions posed by a curious family member through lack of knowledge of the client's rights.

Potential Risk Areas

There are many areas in which there is a serious risk to the client in the area of confidentiality. Many of these risk areas were addressed in the Krever Commission Report after their inquiry into the Confidentiality of Health Information in Ontario.[25] Based on their analysis of these risk areas, the Krever Commission recommended a number of legislative revisions for the protection of the client in such areas as third-party disclosures, storage and destruction of records, staff training, notification of clients when information has been released without a waiver, and so on. Many of the problems discovered in the area of private communications arise from the way in which information is stored (e.g., audio- or videotapes, computerized data banks, cumulative records) and the ease with which information can be released to third parties.

Tapes of Client Contacts. Clients are more at risk with regard to confidentiality if their interviews are either audio- or videotaped. Audiotaping is a fairly frequent occurrence in situations where a therapist is not yet qualified to practice independently and has to be supervised. Typically, the client is informed that the tape will only be heard by the therapist's supervisor and that it will be erased shortly thereafter. When a therapist's clinical experience is part of a course requirement, the therapist may be expected to share the taped client-interactions within the classroom setting. Although clients may give consent for this prior to being taped, there is a much greater risk that their privacy will be violated under these circumstances in that the information will be shared with individuals who are not yet bound by any professional or ethical codes, for example, students. Although some of the risk can be reduced by withholding the client's name, there is still the danger that one of the individuals listening to the tape will recognize the client's voice. Client identification by a third party is even more likely in the case of videotapes. Videotapes have become increasingly popular within the last decade for educational and supervisory purposes as well as for monitoring a client's progress over time. The possibility that a client will be recognized by a third party is significantly increased because the client is visible. In many teaching hospitals and institutions, a client is "expected" to consent to such procedures if he or she wants to be assessed or treated in that setting.

Cumulative Records. Cumulative records also pose a problem regarding a client's privacy. This problem is particularly evident in institutions that provide services to an individual over a prolonged period of time, for example, the educational system. School files, for example, might contain anything from academic grades to sexual problems. A teacher wanting information about a student's academic functioning could potentially have access to more personal information about the student even though such information might be irrelevant for the teacher's purposes. Historically, cumulative records have often served as information dumping grounds "into which any subjective and unverified comments about attitudes, home environment, and so forth" can be filed.[26]

To keep such institutions accountable regarding the accuracy and relevance of information kept in cumulative files, individual records should be open for inspection by the client or guardian so that inaccuracies can be challenged and appropriate modifications made when justified. To reduce even further the problems inherent in cumulative records, it has been recommended that definitions be given of the type of information to be kept in particular files. For example, within the educational system, it might be preferable to restrict a student's file to information relating to academic achievement and school behavior. Information of a more personal nature (e.g., family problems) should not be kept with the academic data but in a separate file that is only accessible with proper authorization.

With regard to psychiatric reports and psychology test results, the boards of education for many states have developed a policy that now restricts the disclosure of mental health information. For example, the Board of Education for the State of Michigan indicates that:

(1) Specific responses to personality tests, projective and nonprojective, shall be adequately safeguarded from becoming accessible to the public. An interpretation summary of test results may be made available by such qualified personnel only to individuals directly concerned with the educational welfare of the pupil. However, specific responses and interpretation summaries may become part of published research findings and reports where the identities of the individuals tested are properly safeguarded.

(2) A transfer of individual personality-test interpretation summaries to other school districts or agencies shall not be made without permission of the parents or guardian expressed in writing and filed with the sending district.[27]

Another danger of cumulative records is that they are typically kept for prolonged periods of time. Information retention for lengthy periods after an individual has terminated contact with a particular facility increases the risk that confidentiality will be violated and should be discouraged. Many institutions as well as professionals now have guidelines regarding how long a client's record should be retained. Once that interval has expired without further contacts with the client, the record should be properly destroyed.

Computerized Data Banks. With the advances of computer technology, there is an increasing likelihood that client information will be stored in data banks as this not only reduces costs, and facilitates data retrieval and data transfer, but also increases the efficiency of many administrative procedures regarding client care. Because of the provincial health insurance plans in Canada, for example, computers are used to facilitate accounting regarding client contacts with medical doctors. It is predicted that a client's complete medical history will soon be available on computers in the larger health facilities. As this happens, it is also to be expected that "unauthorized entry into data banks (will be) more difficult to control as the data becomes more accessible and transferable."[28]

Certain safeguards must obviously be taken to prevent the violation of a client's privacy under such circumstances. For example, to reduce the possibility that unauthorized individuals would have access to private information about another individual, the data could be differentially coded according to certain criteria. For example, demographic information about a client could be accessible by a different code than that used to retrieve more personal information. Only individuals directly involved in the client's health care or those authorized by the client could be provided with the more "personal" code. To reduce further the risk that private information would be easily accesible to improper external sources, it has been suggested that computerized health care data not be merged within larger data banks.

Release of Information. Information from a client's file can be released with or without consent, depending upon the purpose of the disclosure. As outlined in the section Exceptions to Confidentiality Rule, many third parties can gain access to a client's file without the individual's expressed permission. When such release of information is justified, the client should be properly notified of the nature and extent of any disclosure. Even in circumstances where his or her consent is required, there may be a risk to the client if proper procedures have not been followed in obtaining permission. For the client's protection in this area, the Krever Commission has recommended that the following legislative requirements be adopted:

90. That legislation permitting disclosure of health information pursuant to a patient's authorization require that the authorization:
    (a) be in writing and contain the original signature of the subject of the health information as well as the original signature of the witness;
    (b) be dated;
    (c) specify the name or description of the recipient of the information;
    (d) specify the name or description of the person or institution intended to release the information;
    (e) include a description of the information to be disclosed;
    (f) specify the purpose for which the information is requested;
    (g) include an expiration date or time limit for the validity of the authorization; and
    (h) specify that the individual may rescind or amend the authorization in writing at any time prior to the expiration date, except where action has been taken in reliance on the authorization.
91. That a standard form of authorization for disclosure of health information,

in accordance with conditions (a) to (h) of Recommendation 90, apply to all health information maintained by health-care providers, including psychiatric facilities.

92. That when, in the opinion of the health-care provider, the physical or mental condition of a patient prevents him or her from having the ability to understand the subject matter in respect of which consent is requested and from being able to appreciate the consequences of giving or withholding consent, authorization for the disclosure of the information may be given by the patient's nearest next of kin.

93. That the parent or legal guardian of a patient under the age of 16 years may authorize the disclosure of his or her health information to a third person.[29]

Consequences for Improper Disclosure

The client has the option of reporting a particular professional to his or her professional body if the professional has disclosed private information about the client without appropriate authorization. The client may also choose to sue either the professional or the professional's employer under the understanding that the employer can be held legally responsible for the actions of any employee with regard to health care provision. The client might either choose to sue on the basis of defamation of character or invasion of privacy. In the case of defamation, the client must prove that the information revealed by the professional was incorrect as well as unauthorized. In the event that the information released was true but disclosed without consent, the client can sue for invasion of privacy. In this latter instance, the client must demonstrate that the information disclosed was "of such a nature as to offend a person of ordinary sensibilities. Generally, hospital or health data is not sufficiently offensive to be actionable."[30]

RIGHT TO CONSENT

The section on "consent" proceeds from a basic definition of the consent issue to a description of types of consent, criteria for proper consent, situations requiring and not requiring consent, as well as consequences of consent violations.

Society owes individuals the right to refuse or consent to treatment since this right protects them from an intervention that has the power to control their mind, regulate their thoughts, or change their personality. Within the health care field, consent consists of an agreement by one individual to participate in various diagnostic or treatment procedures or both proposed by another individual. "The legal definition of *consent* requires that an individual's permission be given knowingly, intelligently, and voluntarily" although the exact "meanings of these terms are not spelled out in case law."[31] The courts have mandated that every individual has the right to agree to or refuse a particular intervention in that he or she has the right to be free from interference. Violations of this right can lead to severe consequences for the professional or institution or both involved in the care of the client.

Consent to a particular procedure results in a contract between the client and the health care provider. In order to assert that the contract is valid and not voidable in a court of law, the consent must be made by a person defined as capable or competent, and obtained under clearly defined conditions. More specifically, the client must consent to the conditions outlined in the contract voluntarily and with sufficient information regarding the terms of the contract to allow for an intelligent decision. Except in the case of a legally appointed guardian, no other party can consent on behalf of another adult. The law is less than clear in this area with regard to minors.

In the area of capacity, "early English common law said that contracts are based on a 'meeting of minds,' and if a party lacked sufficient mind, there could be no such meeting. . . . Historically, the principal categories of persons having no capacity or limited capacity to contract were married women, infants and lunatics."[32] Married women were granted the right to make contractual arrangements only after the beginning of this century.

At the present time, the right to agree or disagree to an externally imposed procedure is guaranteed by law in Canada and the United States. Canadian and American law are quite similar in the area of consent although Canadian courts are more likely to judge a case on the basis of individual circumstances rather than adopting a specific rule to cover all circumstances that might arise. Many of the difficulties arising from improper consent have been demonstrated through the American court system "since Canadian courts have yet to entertain much serious litigation concerning alleged psychiatric assault (i.e., treatment or physical touching of one's body without valid consent)."[33]

Types of Consent
There are two general classifications of consent, both of which can be legally binding if the consent is obtained according to proper procedure.

Express Consent. This type of consent consists of verbal affirmation by the client, either orally or in writing, to specific recommendations proposed by the client's health care provider. Although an oral consent is, in fact, a valid consent, the professional may still prefer a written one in that it provides tangible evidence that consent was at least discussed with the client. Even though the client has signed a consent form, however, his or her consent is not accepted as valid if proper procedures were not followed in obtaining a signature.

In many health care settings, clients are requested to sign "blanket" consents indicating that they have been sufficiently informed regarding the proposed intervention and that they accept any possible adverse results from this same intervention. The client's signature on "blanket" consent forms still does not mean that the consent was valid if the client can prove that it was not given "knowingly," "intelligently," or "voluntarily."

Some settings utilize two varieties of consent forms. On admission, a client may be asked to sign a "general" consent form agreeing to standard hospital procedures (e.g., blood tests, urine samples) so that individual consents do not have to be obtained prior to each routine procedure. The client should be asked to sign a "specific" consent form as well, agreeing to the "specific" procedures prescribed for him or her.

In addition, the consent form should be dated and duly witnessed by an individual over the age of majority. Having the client's signature witnessed is only relevant if the witness was present when the consent conditions were met. Nurses are often placed in the awkward position of obtaining and witnessing the client's signed "consent" under the assumption that the client's oral consent was given earlier in the presence of the client's doctor. The nurse may be instructed to ask if the client freely agrees to the proposed procedures and is aware of the possible and likely effects of that procedure. If the client indicates that an informed consent was not made, the nurse must notify the proper authorities. The nurse or hospital or both can be held liable if the nurse discovers that the client was not adequately informed, and then makes no attempt to remedy the situation.

Implied Consent. There are times during which consent can be deduced from the client's behavior at the time of the intervention. The most obvious examples are the client who rolls up a sleeve to accept a needle, or holds out a hand to receive medication. Consent must never be implied simply on the basis of the client's physical or psychological condition. It must not be assumed that the client has given implied consent by virtue of accepting admission into hospital. Even though the client may have been admitted voluntarily, the individual may not have sufficient information about the specific treatment procedures within the hospital to make an intelligent or knowledgeable decision about such procedures. In other words, the observation that a client passively complies with various treatment plans does not mean that "proper" consent was given. In most instances, the client is unaware of the right to influence treatment procedures. The responsibility is therefore on the health care provider to ensure that the proper conditions have been met before accepting a client's implied consent as valid.

Criteria for Proper Consent

There are several criteria that must be met before a consent can be considered valid and therefore not void in a court of law. Professionals should be aware of these criteria if they do not wish to be held liable for "forcing" a client into a particular treatment process.

Capacity. A person must be considered "capable" in order to have the right to accept or reject treatment recommendations independently. An individual is only deemed to have this capacity if he or she is legally and mentally competent. Historically, in the case of married people, English common law stated that a husband's consent was required for health care procedures on his wife, particularly in cases where their marital relationship could be affected by the procedure imposed. At the present time, it is accepted that the only consent required by law is that of the client although many agencies out of caution continue to require the consent of the husband as well.[34]

Mental Competence. An incompetent person is not allowed to give consent because of the assumption that "defects in judgment caused by brain damage or mental deficiency may preclude the understanding deemed necessary for contractual capacity."[35] An individual is considered mentally competent if he or she has "the mental capacity to understand the nature and risk of not undergoing the treatment. . . . A person may be mentally ill, but if the mental illness does not affect his decision-making process with regard to consent, he would be considered competent to consent."[36] The client need only understand the treatment in general rather than in technical terms in order to be considered competent from a legal standpoint, and to be granted the right to give or withhold authorization for treatment. There is the danger that individuals continue to confuse mental illness and incompetency. There is also a general tendency to equate "old age" with incompetence and to bypass the elderly person's right to make decisions about his or her body by going directly to that person's children for consent. Such a consent is obviously not legally binding should the elderly, but competent, client choose to challenge it in court.

Even for clients under the authority of a public trustee, "statutes authorizing such trusteeship usually govern property only and not the body of the person. Therefore such a trustee would not have the power to consent to the treatment of the patient."[37] Even when a client is considered incompetent to manage financial affairs (e.g., a hypomanic who may be a compulsive spender), the legal system can still consider the individual to have the competence to give or withhold consent regarding health care matters.

In situations where a client is admitted to hospital "by force" and kept there involuntarily, the client may still have the capacity to decide which type of mental health care is acceptable. Under no circumstances should involuntary status in and of itself classify a client as incompetent. A suicidal client, for example, may be kept in a hospital to control any manifestation of self-destructive behaviors. Despite a desire to commit suicide, the client may still have the mental competence to make informed decisions about his or her own mental health needs.

Incompetence should also not be equated with irrational or unreasonable thinking. "The patient has a right to refuse treatment, even though refusal is based on mistake, fear, caprice, whim or just plain stubbornness."[38] Regrettably, a mental health provider may choose to label a client irrational and thereby incompetent for refusing the recommended form of treatment. The fact that a client may not agree to a useful and recommended procedure does not mean that the client did not comprehend the nature and possible benefits of that procedure. If the client was considered sufficiently competent for the health care provider to ask for consent in the first place, the client must be considered equally competent to withhold such consent. Otherwise, it does not appear that the client has a choice. A conflict of interest obviously exists in these circumstances in that the person with the authority to declare the client as incompetent is typically the same physician who is trying to gain the client's consent for a particular procedure. In declaring a client incompetent, the physician should ensure that the decision is based on reasons other than the client's "irrational" decision regarding a particular recommendation; in other words, the physician should be able to provide an independent measure of the client's incompetence besides the client's refusal to accept treatment. Preferably, the physician should consult with another professional before finalizing any decision.

As a way of assisting the professional in this difficult area, Culver et al.[39] have set out "minimal" criteria that, if met, would indicate that a client had sufficient competence to make a proper consent. They state that

a patient is *competent to decide* about having a particular treatment (such as ECT [electroconvulsive therapy]) when the following are satisfied:

(1) the patient knows that the physician believes the patient is ill and in need of treatment (although the patient may not agree)
(2) the patient knows that the physician believes this particular treatment may help the patient's illness, and
(3) the patient knows he or she is being called upon to make a decision regarding this treatment.

If the client is sufficiently intact to meet these minimal criteria, then the client should be considered sufficiently competent to make an informed judgment for or against a particular intervention. Additionally, treatment decisions made by an individual during an earlier state of competence should be respected even if the individual is later declared incompetent and unable to consent or refuse at that point. Care should also be taken to determine if the state of incompetence is likely to be a temporary condition (e.g., a function of alcohol or drug abuse) or permanent (e.g., a function of retardation or senility).

As Ford (1980) states:

> The theory that a patient committed by the courts must accept treat-
> ment rests on the assumption that he is incompetent to make a decision
> that such treatment is in his best interest; yet this assumption is not
> necessarily correct. At a commitment hearing, *only* the issue of a pa-
> tient's dangerousness (to self or others) or substantial inability to care
> for himself is decided. Such a patient presumptively retains *all other*
> *civil rights*—the right to vote, to freedom of speech and religion, and to
> decide whether to accept medication. . . . Thus, in addition to a finding
> of dangerousness or substantial need for care, a court should ideally
> make a separate finding about a patient's competence to accept or re-
> fuse medication.[40]

Once an individual is declared incompetent to make decisions about
health care needs, the decision-making capacity is given to the individual's next of kin as long as the professional has reason to believe that the
next of kin would act in the client's best interests. If not, the professional
can request that a guardian be appointed by the state to act on behalf of
the client. Guardians are often appointed when a client refuses medication that is considered necessary for his or her improvement. Regrettably,
there are many difficulties inherent in getting a guardian, particularly
since there is not a ready supply available for use. In most circumstances,
a family member is appointed to act as legal guardian for the client, assuming a family member can be found. In many situations, however, family members are part of the overall problem for the client and may have
their own difficulties making fair decisions on the client's behalf. In other
words, the appointment of a guardian may not necessarily solve the problem. In order to act objectively on the client's behalf, the guardian must
be sensitive to many complicated issues including the client's rights and
the difficulties inherent in different treatment approaches.

Even when a court does decide to appoint a guardian for a client, it
does not follow that the court would approve of such forms of medical
intervention as psychosurgery or ECT because of the intrusiveness of
these techniques. As Ford states:

> In addition to considering the intrusiveness of treatment, the court
> should weigh its irreversibility, side effects (such as tardive dyskinesia),
> and efficacy; whether an emergency is involved; whether an inpatient
> or outpatient setting is necessary; and whether less restrictive alterna-
> tives to the treatment in question have been explored and rejected for
> valid reasons.[41]

These variables should have an effect on the guardian's decision-making
powers for a particular client.

When the client is mentally incapable of consenting and has no legal
guardian as yet, Rozovsky suggests that it is

always advisable to obtain consent from spouse or relatives not because they represent the patient, but to prevent them from taking any action to which they might conceivably have a right. It will also weaken any case brought by the patient since it demonstrates the good intentions of the hospital. This could lessen or remove any punitive damages which might be awarded by a court.[42]

Legal Competence. An individual is not generally considered legally competent until he or she reaches the statutory age, under the assumption that an individual cannot make adequate judgments about himself or herself when still developmentally or psychosocially immature. As Grisso states:

> The statutory ages employed, however, are different for various treatment purposes even within a given state, and they vary considerably from one state to another even for a specific type of treatment. For example, various states allow minors to consent to treatment related to pregnancy, without parental consent or knowledge; but in different states, the minimum age allowances are 12, 14, and 15. The ages at which minors may consent to treatment for drug dependency range from various early adolescent ages to no minimum age at all.[43]

Prior to reaching the "proper" age, decisions regarding a minor's health care needs typically fall under the control of the minor's parents, unless it can be proven that the parents are not acting in the client's best interests. On the basis of the *parens patriae* doctrine (i.e., the duty of the state to protect its citizens), the state can make decisions for the minor against the parents' wishes if the state decides that the parents are not providing adequate protection for the child's physical or psychosocial needs or both. Protection for the child is accomplished by having the state appoint a guardian who will then act on the child's behalf.

Many individuals believe that the "mature" minor should be given the right to make independent decisions about health care intervention. In most jurisdictions, the consent of a minor may be accepted as valid if that minor is judged to have sufficient cognitive ability to comprehend fully the nature and possible consequences of the proposed intervention. This possibility is more likely to occur in the case of the emancipated minor. Although there is no specific legal definition for emancipation, the term is generally used in the United States to describe a child who has been freed from the custody of his or her parents and whose parents have given up their legal responsibilities toward him or her. Typically, the emancipated minor is living independently from parents and managing his or her own affairs.

Grisso and Vierling differentiate between three types of "consents" that could be used with minors under the assumption that they would be treated differently within a court of law[44]:

1. A right to "consent to treatment independent of their parents' consent or knowledge"
2. A right to "dissent when their parents have consented to their treatment," in other words, the right to refuse treatment
3. "A 'right to know' or a 'right to participate' when their treatment is being decided"

They also suggest that court authorities pay more attention to relevant developmental research to assist them in making judgments in this difficult area, that is, to help them decide when a minor is mature enough to give his or her own consent. Grisso and Vierling reviewed a number of psychological research studies on cognitive and behavioral characteristics in minors in an attempt to provide some general guidelines as to when a minor is likely to make "mature" decisions about health care. They concluded that

> minors below age 11 generally do not have the intellectual abilities or are too prone to deferent response to satisfy a psychological interpretation of the legal standard for competent consent. . . . In the age range of 11–14 years, existing research suggests caution regarding any assumptions about these minors' abilities to consider intelligently the complexities of treatment alternatives, risks, and benefits, or to provide consent that is voluntary.[45]

Grisso and Vierling further conclude on the basis of their research review that minors 15 and older are as competent to provide consent as are adults.

Voluntary Consent. In order to be considered valid, a consent must be given freely by the client with no external consequences attached to the various choice possibilities. "Similarly, any consent obtained by fraudulent misrepresentation, or after partial administration of anaesthesia, while under the influence of drugs or alcohol or while delirious would also be open to serious question."[46] Rozovsky[47] refers to a case in Quebec in which consent was considered invalid because it was given by the client after he had been administered a sedative and was therefore not necessarily given voluntarily.

In hospital situations, a client is typically under the influence of psychotropic medication that, in some circumstances, significantly interferes with the ability to think clearly and coherently; and, in others, makes the client sufficiently tranquil to suppress any realistic anxiety about a particular intervention. On the other hand, clients who are not receiving medication or other forms of intervention may be in such a state of psychological distress (e.g., depression, anxiety, drug or alcohol withdrawal) that they are willing to "agree" to almost anything proposed to them. This situation poses a serious dilemma for the professional in that either of these fairly common conditions (i.e., presence of extreme distress or intrusive, external influences) makes it difficult if not impossible to obtain a valid "voluntary" consent from psychiatric clients.

Under no circumstances should a client be persuaded to make a specific choice as a result of an expressed or implied threat of punishment or a promise of reward. In other words, consent cannot be accepted as free or voluntary if the client has reason to believe, for example, that refusal would result in a loss of privileges, seclusion, or a change to incompetent or involuntary status.

The need for voluntary consent is obviously difficult to obtain in most institutional settings in that clients are likely to be overly dependent on the service providers to alleviate their symptoms and therefore may be afraid to refuse anything out of the fear, real or imagined, of reprisal. Many clients who have been voluntarily admitted may be confronted with pressure, subtle or otherwise, to remain in a hospital even though they have the legal right to sign themselves out. This problem is magnified by the fact that many institutional staff are not fully aware of a client's right to withhold consent and may therefore show disapproval toward clients for "resisting" their attempts to help. A classic example is the misuse óf behavior modification techniques to "motivate" clients to change their behaviors in accordance with an externally imposed treatment plan. This type of manipulation is fairly common within mental health facilities and the prison setting. For example, the Project on Law and Behavior describes the Michigan Intensive Program Center in Marquette in which a program was developed to modify prisoners with behavior management problems, for example, fighting. When the program was first developed, prisoners were transferred to this facility involuntarily and not told the goals of the program. "'Consent' to enter the program is engineered by giving inmates an option between segregation with no amenities and the token economy program where privileges are earned."[48] Behavioral incentives obviously interfere with a client's free choice if they are used to influence a person's choice *between* treatments rather than to assist an individual in reaching goals *within* an agreed-on treatment program.

Informed Consent. In order to give a valid consent, a client must have sufficient information about a particular procedure and its possible consequences to make a rational decision for or against it. A client also must be informed that he or she has the right to withhold consent to a recommended procedure and also that he or she can later withdraw a previously given consent at any time.

First of all, a fair and reasonable description of the proposed intervention must be provided to the client in language that the individual can understand and at the level of complexity that the client requests. Therefore, the explanation of the proposed procedures must be individualized according to the needs of the client, that is, a different explanation would have to be given to an uneducated or illiterate client than to one with a medical or psychosocial background. In the area of medical intervention, "the physician has a duty of disclosing as much information as the average reasonable person, in the same set of circumstances as the patient, needs to decide if he wants to accept or refuse the proposed surgery or procedure."[49]

It is generally accepted that the description given to the client should consist of the following elements: diagnosis of the client's presenting problem(s), a description of the recommended treatment approach, benefits that should result as well as the probability of such benefits, possible adverse effects that could follow from the intervention with an estimation of their likelihood, alternative treatment approaches with their incumbent risks and benefits. Risks that are considered remote need not be disclosed. Clients should be advised if the approach recommended is relatively novel and if it can have any possible adverse effects on their physical functioning, sexual capacity, or fertility. The process of informing the client must also allow adequate opportunity for discussion on the proposed procedure so that the client is able to obtain clarification or elaboration on specific points.

In the United States, there is generally more emphasis on warning a client of potential risk areas than there is in Canada. "The rule in Canada for informed consent is very flexible. The doctor must give the patient a reasonable amount of information that would enable him to understand the nature and risks of undergoing the procedure or not undergoing it. What is reasonable depends on the circumstances of the case and on the particular patient."[50]

In general, there are a number of problem areas related to informed consent that are common to most jurisdictions. In the first place, the client is overly dependent on the professional to provide adequate and accurate information. Since professionals are likely motivated to have clients agree with their recommendations, there is the inherent danger that the professionals' own choice of treatment may be overemphasized and other alternatives underestimated. Standardized descriptions of all common therapeutic interventions might help to offset this possibility.

Second, although therapists are always obligated to indicate possible side effects of the treatment proposed, "psychotherapy outcome studies do not typically examine the effects of therapy or important beliefs and social relationships that are not targeted for change. Questions can therefore be raised as to whether psychotherapists can provide the minimal information necessary for clients to make informed decisions."[51] Historically, legal regulations regarding consent have applied only to physical forms of intervention (e.g., medication, psychosurgery, ECT) rather than psychotherapy. "Just as it is said that 'sticks and stones may break my bones but names will never hurt me,' only the physical therapies—never psychotherapy—are challenged. In fact, however, wild psychotherapy can be as devastating as wild physical therapy."[52] Lack of definite rulings in the area of psychotherapy leaves clients rather vulnerable from a legal standpoint, although they would still have the option of complaining to the therapist's professional body if they were to believe that the therapist had acted improperly in this or other areas.

Another problem in the area of consent results from the need to describe side effects of a particular treatment to a client. Sharpe[53] refers to the specific difficulties confronting physicians who are required to "keep abreast of the 'normal' reactions and side effects connected with new drugs," especially in view of the speed with which drugs are currently being introduced into the market. Physicians have generally become overly dependent on the drug companies for such information despite the obvious danger that the drug companies have a vested interest in promoting their products.

In view of these difficulties, professionals are encouraged to explain recommended procedures personally rather than delegate that responsibility to auxiliary staff. Otherwise, there is the risk that the client will be misinformed, thereby negating the consent. When the prime therapist communicates this information to a client, however, a problem may still arise in getting informed consent because of the specific relationship existing between the client and his or her therapist. In other words, a client may have so much trust in a therapist that he or she will accept recommendations without adequate information on which to base a decision. Moore describes a research study showing that only half of the subjects studied were truly informed, even though they were given both oral and written explanations of the proposed intervention. "Either the subjects could not or were not motivated to be informed, the concept was too complex or too frightening, or they trusted the physician."[54] To guard against this possibility, Martin recommends that a test be administered after an explanation has been given to ensure that the client has attended to and understood the salient points of the description offered.[55]

Another possible danger for the client arises because the professional is given much "therapeutic discretion" regarding how much to disclose to a client. In the area of medical intervention, for example, the physician may decide that disclosure of any information to the client would not be in the client's best interests. Under such circumstances, physicians will often disclose the necessary information to the next of kin, even though this might be construed as a violation of the client's right to privacy. In American courts, the physician's right to withhold all or part of the treatment information from the client is called "therapeutic privilege." Therapeutic privilege is exercised if the therapist believes that certain disclosures would be detrimental to a client's emotional or physical state or both. In Canada, such decisions are recognized as the "discretionary" right of physicians. The danger to the client when discretionary privilege is exercised is that it provides the physician with justification for withholding information on the basis of the client's best interests. The underlying assumption in such a policy appears to be that the doctor knows best what the client needs. A client's supposed fragility appears to be too convenient an excuse for withholding information and can be too easily overestimated. This seemingly paternalistic approach to disclosure implies that the client needs to be protected from himself or herself by a higher authority who may present information in a "palatable" fashion in order to minimize the client's likelihood of refusing. The doctrine of paternalism dates back to the 18th century and "is founded on the notion that those who need to be protected are incompetent. . . . These attitudes may take on the character of self-fulfilling prophecies: if you expect a person to be incompetent and you treat him as incompetent and he knows he is supposed to be incompetent, then you should not be surprised to find him to be incompetent."[56] An added complication related to the paternalistic approach to disclosure is that the authority figure in question has a vested interest in the client's compliance and yet is typically the one deciding to "protect" him or her from a poor decision by withholding information.

Situations Not Requiring Consent

In a "true" emergency (e.g., lethal overdose of drugs), a medical procedure can be applied to an individual without consent. In order to qualify as a true emergency, the situation must meet four criteria. First, the danger to the client must be immediate. Second, the individual must be either unconscious or too incapacitated to give or refuse consent. Third, the treatment must be considered essential to prevent the client's death or serious bodily harm. Finally, the client must not have refused consent for the intervention prior to the emergency. Under emergency circumstances, the physician is encouraged to keep the client's next of kin informed, if they are available, and to ask permission for proceeding even though this is not legally essential.

Situations Requiring Consent

Transfer of Information. In the area of privileged communication, informed consent must be given by the client before the therapist can disclose information about the client in court. Outside the courtroom, the professional is not allowed to share information about a client with other parties without the client's informed consent. If the therapist, however, believes that it would be in the client's best interests to share confidential information with the client's family, for example, he or she must obtain the client's informed consent to waive his or her right to confidentiality. Del Rio[57] believes that clients generally cannot make an informed consent about waiving confidentiality of their records. "The patient never knows what he is waiving, what information has been written or in what particular way, nor has he the knowledge that the physician has of the highly technical language in which such records are usually written. Patients must be dutifully apprised of the full connotations of waiving the privilege of privacy," although it is unlikely that this can ever be done sufficiently to meet the three criteria for informed consent.

The independent practitioner wishing to disclose information about a client should provide a rationale for making this recommendation, exactly what information he or she proposes to reveal and to whom, expectations of the outcome of this disclosure, and any possible negative consequences for the client. The practitioner's explanation should also include the advantages and disadvantages of not waiving confidentiality. By outlining the pros and cons, the client may be reassured that the therapist does see advantages to both options, possibly alleviating any anxiety the client may have over possibly disagreeing with the therapist's proposal. To avoid manipulation of the client's decision, the therapist must not imply that approval or disapproval will follow from any specific choice made by him or her.

Diagnostic Intervention.   In order to give a valid consent, a client should be apprised of the reasons for a specific diagnostic investigation, the exact procedures to be followed, the degree of intrusiveness of the procedures, the nature of the results, and the possibility of any negative consequences resulting from the investigation. In the case of psychological tests, for example, the client should be aware that the diagnostic results could be subpoenaed and used against him or her in court. Written consents are typically not obtained for routine diagnostic procedures, particularly if the procedure is relatively simple and the possibility of adverse effects are extremely remote. The client's consent is often implied by participation in the assessment process. The fact that no oral consent was obtained, however, may suggest to a court of law that no discussion was held with the client to inform the individual about the assessment procedure.

In the case of minors, permission for diagnostic investigations should typically be obtained from the child's parents or guardian. This requirement may pose particular difficulty for the psychologist within the school system, for example, in that he or she must therefore obtain written consent from each student's parent or guardian prior to administering any personality or intellectual tests or both.

Another difficulty within the diagnostic field arises in the area of behavior modification, not only with regard to pretreatment manipulation of an individual's choice of treatment options as previously discussed, but in the area of pretreatment behavioral assessment. A behavior modifier is typically required to obtain baseline (preintervention) data before introducing a treatment variable in order to be able to make com-

parisons in the frequency or intensity of a specific behavior before and
after the introduction of the treatment variable. It is a fairly common
practice for professionals operating as behavior modifiers to observe clients in their "natural" environment (e.g., ward sitting room, classroom),
in order to determine the presence of a particular problem. The therapist
may be disinclined to obtain consent from a client until he or she knows
which of the clients observed would likely require the treatment program
and because there may be some concern that the clients would not act
"naturally" if they knew why they were being observed. Clients should
have the right to give informed consent when measures are being taken
of their behavior. Kerlinger disagrees with this position, even when those
observations are being taken for research purposes. Kerlinger states:

> When a researcher observes members of a group interacting, even with-
> out the knowledge of those observed, there is no invasion of privacy.
> The individuals involved, even if they do not know that they are part
> of a research situation, are in a public or semipublic situation and are
> thus not "in private." Privacy means individual, personal, confined to
> one or a few persons. It means secluded from the sight and hearing of
> others because of the essentially personal nature of so-called "private
> activities."[58]

Other professionals might consider this position debatable, particularly
when dealing with institutionalized clients who have little input as to
where they spend their time.

Treatment Intervention. Clients have the right to accept or reject a particular mode of treatment. Much of the earlier discussion on consent con-
centrated on specific difficulties in meeting consent criteria in the area of
treatment intervention. In dealing with clients suffering from various
forms of psychological distress or cognitive disability or both, there is an
increasing risk that consent cannot be properly given. For inpatients in
particular, it is difficult to prove that consent was voluntarily given or
that the client was sufficiently calm and "clear-headed" (e.g., not under
the influence of drugs) to attend accurately to and comprehend any information given to him or her. A client's need to alleviate acute distress
symptoms (e.g., depression, anxiety) may also make the client overly dependent on a therapist's recommendations, thereby avoiding the effort of
making an independent decision. On the professional's part, there is the
difficulty of either having too little information to give the client about
side effects or too much. As a consequence, the professional may not be
able to provide sufficient information about the recommended procedure
and alternatives to permit the client to give an informed consent.
    Within the general area of consent for treatment, however, the pro-
fessional does not need to be as concerned about the problems attached

to informed consent if he or she is "counseling," rather than "treating" the client. Although these terms may be used interchangeably within the mental health field, they are differentiated in a court of law in that treatment is typically used to refer to medical intervention. Generally, informed consent is only critical when medical treatment is involved. "The law and practice that relates to consent to treatment does not apply as such to counseling,"[59] although many counselors continue to obtain such consent for ethical and professional reasons.

Within the area of medical treatment, there is much controversy over a client's right to refuse medication when the right conflicts with the right to treatment. A study by Appelbaum and Gutheil[60] found that most inpatients who refuse their medication do so for "delusional" rather "rational" reasons.

Stone recommends the following "tests for determining when a client's refusal of medication should be respected."[61]

(1) There should be a burden on the reliably diagnosed severely ill person to articulate a reason for refusing treatment.
(2) Those patients who are unwilling or unable to consent, or object (the so-called nonprotesting patient), should be considered as having made an incompetent refusal.
(3) If the alleged patient is able or willing to state a reason for objecting to confinement, the psychiatrist should be asked to demonstrate that the refusal is irrational and is based on or related to the diagnosed illness . . .
(4) If the patient has a reason which is not a product of his illness, e.g., "I have been a Christian Scientist all my life: I do not believe in medicines or physicians." Even though a physician might consider this irrational, it is not based on his current misperception of reality, and it should therefore be considered a competent refusal.

Experimental Intervention. As a general rule, stricter criteria must be met before a client is judged to have made an informed consent regarding proposed experimental procedures. Individuals choosing to participate in any form of medical research must be given as much information as a "reasonable person" might require in order to reach an informed decision.

In the area of drug experimentation, the American Medical Association has provided the following instructions to physicians wishing to administer an experimental drug. As stated by Sharpe:

> Generally, drugs under clinical investigation should be administered only where: (1) the informed consent of the patient or his authorized representative has been obtained; (2) the physician is convinced of the reasonable accuracy of his diagnosis and, if necessary has confirmed it by adequate consultation; and (3) existing methods of treatment have proven unsatisfactory. The voluntary participation of the patient will not excuse a deviation from the physician's obligation to exercise his best skill in rendering the care required of a reasonable practitioner.

Furthermore, the physician is advised to confine his clinical investigations of new drugs to those furnished by reputable sources who have
supplied him with comprehensive written information concerning: (1)
animal experimentation; (2) previous clinical investigations, if any; (3)
recommended dosages; (4) contraindications; (5) possible side-effects to
be watched for, and (6) the safety and possible usefulness of the drug,
from existing data.[62]

In the area of psychosocial research, similar guidelines apply so that the
clients are not misled into giving their consent because of insufficient
data.

Consequences of Consent Violations

If an intervention (e.g., ECT) is imposed on an individual without valid
consent, that individual can charge the professional directly involved or
the professional's employer or both with assault and battery. A person
can be charged with an assault if "without the consent of another person
or with consent, where it is obtained by fraud, (a) he applies force inten-
tionally to the person of the other, directly or indirectly, or (b) he attempts
or threatens, by an act or gesture, to apply force to the person of the
other, if he has, or causes the other to believe upon reasonable grounds
that he has, present ability to effect his purposes."[63]

The professional cannot attempt to justify the failure to get consent
on the basis of the client's treatment needs or on the basis that the client
did, in fact, benefit from the forced intervention. In a legal proceeding,
evidence regarding the client's need for treatment or the quality of treatment imposed would not be considered relevant in this instance in that
the legal issue centers on the client's rights and not needs.

The charge of assault and battery may be made for violation of any
one of the criteria specified for consent. Sharpe[64] gives an example of a
case that could result in charges, that is, when a professional accepts a
consent from an individual legally incompetent to give it. For example, if
a 15-year-old girl should consent to a medical examination in a hospital
emergency department for evidence of rape, the parents might later
charge the physician with assault and battery on the grounds that their
child was not sufficiently "mature" to appreciate the nature of the procedure and any possible risks attached to it.

In the event of implied or orally expressed consent, the onus is typically on the professional to prove that a proper consent was, in fact, obtained. If the client admits to giving consent, the burden is then on the
client to prove that the consent was not given "knowingly," "intelligently," or "voluntarily." In a courtroom, if a client claims that he or
she did not have sufficient information on which to base a decision, jury
members might be asked to determine whether the information would
have been sufficient if they had been the client, under the assumption

that the jury member constitutes the "average" person. It has generally been accepted that clients vary in their ability to comprehend technical explanations. Therefore, what is "reasonable" for one client need not be "reasonable" for another. Because of their individual variations, it may not be fair to make decisions on the validity of an informed consent by comparing the information required by one individual with that necessary for "the average reasonable person." Sharpe further indicates that a physician may not be held liable if the disclosures made by him or her do not differ significantly from "those disclosures which a reasonable medical practitioner would make under the same or similar circumstances."[65]

RIGHT TO ADEQUATE TREATMENT

A client has the right to receive "adequate" treatment. This right should apply regardless of the client's status (i.e., inpatient vs. outpatient; involuntary vs. voluntary; competent vs. incompetent). A client also has the right to receive proper treatment regardless of any special group to which he or she may belong (e.g., minor, mental retardate, criminal). The following sections provide a review of the basic issues involved in providing adequate treatment to different client groups.

Inpatients

Clients may admit themselves to hospitals voluntarily or may be forcibly detained if admitted on an involuntary basis. Voluntary and involuntary clients have the same rights regarding adequate health care provision. In addition, competent and incompetent clients have the same health care rights although, in the case of the incompetent client, a guardian should be appointed to safeguard that person's rights and to make required health care decisions.

In the case of involuntary commitment, the client is typically forced to receive treatment under the assumption that he or she is unwilling to accept health care intervention voluntarily. The right to commit mentally disturbed individuals against their will has existed for approximately 100 years. Prior to that time, mentally disturbed individuals were simply allowed to roam the streets.[66]

In most jurisdictions, involuntary commitment is justified if a person is considered actively dangerous to self or others. Another justification for involuntary commitment is society's obligation to provide treatment to persons in need of such intervention (i.e., the *parens patriae* doctrine). In accordance with the *parens patriae* doctrine, society has an obligation to protect its citizens, either from themselves or from others. This doctrine has been interpreted to mean that society must offer treatment to mentally disordered individuals who are in need of such treatment. This obligation has been used to justify forced treatment under the assumption that treatment is in the client's best interests. Although society has accepted the obligation to treat individuals who need such services and although they have developed institutions to satisfy this need, clients are typically not receiving the kind of care needed to alleviate their problems because of understaffing as well as low quality personnel. For example, Slovenko indicates that

> only fifteen states have more than 50 percent of the total number of physicians necessary to staff the public mental hospitals according to the minimum standards of the American Psychiatric Association. On the national average, nurses are calculated to be only 19.4 percent adequate. As a consequence, the best that can be done is to give a physical examination and make a psychiatric note once a year.[67]

He also indicates that the "native born physician who works in the state mental hospital is usually there because he is on probation on account of narcotic addiction or alcoholism."[68] If treatment facilities are unable to provide the treatment necessary to help their clients, what right does society have to deprive such individuals of their liberty under the justification of "need for treatment"? Kittrie[69] accuses society of having taken on too much power in the therapeutic arena without the knowledge, resources, or research background to properly exercise that power.

In the United States, the courts have frequently supported a client's right to be released when the client can prove that he or she has not received adequate treatment within a particular facility. A client has the right to a hearing if he or she is in a facility that is merely satisfying a custodial rather than treatment function. If treatment is being provided, the health care facility must then be able to prove that the treatment is in accordance with the client's psychological needs rather than in line with the management needs of the facility. In other words, therapy that is being provided to keep the client docile and cooperative within the treatment setting is not necessarily satisfying the client's needs for therapy unless these are the same behaviors that the client needs to develop in order to function more appropriately in the outside community.

In 1960, Morton Birnbaum, a physician and attorney in the United States, was the first person to advocate an enforceable right to treatment. Since that time, a number of court cases have resulted to test out this right. One of the most influential cases, *Wyatt v. Stickney*,[70] sensitized the public to the inhumane way in which many clients have been treated under the auspices of mental health care. The case arose when 90 staff members who had been fired from a state mental institution hired a lawyer (G. W. Dean, Jr.) to help them get their jobs back. The argument Dean chose to justify their rehiring was based on the need for sufficient staffing to satisfy society's obligation to provide adequate treatment. In the course of presenting his case, Dean broadened his investigation to include other health care facilities in Alabama. He discovered many atrocious circumstances in these facilities, including excessive and cruel confinement. For example, it was discovered that "one girl had been in a strait jacket for nine years, because she sucked her hands and fingers."[71] In addition, there was much evidence of physical abuse, filthy living conditions (e.g., insect infestations, excrement on the floors), extreme overcrowding, poorly qualified staff, and so on. As a consequence of this investigation, extensive rulings regarding "adequate" mental health care were established. In general, three major requirements regarding institutional care were delineated:

(1) a humane psychological and physical environment
(2) qualified staff in numbers sufficient to administer adequate treatment
(3) individualized treatment plans[72]

With regard to the first requirement, standards were provided regarding the client's right to refuse experimental procedures, to receive proper nutritional and medical care, to interact with the opposite sex on a reasonable basis, and to live under adequate living conditions (e.g., standardized levels of heating and ventilation, adequate garbage disposal, fire precautions, accessible toileting and bathing facilities, adequate living space). In addition to not having to participate in experimental procedures and not having to take excessive or unnecessary medication, the judge for the *Wyatt* case also ordered that "patients have a right not to be subjected to treatment procedures such as lobotomy, electroconvulsive treatment, adversive reinforcement conditioning or other unusual or hazardous treatment procedures without their express and informed consent after consultation with counsel or interested party of the patient's choice."[73] In addition, the judge indicated that clients could only be restrained or isolated if they posed an acute danger to themselves or others and if other less intrusive forms of restraint were not possible. Time limits were imposed on the amount of time such clients could be restrained. To ensure that such regulations were carried out, the judge in the *Wyatt* case appointed a human rights committee to act as a standing committee for each of the facilities involved in the case. The purpose of this committee was first, to ensure that clients' standards were being upheld, second, to advise clients regarding their rights, and third, to review all treatment and research plans.

In terms of staffing requirements, the court ordered that "every 250 patients must be served by a staff of 207, including two psychiatrists, four registered physicians, four psychologists, twelve registered nurses, seven social workers, ninety-two orderlies, aides and supporting staff."[74] These figures were derived from standards proposed by a number of different professional organizations: American Orthopsychiatric Association, American Psychological Association, Civil Liberties Union, and

American Association on Mental Deficiency. At times of economic restraint, however, such standards are difficult to achieve.

The court further ordered that individualized treatment plans be available on each client. Although hospitals could easily learn to comply with this particular regulation, this does not necessarily mean that their formally defined treatment plans would correspond to what was actually being done with a client. At the same time, the necessity of having such a plan on file would at least force staff to be thinking in terms of treatment needs for a particular client and would make it easier for staff to develop some consistency in their approach to a particular client once a treatment plan for that client had been formally and objectively stated.

Despite the example set by the Wyatt case, much variation still exists regarding quality of care and the type of client rights that is recognized or respected. As more and more clients fight for their rights in court, however, the greater the likelihood that health care providers will respect their clients' rights to adequate treatment, particularly if these legal struggles result in economic disadvantages to the professional or institution involved. In *Donaldson v. O'Connor and Gumanis,*[75] for example, the plaintiff was awarded $38,500 for being confined for several years without adequate treatment. In this case, "the judge told the jury that the patient did not have to prove the defendants acted in bad faith but merely that they realized he was nondangerous and knew he was receiving only custodial care."[76]

Most of the cases related to a client's right to adequate treatment have been held in the United States. This issue has not been fully tested in Canada as yet, although Canadian courts do support the notion that hospitals have an obligation to provide a client with treatment as well as reasonable care (*Cassidy v. Ministry of Health,*[77] *Bernier v. Sisters of Service*[78]). Most of the cases in Canada have arisen because of negligence and improper care within a particular health care facility rather than lack of adequate treatment.

Outpatients

Outpatients have the same rights regarding health care provision as inpatients. One of the greatest difficulties in the area of outpatient treatment is providing sufficient and adequate treatment resources in the community. This is particularly a problem when a person becomes an outpatient as a consequence of the deinstitutionalization process. For many years, there has been a political move away from large institutions to community-based facilities. Although many of the larger institutions have drastically reduced their numbers, there has not been an equivalent increase in services available on an outpatient basis. Society owes the deinstitutionalized client the right to adequate aftercare to facilitate adjustment to community living and to assist the client in maintaining any therapeutic gains made in a hospital.

Specialty Groups

Individuals who are legally or mentally incompetent are more likely to have problems in obtaining adequate treatment than the "average" person in that they are not given the opportunity to make their own health care decisions and are dependent on other people to do so. Although safeguards are available to protect such individuals (i.e., appointing a guardian), these safeguards are frequently not exercised. Not providing such clients with a guardian could potentially result in a failure to provide them with adequate treatment. This is particularly the case with minors who have the added burden of being mentally retarded. For example, over a 20-year period, 27 children were apparently allowed to die in an Ontario hospital for sick children because parents did not give permission for a simple operation that could have alleviated a dangerous physical problem.[79,80]

Regardless of the lower intellectual level of such individuals, they still have the right to receive humane and adequate treatment. In the past, many of the institutions for the mentally retarded have been found to be a haven for mental, physical, and sexual abuse. In dealing with a mentally retarded adult, many staff also assume that the client is incompetent in all areas if the person is found to be incompetent in one. A person who is found intellectually incompetent to make a contract in the business area, however, may still be sufficiently competent to get married or drive a car. As stated earlier, an individual should not automatically lose all civil or political rights by virtue of losing one. Health care professionals working with such a client population should be sensitized to these issues so that they can guard against abusing their clients' rights.

Another specialty group is the elderly, a proportion of whom does suffer from some variety of mental impairment. Because of their age, however, little if any effort is directed toward assisting them with their "mental" problems. Instead, they are typically given only custodial or physical care or both.

Another difficult population group is made up of those individuals who are labelled "sociopathic personalities." Sociopaths, particularly those diagnosed as sexually deviant, have difficulty obtaining adequate treatment since professionals generally believe that such clients are untreatable. Because of preconceived biases regarding their treatability, they may be placed in a mental health facility primarily as a protection for the general public rather than as a way of assisting them with their problems. Despite the potential for danger from this population group, a mental health facility has no right to detain sociopathic individuals unless attempts are being made to rehabilitate them. If they are under sentence, they should be returned to a penal institution and, if there is no sentence outstanding, they should be simply discharged.

For criminals in general, there may be some tendency to ignore their mental health needs. From a legal standpoint, mental health care must be made available to any prisoner suffering from a mental disorder. Administrative staff in a prison are often given the authority to transfer an emotionally disturbed prisoner from a prison setting to a mental health facility in order to provide an opportunity for adequate treatment. The prisoner may be required to stay within such a facility until such time as the appropriate authorities are convinced that the person has recovered, at which point the prisoner can either be released or returned to prison if he or she still has a sentence to complete. This health care provision applies not only to prisoners who have developed a mental disorder while in prison but also to individuals who cannot be tried because of mental disorder or who have been tried and found not guilty by reason of insanity.

RIGHT TO THE LEAST INTRUSIVE TREATMENT

In *Lake v. Cameron*,[81] it was decreed that a client not only has a right to adequate treatment but also to the least intrusive treatment necessary to alleviate a particular problem. In determining the degree of intrusiveness of a particular intervention, the professional should take into consideration a number of different factors. First of all, the therapist should consider the permanence of any change that could result from a particular procedure. Treatment effects that may be reversible are considered less intrusive than those that are permanent, for example, psychotherapy versus psychosurgery. Another characteristic to consider is the "foreignness" of the change to the client, that is, the degree to which the modified behavior differs from the behaviors typically manifested by that client. The therapist should also consider the scope of behaviors that could possibly be changed as a result of the proposed intervention, the speed with which such changes are likely to occur, the duration of the change, and the client's ability to resist such changes. More intrusive procedures should only be recommended after less intrusive techniques have been tried and found ineffective.

RIGHT TO CHOOSE BETWEEN TREATMENTS

As outlined in the section Informed Consent, a client has the right to refuse a particular form of treatment (e.g., ECT or medication). The refusal of one form of treatment should not negate the client's right to be offered alternative forms of intervention and does not satisfy an institution's legal obligation to offer adequate treatment. The client should be advised of the different alternatives available, together with the possible benefits and potential harms related to each alternative, so that the individual can make an informed choice. In attempting to make a treatment decision, the client has the right to request a second opinion on his or her "mental" condition and on alternative forms of intervention. Professionals are ethically bound to respect and facilitate such requests for external opinions rather than show disapproval or reluctance.

RIGHT TO BE INFORMED

Many facilities attempt to inform clients of their rights by posting written material on the various wards. An ombudsman may also be available to advise clients of their rights. Otherwise, the responsibility for keeping clients informed of their rights lies with the health care providers. In the social work area, for example, if a client on welfare "is unaware of his right to a clothing allotment and therefore does not claim it, it is the social worker's ethical responsibility to tell him about the allotment and facilitate his acquiring it, whatever the inconvenience for the worker or his employing agency."[82]

As a further example, in the area of client–therapist communications, the therapist should inform clients if their disclosures would not be privileged in a courtroom. With the exception of a few conscientious professionals, most health care providers neglect this responsibility until such time as a problem has arisen (e.g., after the professional has been subpoenaed to testify in court).

In addition, clients should always be informed that they have the right to appeal any decisions that might interfere with any of their rights. They should also be notified how they should proceed in making such an appeal should it be necessary.

RIGHT TO FREEDOM OF MOVEMENT

Only outpatients and voluntary inpatients maintain this right although restrictions are often placed on voluntary clients in terms of within-hospital, and "ground," privileges. Involuntary clients as well as prisoners no longer have this freedom assuming due process of law has been followed in establishing their institutional status.

RIGHT TO RESIST INSTITUTIONAL PEONAGE

Many clients have been "coerced" into providing free labor as part of their confinement in a health care facility. Offir gives as an example a female client (Mrs. Dale) with an IQ of 134, who was persuaded to do menial chores to avoid being denied ground privileges. The client in question was expected to "bathe and clean up after aged patients who soiled their linen, work long hours in the dining room and laundry, polish floors and clean offices. . . . People like Mrs. Dale forfeit not only wages, but also workmen's compensation, state retirement plans, social security, and other benefits of being employed."[83]

On the basis of the *Wyatt v. Stickney* case, it was stated that "no patient shall be required to perform labor which involves the operation and maintenance of the hospital or for which the hospital is under contract with an outside organization. . . . Patients may voluntarily engage in such labor if such labor is compensated in accordance with the minimum wage laws of the Fair Labor Standards Act."[84] When the institution can demonstrate that the work assignments are an integral part of the client's treatment and in situations when the client is free to stop working at any time without threat of punishment, the court is unlikely to recognize a client's claim that he or she has been subjected to involuntary servitude (Henry v. Ciccone).[85]

RIGHTS REGARDING TRANSFERS

Transfers are frequently conducted if a province or state other than the one in which the client is committed is financially responsible for that client's care because of legal residency requirements. In the event a client objects to being transferred, he or she should have the right to make a formal objection in the presence of a review board. In general, a client should not be forced to accept a transfer from one health care facility to another if he or she was admitted to the facility voluntarily.

RIGHT TO OPERATE A MOTOR VEHICLE

From a constitutional point of view, the opportunity to operate a motor vehicle is not considered a civil right but a privilege granted by society under certain prescribed conditions. Most provinces are obliged to withhold a driver's license from an individual who has a mental disorder that could potentially interfere with driving ability. For example, the Highway Safety Act of Manitoba (R.S.M. 1970)[86] states:

> The Registrar shall not issue a driver's license to a person who is a mentally disordered person within the meaning of *The Mental Health Act* (s.23). The Registrar may require an applicant or holder of a license to undergo a medical examination and produce a certificate of a medical practitioner that the holder or applicant is not suffering from any disability that would render him a source of danger. (s.26)

As in other areas where a client's rights are suspended by reason of mental disorder, there are no clear standards for determining what constitutes a mental disorder or for determining whether a particular disorder could affect the client's ability to function in a particular area. Swadron and Sullivan recommend that specific criteria be developed for individuals having the following problems so that fair decisions can be made regarding the issuance or suspension of an individual's driver's license: "sensory defects, disturbances of motor control, intermittent disturbances of consciousness, defects of emotional stability, defects of judgment, ideation and thought."[87]

The Canadian Medical Association[88] has published a guide for physicians listing various physiological and psychological variables affecting a person's fitness to drive. Clients may be discouraged or forbidden from driving if they have consistent difficulties with concentration or behavioral control as a result of a particular mental disturbance. Various psychotic or emotional symptoms could also interfere with an individual's ability to drive safely, not to mention the physiological effects produced by any medications being used. Individuals receiving ECT may also be prohibited from driving as a result of "impaired mental/motor reflex."[89] Most of the symptoms in this guide are not clearly defined, however, and are left to the discretion of the client's attending physician.

RIGHT TO MANAGE BUSINESS AFFAIRS

A client has the right to manage his or her estate, dispose of property, or write a will, for example, unless the individual is declared incompetent to do so.

> A person's competency may vary according to the activity anticipated. Thus, criteria for incompetency to execute a will may differ from criteria for competency to enter into a contract or to consent for medical treatment. For example, testamentary capacity may depend upon whether the person assessed knows what property he has and which relatives he has who would be the natural objects of his bounty. Competency to enter into contracts would include his ability to comprehend the nature and terms of the particular transaction.[90]

Involuntary institutionalization is not sufficient cause to deprive a client of this right although health care staff that are naive regarding clients' rights may operate under this erroneous assumption and regrettably reinforce this attitude in the client and his or her family. When a client demonstrates that he or she is incapable of making reasonable decisions regarding business affairs, the client may be declared incompetent in this area and decision-making rights transferred to an appointed guardian. A client has the right to appeal such an incompetency order although the length of time between appeals may vary from one location to another. Most appeal periods are 1 year although the revised Mental Health Act in Ontario[91] now allows for appeals after a 6-month period. If at any point, however, the client's attending physician no longer considers the client incompetent to manage his or her affairs, the incompetency status can be revoked after due procedure.

RIGHT TO VOTE

A client's right to vote may be removed if the person is either declared incompetent or is institutionalized involuntarily. Depriving a client of this franchise does not appear justified if the person's mental disorder does not interfere with making reasonable decisions in this area. "It should not be expected . . . that the decision to hospitalize or declare a person incompetent respecting his property should precisely reflect his competence in relation to exercising the right to vote."[92] There also seems no rational justification for depriving such clients from exercising their franchise simply on the basis of institutional status alone. Although voluntary clients certainly have the option of discharging themselves in order to vote, it would seem more reasonable to make provisions for voting within the facility rather than forcing a client to discharge himself or herself prematurely in order to exercise this right. Mental health facilities vary widely in their willingness to accommodate clients with voting rights, suggesting the need for formal guidelines in this area.

RIGHT TO PRACTICE AN OCCUPATION

A client's right to practice a particular occupation may be prevented as a result of mental disorder. The right to prevent an individual from obtaining a professional license as well as the right to revoke or suspend an existing license is addressed in statutes governing the practice of many different professional groups. The major flaw in such statutes is their failure to provide a clear and comprehensive definition of the varieties of mental disorder that would interfere with the client's ability to practice a profession. In addition, no mention is usually made of the process by which the professional body would determine whether a particular person is mentally incapable of practicing a profession. Because of the lack of clearly specified criteria, there is always the danger that involuntary admission in and of itself would be used as the basis for this decision.

Even when a client is once again declared competent to manage business affairs, the respective professional body may not allow the individual to practice a profession. For example, in *Hubbard v. Washington*,[93] the state medical disciplinary board stated that: "there is a distinction between a practitioner (i) being mentally incompetent to make contracts and to transact business in the usual manner, and (ii) being mentally incompetent to practice medicine and perform surgical operations. The fact that he has been found by the court to be competent to make contracts and engage in the ordinary business transactions incident to the management of his personal affairs does not *ipso facto* restore his qualifications to practice medicine and surgery."[94]

For the protection of the client, there should be standards developed regarding career rights with clearly delineated criteria for professional reinstatement. The individual should also have the right to appeal negative decisions made by his or her licensing body in a regular court of law.

RIGHT TO COMMUNICATE

Mental health regulations typically provide some guidelines regarding a client's right to communicate with agencies or individuals outside the health care facility. For example, the Mental Health Act of Ontario (R.S.O. 1970, c.269) states:

19—(1) Except as provided in this section, no communication written by a patient or sent to a patient shall be opened, examined or withheld, and its delivery shall not in any way be obstructed or delayed.

(2) Where the officer-in-charge or a person acting under his authority has reasonable and probable cause to believe
   (a) that the contents of a communication written by a patient would,
     (i) be unreasonably offensive to the addressee, or
     (ii) prejudice the best interests of the patient; or
   (b) that the contents of a communication sent to a patient would,
     (i) interfere with the treatment of the patient, or
     (ii) cause the patient unnecessary distress,
     the officer-in-charge or a person acting under his authority may open and examine the contents thereof and, if any conditions mentioned in clause (a) or (b) as the case may be, exist, may withhold such communication from delivery.

(3) Subsection 2 does not apply to a communication written by a patient to, or appearing to be sent to a patient by,
   (a) a barrister and solicitor;
   (b) a member of a review board or advisory review board under this Act; or
   (c) a member of the Assembly.[95]

Insulating a client from a difficult and often hostile environment is the compelling reason for the practice of mail and telephone censorship. Censoring the client's outgoing and incoming communication provides control over the kind of stimuli that the client can successfully cope with.

As previously described, the only justification for interfering with a client's private contacts with others is that such communication would be antitherapeutic or would likely interfere with the person's later acceptance into the community. For example, a client sending threatening letters to an employer may jeopardize the opportunity to return to that job following discharge. The danger to the client in such cases, however, is that the institution can only determine if communications relating to a client are antitherapeutic after the fact, that is, after the communication has been examined. Potentially, all clients could have their communication screened on the assumption that it could possibly have adverse effects on them, thereby justifying the institution's right to interfere with the client's privacy. To provide some protection for the client in this area, some guidelines were developed as a result of the *Wyatt* case, that is:

> patients have an unrestricted right to send sealed mail, and they have a right to visitation and telephone communications and to receive sealed mail except to the extent that the qualified mental health professional responsible for formulation of the particular patient's treatment plan writes an order imposing special restrictions. Such an order must be renewed after each periodic review of this treatment plan.[96]

To provide further protection to the client and to force some accountability on the part of the health care facility, it is also recommended that a notation be placed in the client's file each time the facility interferes with a client's right to communicate, with the rationale for doing so clearly outlined.

RIGHT TO FEEDBACK

The client's bill of rights published by the American Hospital Association specifies that clients be given feedback from their health care providers regarding their state of health, that is, "the patient has the right to obtain from his physician complete current information concerning his diagnosis, treatment, and prognosis in terms the patient can be reasonably expected to understand. When it is not medically advisable to give such information to the patient, the information should be made available to an appropriate person in his behalf."[97]

An obligation to provide feedback to a client is also delineated in the ethical codes of many professional groups. For example, within the profession of psychology, the psychologist has a duty to communicate test results to a client in language that can be understood, even though the client is not allowed access to "raw" psychological data. Under most circumstances, the client is provided with an oral interpretation of the results rather than a written report because of the risk of misinterpretation.

RIGHT TO EXAMINE RECORDS

Although many facilities may discourage a client from doing so, it is generally believed that a client has the right to examine his or her records unless there is good reason to believe that access to the record is not in his or her best interests. This access does not apply to any personal notes written by the therapist on a client. If it is believed that the information in the record would have a psychologically detrimental effect on the client, such access may be refused. "If an impasse is reached, medical and legal advice should be sought prior to showing the patient his record."[98] A notation should always be made on the client's file when such access has been granted or when it has been requested and refused for particular reasons. If the client is given permission to see the record, it is quite important to have the appropriate professional(s) available at the time of examination to assist the client in understanding the information and to answer any questions. If a client is denied the right to examine personal records, he or she still has the option of having a copy of the file sent to a third party (e.g., a lawyer), thereby gaining access to the file indirectly. The following quote serves to communicate the apparent irony of such a process:

> "I find it perverse that although I am denied direct access to my own files, I can authorize others to examine them."—Anonymous client[99]

According to Roth et al.,[100] "only about one third of the states now have statutes that permit some sort of direct patient access to records and half of these afford only very limited rights." The Krever Commission Report[101] points out a similar situation in Ontario. On the basis of their inquiry, however, the commission recommended:

82. That legislation be enacted to express the general rule that an individual has a right to inspect and receive copies of any health information, of which he or she is the subject, kept by a health-care provider.

. . . .

85. That, after inspecting or receiving the health information, an individual has a right to request that the information be corrected. The health-care provider shall make the correction as requested or inform the individual of the reasons for the refusal. In the event of a refusal, the individual may apply to the Health Commissioner for review of the refusal. The decision of the Health Commissioner should be subject to an appeal to the county or Supreme Court.

When it is believed that access to health information is not in the client's best interests, the Krever Commission further recommended:

83. That a Health Commissioner, a well-respected, non-member of the

health professions, be appointed, whose responsibilities would include receiving applications by health-care providers for an exemption from the obligation to disclose information to a requesting subject, receiving applications by an individual for corrections to his or her health information, making a decision on the applications, and informing the health-care providers and the subjects of the decision.

84. That when, in the opinion of the health-care provider, disclosure of the information is likely to have a detrimental effect on the physical or mental health of the requesting individual or other person, an application may be made by the health-care provider to the Health Commissioner for an exemption from the obligation to disclose that information. The decision of the Health Commissioner should be subject to an appeal to the County or Supreme Court.[102]

Individuals in favor of a client's access to formal records believe that the client has the right to know what is being said about him or her to encourage accountability in the area of diagnosis and treatment planning and to promote greater accuracy and caution in record keeping. Access to the record potentially assists the client in learning about his or her health care needs and in understanding prescribed treatment procedures.

The therapeutic disadvantages that could result from having a client examine records has often been used as a blanket justification for withholding such material from almost everyone. Professionals speculate, for example, that the client could be adversely affected by reading about himself or herself in the third person and in terms that are occasionally derogatory. For example, clients may be described in such terms as attention-seeking or manipulative. Clients reading this interpretation of their behavior could understandably become upset by learning of others' perceptions of them, either because of the unfairness of a particular interpretation or because they are unwilling to recognize that particular characteristic in themselves. In any event, a likely consequence is that the relationship with the therapist may be adversely affected and that the client may become less receptive to professional assistance.

Another argument that has been used to justify withholding hospital records is the high risk of misinterpretation. Such misinterpretation could be based partly on the client's naivete regarding professional terminology, for example, or because of selective attention to specific aspects of the report. For example, clients may only attend to the negative comments directed toward them and ignore some of the more positive comments because of the hurt that may arise from reading something critical.

In addition, a hospital may be reluctant to allow the client direct examination of the file because it may contain information from other individuals (e.g., relatives) who might not want the client to know what they said about him or her because of the possible repercussions. In many situations, information regarding a client's behavior has been volunteered by the client's family. Out of fear or concern regarding their future interactions with that person, family members might be unwilling to provide such information if they realized the client would be able to read what they said.

A study by Roth et al.,[103] however, did not generally find any adverse effects resulting from letting clients examine their records when done in the presence of a professional who could answer any questions regarding their file. Although further research in this area would be warranted because of the small number of clients included in the study, the findings certainly suggest that the concerns regarding client access to records may be grossly overestimated.

RIGHT TO DUE PROCESS

As previously described, society has often felt justified in depriving an individual of certain rights. Some of the most common rights that are removed include the right to freedom of movement (e.g., involuntary psychiatric clients, prisoners), the right to refuse treatment, the right to have children, and the right to manage business matters. There are three possible justifications given for interfering with an individual's rights: first of all, to protect the client from hurting himself or herself as a result of whatever mental disorder may exist (e.g., through self-destructive behavior, incompetent business transactions); to protect other individuals who could be specifically affected by their relationship with the client (e.g., a spouse, children); and, to protect the general public from "actions and deeds arising from the nature of the illness, e.g., voting, acting as a judge, juror, physician, lawyer, chartered accountant, teacher, trustee, as operator of a plane, ship, car or train, etc."[104]

For all of these possibilities, there must be sufficient cause to believe that the removal of a specific right is justified. To demonstrate sufficient cause, due process of law must be followed. The right to due process is guaranteed to every citizen as a protection against unfair external interference with his or her constitutional rights. In the case of the alleged mentally disturbed individual, however, the right to due process has often been ignored or only given token homage. Nevertheless, it has been generally recommended that certain procedures be followed when challenging a client's rights in order to reduce the possibility that a specific right will be removed unjustly. These procedures include adequate notice, right to counsel, a fair hearing, and the opportunity to appeal any negative decision. If any of these procedures are not followed, the client has the right to challenge the process by which his or her rights were removed in court. Such procedural safeguards are important not only to protect the individual's freedom, but also to safeguard him or her from any scheming relative or the danger of "public haste, neglect and negligence."[105] According to Kittrie,

The demonstrated laxity of criteria in the therapeutic realms require even greater than usual emphasis on fair procedures to help decide, for example, whether a given juvenile committed the acts that would denominate him a delinquent, whether the mentally ill person is actually dangerous to himself or others, whether the alleged psychopath does indeed have a record of past violations and in fact demonstrates a propensity for further crime, and whether procreation by the patient for whom sterilization is requested is likely to produce defective children.[106]

Notice

First, clients should receive adequate written notice of the hearing to allow them sufficient time to develop a defense. In order to do this, the client also needs to be informed regarding the purpose of the hearing and any allegations that have been made. It is necessary for such a notice to include the time and place of the hearing as well as any procedural rules to be followed. When it is believed that the client may be incapable of understanding the nature or consequences of the proposed hearing, an attempt should be made to secure an attorney for the client or a legal guardian so that the notice can be served to a competent party willing to act on the client's behalf. Generally, it is not considered sufficient to notify only the client's family in these instances, as family members may have a conflict of interest regarding the client that could interfere with their acting in his or her best interests.

In the case of an emergency, no notice or hearing is generally required to admit a client to an institution involuntarily. In most jurisdictions, however, criteria for emergency admission have been established in order to provide some protection for the client in question. In most states, individuals can be committed involuntarily on the certification of two physicians. On the basis of their certification, they must indicate that they have examined the individual and that, on the basis of this examination, they have concluded that the client is mentally disordered and a danger to self or others. The criteria of dangerousness have been challenged, however, in that professionals have not been "clinically able to predict dangerousness even with 50% accuracy."[107] Because of "a strong tendency to overpredict dangerousness . . . commitment based only on a prediction of dangerousness would thus involve a potentially large percentage of false positives."[108]

In spite of the lack of hard data to support commitment decisions, the client is still not given an opportunity to challenge his or her commitment in emergency situations, although this can be done after his or her freedom has been removed. Even in the case of a nonemergency civil commitment, many statutes do not provide for notice prior to commitment proceedings although notice may have to be given to the client's immediate family. Many states either ignore the need for adequate notice or suggest that such a notice could have an adverse effect on the client's psychological state, thereby justifying their withholding it. Even in states where a notice is given, the minimum notice required is often a mere 24 hours, therefore diminishing the client's opportunity to prepare and present an adequate case in his or her defense.

Fair Hearing

As previously described, clients should have the opportunity to challenge the allegations made against them or to present alternative, less intrusive, forms of intervention in the presence of an impartial judge or committee. As part of a defense, clients also should have the right to be present at the hearing, to have access to the information being used against them, to present witnesses in their defense, and to confront and cross-examine witnesses testifying against them. In addition, they should be entitled to counsel to assist them in this process because they are likely to know very little about commitment proceedings and how to defend themselves properly. Furthermore, clients should not be obliged to provide information about themselves that could be incriminating. In many instances, there is much variation in the degree to which various authorities adhere to these particular due process requirements. In the case of involuntary commitment proceedings, for example, "the courts divide on the question of whether a pre-hospitalization judicial or other independent hearing is a requirement of due process."[109] In places where a prehospitalization hearing is not granted, the client has the right to request a posthospitalization hearing or to file a writ of habeus corpus in which the institution is obliged to justify its reasons for depriving an individual of liberty or else to release him or her. Even in places where hearings are required, however, they are often just a formality. Cohen refers to this process as assembly-line justice and states, for example, that "in Texas, a total of seventy-five minutes was devoted to the hearing of forty cases (or 1.8 minutes per patient)."[110]

More specifically, the rights that a client should be granted in order to satisfy due process requirements in the course of the actual hearing include the following ones.

Right to Counsel. Counsel is important in helping the client prepare and defend his or her case by collecting relevant information, challenging information presented by witnesses acting against the client, and so forth. Even though this is a recommended procedure, many states do not provide the client with this opportunity, that is, there are only 42 states that even recognize the client's right to counsel, and only 24 states that recommend a counsel be appointed when the client is indigent or unrepresented.[111,112] Even when a counsel is present, the client's attendance may be irrelevant. "Unless the proceeding is adversary in nature . . . the attorney does not engage in any preparation and does not effectively participate in the hearing. . . . The consequence is allocation of effective decision making to the medical, more particularly the psychiatric, profession with the legal process and the attorney assuming a ceremonial function."[113]

Right Not to Incriminate Oneself. When being examined with regard to mental status (e.g., in commitment proceedings), the client should be advised of the purpose of the psychiatric examination so that he or she has the choice of withholding information that might incriminate himself or herself. In other words, "the patient should be told by counsel and the psychiatrist that he is going to be examined with regard to his mental condition, that the statements he may make may be the basis for commitment, and that he does not have to speak to the psychiatrist" (*Lessard v. Schmidt*).[114]

Right to Information. In order to prepare an adequate defense, it has been recommended that clients be given access to pertinent information in their file (e.g., diagnosis, psychiatric and social history, psychological assessment findings) under the assumption that they should know what is being said about them in order to prepare a defense. The right to have access to relevant information has also been recommended by the Krever Commission in situations where restrictions regarding a client's rights are being reviewed by a review board, that is, "for the purposes of a hearing before the Advisory Review Board, the patient or his or her counsel has a right to inspect the patient's clinical record."[115]

Right to Appeal

After an individual has lost a specific right (e.g., freedom of movement), he or she should have the opportunity to appeal the decision in a higher court or to request a periodic review of the decision in order to prevent unnecessarily prolonged deprivation of this right. For example, a client has the right to an appeal if it is felt that he or she (1) is not receiving adequate treatment, (2) has been committed unfairly, (3) is being transferred against his or her will. The period that must elapse before the client has the right to request a review of past decisions varies across issues and across locations. For such issues as incompetence, the review period typically ranges from 6 months to a year. In the case of involuntary institutionalization, the review period may vary from a few days to several months, depending on the length of time that has elapsed since the last review and since the client's involuntary admission.

Right to Due Process: Specialty Groups

Specific difficulties may arise when the intervention proposed produces a permanent and irreversible change, thereby not allowing the individual a chance for periodic review of the suspension of a particular right. This problem occurs, for example, when a request is made to prevent a mentally retarded individual, through sterilization, from having children. The following procedures have been recommended to protect the client from unnecessary interference with parental rights (*Buck v. Bell*):

1. *Commencement*—The superintendent of the institution in which the patient is committed files a petition, accompanied by affidavit, stating the facts which led to his conclusion that the welfare of society would be enhanced if the individual were sterilized.
2. *Hearing Agency*—A special board receives the superintendent's petition and holds a hearing on the matter. All evidence and findings of the board must be reduced to writing.
3. *Notice*—Notice of the petition and of the hearing are to be given to the individual and to his guardian. If there is no guardian, the superintendent must have one appointed by the county court.
4. *Hearing*—The individual may attend the hearing if he or his guardian so desire.
5. *Appeal*—If sterilization is ordered by the board, the inmate or his guardian may appeal the decision to the county court. The court may review the order of the board upon its record and may hear any other admissible evidence. The court may revise, affirm, or reverse the order. An appeal from the county court may also be taken to the Supreme Court of Appeals, but unlike the appeal from the board's decision, granting this appeal is discretionary with the Supreme Court.[116]

The right to due process also has been frequently ignored in the case of minors. Although the right to due process has been recently challenged and won (*Bartley v. Kremens*),[117] traditionally a minor could be committed to an institution by his or her parents without recourse to a hearing or an appeal. Kittrie refers to the specific problems arising in the case of the juvenile who is likely to be adjudicated a delinquent without recourse to due process of law, even though the consequences of being so labeled may result in greater restrictions for the juvenile than for an adult accused of the same misbehavior. "If an adult, for example, were arrested by the police in a public street in the early hours of the morning, he would be hastily released in the absence of any criminal charges. If a juvenile is apprehended under similar circumstances, he can be committed to an institution for being in an unsuitable environment and beyond the control of his parents."[118] The discriminatory way of dealing with this same type of misbehavior suggests that due process may be even more important in the case of minors.

REFERENCES

1. Cobb, H. V. (1973). Citizen advocacy and the rights of the handicapped. In W. Wolfensberger & H. Zauha (Eds.), *Citizen advocacy and protective services for the impaired and handicapped* (p. 150). Toronto: Mental Institute on Mental Retardation.

2. Ibid.
3. Ibid., 151.
4. Ibid.
5. Smith, S. J., & Davis, A. J. (1980). Ethical dilemmas: Conflicts among rights, duties and obligations. *American Journal of Nursing, 80*(8), 1463.
6. Swoboda, J. S., Elwork, A., Sales, B. D., & Levine, D. (1978). Knowledge of and compliance with privileged communication and child abuse reporting laws. *Professional Psychology, 9*(3), 448.
7. Tancredi, L., & Clark, D. (1972). Psychiatry and the legal rights of patients. *American Journal of Psychiatry, 129*(3), 104.
8. Ralph Nader's Center for the Study of Responsive Law. *Hearings on Constitutional Rights of the Mentally Ill before the Subcommittee on Constitutional Rights of the Senate Committee on the Judiciary,* 91st Congress, 2nd session, 396 (1970).
9. Coburn, D. (1978). Patients' rights—what is it they want? *Health Care in Canada, 20*(12), 45.
10. Ibid.
11. Westin, A. F. (1976). *Computers, health records and citizen rights.* NBS Monograph 157. Washington, DC: U.S. Department of Commerce/National Bureau of Standards.
12. Sharpe, G. (1972). Privileged communications between physician and patient (Part 2). *Ontario Medical Review, 39*(9), 539.
13. The Mental Health Act (Revised Statutes of Ontario 1970). Ch. 269 as amended by 1978, Ch. 50 and Regul. 576 as amended to 0. Reg. 685/80 and Reg. 577 as amended to 0. Reg. 406/80.
14. Swoboda, Knowledge and compliance, 449.
15. Ibid.
16. Slovenko, R. (1973). *Psychiatry and the law* (p. 61). Boston: Little, Brown.
17. Ibid., 71.
18. Jagim, R. D., Wittman, W. D., & Noll, J. O. (1978). Mental health professionals' attitudes toward confidentiality, privilege and third-party disclosures. *Professional psychology, 9*(3), 462.
19. Foster, L. M. (1980). State confidentiality laws: The Illinois Act as model for new legislation in other states. *American Journal of Orthopsychiatry, 50*(4), 663.
20. Gilmore, A. (1978). Health records confidentiality: The rights of the individual and society. *Canadian Medical Association Journal, 119,* 1100.
21. American Hospital Association (1979). *Institutional policies for disclosure of medical record information* (p. 4). Chicago: American Hospital Association.
22. Foster, State confidentiality laws, 663.
23. Kirk, W. E. (1978). Informed consent is the problem. *Michigan Psychiatric Society Newsletter, 21,* 4.
24. Foster, State confidentiality laws, 662.
25. Krever, Honourable Justice H. (1980). *Report of the commission of Inquiry into the Confidentiality of Health Information* (Vols. 1–3). Toronto: J. C. Thatcher, Queen's Printer for Ontario.
26. Martin, R. (1975). *Legal challenges to behavior modification* (p. 122). Champaign, IL: Research Press.

27. Slovenko, *Psychiatry and the law*, 455.
28. Tiberius, R. (1979). Medical ethics in the next 25 years. *Canadian Family Physician, 25*, 74.
29. Krever, *Commission of inquiry*, 32–33.
30. Hemelt, M. D., & Mackert, M. E. '1978). *Dynamics of law in nursing and health care* (p. 109). Toronto: Reston Publishing Co.
31. Grisso, T., & Vierling, L. (1978). Minors' consent to treatment: A developmental perspective. *Professional Psychology 9*(3), 415.
32. Slovenko, *Psychiatry and the law*, 313.
33. Page, S. (1977). The psychiatric patient: Commitment, consent, competence. *Ontario Medical Review, 44*(11), 547.
34. Gray, C. (1979). The law and informed consent. *Canadian Medical Association Journal, 120*, 43.
35. Slovenko, *Psychiatry and the law*, 321.
36. Rozovsky, L. E. (1974). *Canadian hospital law* (p. 36). Ottawa: Canadian Hospital Association.
37. Rozovsky, L. E. (1979). *Canadian hospital law: A practical guide*, 2nd ed (p. 44). Ottawa: Canadian Hospital Association.
38. Springer, B. W. (1979). Consents from mentally ill patients. *Hospital Topics, 51*(4), 39.
39. Culver, C. M., Ferrell, R. B., & Green, R. M. (1980). ECT and special problems of informed consent. *American Journal of Psychiatry, 137*(5), 587.
40. Ford, M. D. (1980). The psychiatrists' double bind: The right to refuse medication. *American Journal of Psychiatry, 137*(3), 333–334.
41. Ibid., 334.
42. Rozovsky, *Canadian hospital law*, 2nd ed., 45.
43. Grisso, Minors' consent, 415.
44. Ibid., 413–414.
45. Ibid., 423.
46. Sharpe, G. (1971). Medicine and the law. *Ontario Medical Review, 38*(11), 576.
47. Rozovsky, *Canadian hospital law*, 2nd ed., 37.
48. Project on Law and Behavior. (1977). *Law and Behavior, 2*(3), 3.
49. Hemelt, *Dynamics of law*, 98.
50. Rozovsky, L. E. (1977). Consent to treatment: who holds it? *Canadian Family Physician, 1047*, 57.
51. Coyne, J. C. (1976). The place of informed consent in ethical dilemmas. *Journal of Consulting and Clinical Psychology, 44*(6), 1016.
52. Slovenko, *Psychiatry and the law*, 251.
53. Sharpe, G. (1972). The physician-patient relationship: Part IV patient disclosures. *Ontario Medical Review, 39*, 676.
54. Moore, R. (1978). Ethics in the practice of psychiatry—origins, functions, models and enforcement. *American Journal of Psychiatry, 135*(2), 159.
55. Martin, *Legal challenges*, 30.
56. Ladd, J. (1980). Medical ethics: Who knows best? *The Lancet*, 1127–1128.
57. Del Rio, V. B. Y. (1975). Psychiatric Ethics. In A. M. Friedman, H. I. Kaplan, & B. J. Sadock (Eds.), *Comprehensive textbook of psychiatry II*, 2nd ed. (p. 2546). Baltimore: Williams & Wilkins.

58. Kerlinger, F. (1972). Draft report of the A.P.A. Committee on Ethical Standards in Psychological Research. *American Psychologist, 29*, 894.
59. Reid, R. (1971). Legal considerations in counselling young people. *Addictions, 18*(2), 8.
60. Appelbaum, P. S., & Gutheil, T. G. (1980). Drug refusal: A study of psychiatric inpatients. *American Journal of Psychiatry, 32*(3), 340.
61. Stone, A. A. (1975). *Mental health and law: A system in transition* (p. 68). Rockville, MD: National Institute of Mental Health.
62. Sharpe, Physician-patient relationship, part IV, 679.
63. Page, S. (1973). *Mental patients and the law* (p. 51). Toronto: Self-Counsel Press.
64. Sharpe, Medicine and the law, 576.
65. Sharpe, Physician–patient relationship, part 4, 671.
66. Peck, C. L. (1975). Current legislative issues concerning the right to refuse versus the right to choose hospital and treatment. *Psychiatry, 38*, 303.
67. Slovenko, *Psychiatry and the law*, 235–236.
68. Ibid., 236.
69. Kittrie, N. N. (1971). *The right to be different: Deviance and enforced therapy.* Baltimore: Penguin Books.
70. *Wyatt v. Stickney,* 344 F. Supp. 373, 344 F. Supp. 387 (M.D. Ala 1972) aff'd. *Sub. nom Wyatt v. Aderholt* 503 F. 2d, 1305 (5th Cir. 1974).
71. Offir, C. W. (1974). Civil rights and the mentally ill—revolution in Bedlam. *Psychology Today, 8*(5), 62.
72. Slovenko, *Psychiatry and the law*, 234.
73. Ibid., 250.
74. Ibid., 236–237.
75. *Donaldson v. O'Connor and Gumanis,* 493 F. 2d. 507 (5th Cir. 1974).
76. Offir, Rights and the mentally ill, 63.
77. *Cassidy v. Ministry of Health,* 1951 2 K.B. 343.
78. *Bernier v. Sisters of Service,* 1948 2 D.L.R. 468.
79. Garner, J. (1979). Withholding treatment from the retarded: Canadian Psychiatric Association studies legal/medical aspects. *Canadian Medical Association Journal, 120*, 716.
80. Swadron, B. B., & Himel, S. G. (1979). Legal opinion on position paper: Withholding treatment. *Canadian Journal of Psychiatry, 24*(1), 81.
81. *Lake v. Cameron,* 364 F. 2d. 657 (D.C. Cir. 1966).
82. Levy, C. S. (1976). *Social work ethics* (pp. 132–133). New York: Human Sciences Press.
83. Offir, Civil rights, 64.
84. *Wyatt v. Stickney.*
85. *Henry v. Ciccone,* 315 F. Supp. 889 (W.D. Mo 1970).
86. Highway Safety Act of Manitoba, R.S.M. 1970, C. no. 60 as amended by S.M. 197, C. 71.
87. Swadron, B. B., & Sullivan, D. R. (1973). *The law and mental disorder.* Toronto: Canadian Mental Health Association.
88. Canadian Medical Association (1977). *Guide for physicians in determining fitness to drive a motor vehicle.* Ottawa: CMA
89. Ibid., 12.5.1.

90. Sharpe, G. (1977). Consent and competency. *Canadian Medical Association Journal, 117,* 1215.
91. Mental Health Act of Ontario, R.S.O. (1970).
92. Swadron, *Law and mental disorder,* 79.
93. *Hubbard v. Washington State Medical Disciplinary Board,* 348 P. 2d 981 (1960).
94. Swadron, *Law and mental disorder,* 93.
95. Mental Health Act of Ontario, R.S.O. (1970).
96. Slovenko, *Psychiatry and the law,* 252.
97. Hemelt, *Dynamics of law,* 66.
98. Rozovsky, *Canadian hospital law,* 2nd ed., 95.
99. Roth, L. H., Wolford, J., & Meisel, A. I. (1980). Patient access to records: Tonic or toxin? *American Journal of Psychiatry, 137*(5), 592.
100. Ibid.
101. Krever, *Commission of inquiry,* 30–31.
102. Ibid.
103. Roth, Patient access, 592.
104. Swadron, *Law and mental disorder,* 32.
105. Kittrie, *Right to be different,* 368.
106. Ibid.
107. Kahles, L. R., & Sales, B. D. (1978). Attitudes of clinical psychologists toward involuntary civil commitment law. *Professional Psychology, 9*(3), 435.
108. Ibid., 430.
109. Kittrie, *Right to be different,* 88.
110. Cohen, F. (1966). The function of the attorney and the commitment of the mentally ill. *Texas Law Review, 44,* 430.
111. Kittrie, *Right to be different,* 404.
112. Stone, *Mental health.*
113. Cohen, Function of the attorney, 424–425.
114. Lessard v. Schmidt, 349 F. Supp. 1078 (E.D. Wis. 1972).
115. Krever, *Commission of inquiry,* Rec. 88.
116. *Buck v. Bell,* 274 U.S. 200 (1927).
117. *Bartley v. Kremens,* 402 F. Supp. 1039 (E.D. Pa 1975), Prob. Juris. noted, 96 S. Ct. 1457 (1976).
118. Kittrie, *Right to be different,* 117.

Third-Party Transactions

4

CONFLICTS OF INTEREST

Conflicts are a major ethical concern in third-party situations and seem more likely to arise when more than one party has the right to make demands on the mental health professional's behavior. Since these demands are often made by individuals or organizations with a different perspective and background, they may be perceived by the mental health professional as ambiguous and confusing. The presence of ambiguity increases the possibility that the different parties will have conflicting views regarding the professional's loyalties and what they expect from the service. Not only is it frequently unclear what services are being requested but also what responsibilities and obligations the professional should have to each of the parties involved. The confusion and complexities created by such conflicts increase the risk of improper professional conduct and raise a number of ethical concerns which will be highlighted in the following sections: Conflict in Expectations, Conflict in Values, Conflict in Responsibilities, and Variability in Roles.

Conflict in Expectations

One of the most common sources of conflict develops because the various parties involved with the mental health professional have different views as to what the service will provide or what the professional is even capable of providing. In the court system, for example, "a typical unrealistic expectation portrays the psychiatrist as a human lie detector, able to detect insincerity, fabrication, or malingering on the basis of an examination."[1] The professional who fails to acknowledge his or her human limits helps to promote such a myth until such time as reality demystifies such a stance and reduces professional credibility.

In many situations, a discrepancy in views arises as early as the referral question. There are many reasons for this. First of all, the referral question itself may be overly vague, incomplete, or ambiguous. Monahan[2] refers to an unpublished study by Farmer (1977) in which he found that "in over 95 percent of the referrals to psychologists and psychiatrists, judges consistently fail to communicate their objectives and questions to the examiner." Despite this lack of clarity regarding what is being asked, it is fairly common for mental health providers to make assumptions about the referral question and to make an assessment according to these assumptions without seeking prior clarification. In any situation, however, when a professional allows himself or herself to operate according to assumptions, there is room for error, particularly when third parties are involved. More often than not the referral source has a different orientation and training background than the mental health professional (e.g., lawyers, teachers, managers). This diversity in background is bound to be reflected in different forms of expression with different meanings attached to various concepts. For example, when mental health services are provided to the court it is not uncommon for the issue of competency to be confused with the existence of psychosis. Legal terms are often alien to the mental health professional, who may deal with them naively and inaccurately by equating them with specific mental health terms. The same is true of the legal professional when trying to understand psychological terminology. Hardisty has pointed out the implications of these language difficulties for the court system in the following statement:

> Many judges and legislators fail to realize that 'mental disease' no
> longer has an accepted psychiatric meaning. . . . Thus, testifying psy-
> chiatrists attempt to define 'mental illness' by reference to legal and
> social rather than medical guidelines. Yet, at the same time, the medical
> connotations of 'disease' cause lawyers to falsely assume that in legal
> tests the term 'mental disease' has a medically accepted meaning. This
> terminological confusion exacerbates the general tendency of psychiat-
> ric witnesses and lawyers to misunderstand each other.[3]

Some of these difficulties have arisen because the mental health professional has gone along with the demand characteristics imposed by the
referring party without attempting to question or correct misconceptions.

In other words, in dealing with third parties there is the increasing
risk that the referral question will be misunderstood and an inadequate
service provided. The implications of this type of transaction are multidi-
mensional and include potential harm to the recipient of the service; dissatisfaction of the referring party; a tarnished reputation for the professional or the professional body the person represents; and a disservice to
society in terms of the potentially adverse side effects of an inadequate
service and the costs. As an example, Gutheil[4] refers to lawyers' growing
lack of respect for the psychiatric profession because of the naive expectation that psychiatrists could "lend scientific certainty to many of the
most difficult problems faced by the law" and provide data as concrete
as that provided by ballistics experts. This faulty expectation is destined
to result in disappointment and a growing disrespect for the mental
health field for a number of reasons. First of all, there is no scientific
certainty when dealing with the majority of mental health matters, particularly when trying to interface mental health with legal concerns. In
addition, too many misconceptions arise between the various parties regarding the nature of the service that is to be provided. A typical shortcoming on the part of the mental health professional is his or her failure
to determine exactly what is being asked or to decide whether he or she
can actually (or ethically) provide such a service. In other words, the professional fails by continuing to operate in a state of ambiguity and confusion in a situation that is typically fraught with negative implications for
all parties.

Not only do false expectations often exist between the mental health
professional and the third party (referral source) but also with the recipient or consumer of the service (typically referred to as the client). Most
individuals have been brought up with the view that mental health professionals are there to help them. This perception is obviously problematic when the professional is acting as an agent for a third party, particularly when the client's involvement with the professional can have
potentially negative consequences for the client's future. This problem

becomes even more serious when working with individuals who are emotionally disturbed or vulnerable as a function of the situation they are presently in. For example, in situations of voluntary commitment to a psychiatric facility, clients may agree to be admitted because of the high degree of distress they are experiencing and the expectation that they will obtain better assistance with their problems once they are in a therapeutic milieu. Clients who have never been admitted to such a setting are rarely prepared for what confronts them. It is fairly common, for example, for clients to have their belongings searched and to be deprived of certain personal possessions brought with them (e.g, belts, shoelaces, shampoo) because of administrative policies above and beyond the control of the therapist recommending admission. Once the individual is on the unit the need for efficient delivery of services (e.g., medication, meals) forces the inpatient to alter his or her own preferences for doing things in order to fit within a regimented system. In other words, the therapeutic needs and expectations of the client are bound to clash with the organizational and security needs of the institution. Inpatients are also rarely prepared for the limited amount of time they are allowed to spend with their respective therapists. Typically, a large majority of their time involves interactions with individuals who are more disturbed than they are. At other times they may feel bombarded by other members of the health team who consider it their right to invade the clients' private thoughts. Clients who expected (and prefer) to talk only with their therapist may find the "team" approach intrusive. If sufficiently assertive to resist such pressures, they may also have to deal with "subtle" disapproval regarding their lack of cooperation. In other words, the reality of inpatient treatment can vary drastically from the client's expectations and certainly runs the risk of antitherapeutic consequences for some individuals. Therapists rarely try to explore or correct such misconceptions regarding inpatient treatment, thereby providing a disservice to their clients.

Similar misconceptions also arise in the case of court-referred clients. "The mentally ill person sent from the court may turn to the evaluator as parent, lawyer, savior, advocate, ally or simply 'my clinician'."[5] The vulnerability created by the client's legal situation combined with his or her emotional state may add to the client's distorted perception of the mental health professional as someone who is there to help. Even when the client has been fully apprised of the professional's role (e.g., to assess the possibility of malingering or emotional concomitants of his or her physical injury) and is warned that the information could potentially be used to the client's detriment, any existing set to perceive mental health professionals as helpers is likely to lead to periodic lapses in "cautious" responding as the evaluation proceeds. The professional in such a situation faces a serious dilemma and may prefer to behave as though it doesn't exist because of the lack of any easy solution to the problem.

Conflict in Values

Assuming that all parties involved with the mental health professional have clear expectations regarding the service to be provided, problems are still likely to arise if the values of the various parties differ significantly. Professionals who believe that their services or relationships are value-free are deceiving themselves and have a greater risk of providing services that are distorted in accordance with that value system. In the court system, for example, "seldom or never is an expert witness . . . unaffected by values and biases, and least of all by his own subjective view as to how the case should be decided."[6] Unless professionals examine "their own value priorities and, consequently whether their loyalties lie with professional, institutional, or societal interests,"[7] they increase the likelihood that their personal ideologies will significantly bias the content of their work. The risk of having values intrude into service provision inevitably increases as the number of recipients to the service increases since each party is likely to enter the transaction from a different value perspective.

On an inpatient setting, for example, a serious conflict of values could seriously interfere with client care, particularly when a team approach is used to provide treatment. Traditional medical staff (e.g., psychiatrists, nurses) may have strong values regarding the provision of service to clients, with the view that psychotropic treatment is the only critical treatment variable operating with a particular client. The existence of a strong "medical model" value system could potentially interfere with medical staff respecting or cooperating with other forms of treatment intervention (e.g., group therapy, individual counseling). In the case of nursing staff, for example, the presence of such biases could reduce the likelihood that particular clients will be directed to their counseling sessions on time, if at all, even though appointments for medical procedures are rarely missed. From the reverse viewpoint, social workers or psychologists with antimedication viewpoints may subtly (or blatantly) encourage their clients to resist such intervention. Even professionals who are aware of such biases may not recognize the intrusion of these biases on the service they provide and the conflict this inevitably creates for their client and other parties to whom they owe an allegiance (e.g., other health team members).

When mental health professionals are involved with the legal system, there are bound to be significant differences in their respective philosophies and orientation to client transactions. For example, the legal profession is obliged to look at the world in "black and white" while mental health professionals have to take into account the variability and unpredictability of human behavior under different circumstances. Such divergent attitudes may occasionally lead to a communication gap as well as frustration between these two different professional groups.

In general, value systems are more likely to intrude on service provision when human life is involved (e.g., in the case of a murder trial), particularly if the professional has strong feelings against specific outcomes (e.g., for or against capital punishment). Professionals working within a military system have similar problems, especially at times of active warfare when they are required to treat combat fatigue and thereby be responsible for returning an individual to active duty with the high risk that the individual may die for his or her country.

Other value problems can arise when the values of the third party agree in theory with those of the professional but not in practice. For example, the mental health consultant working within an industrial setting may have been hired with the view of helping the worker but in reality is trying to resolve managerial problems by reducing absenteeism and increasing the production rate.

Conflict in Responsibilities

One of the greatest sources of conflict when dealing with third parties derives from the multiple responsibilities falling on the professional and the different allegiances that subsequently develop. In situations when all parties are working toward the same goal, these multiple allegiances are not likely to be a problem. More frequently, professionals are forced to satisfy one party at the expense or dissatisfaction of another party. An even greater difficulty arises when the service provider is not even aware that such a dilemma actually exists. Vann and Morganroth[8] refer to interviews with psychiatrists acting as consultants to the court system in which

> it was found that they were not clear whose agent they were. Some of the psychiatrists considered themselves to be the agents of the hospital director who had technically appointed them at the request of the court. Other psychiatrists considered that when they made evaluations of persons accused of crime, they were the direct agents of the court. Indeed, one of the psychiatrists felt confused on this point and did not know whose agent he was, while another considered that he was simply his own agent and felt no responsibility to any other parties. . . . it is highly significant that none of the psychiatric experts conceptualized their activity to be the agents of value-free "science" or, for that matter, of the patient or prisoner himself.

Employer versus Client. The mental health professional frequently has different responsibilities to the institution that employs him or her than to the clients with whom he or she has direct contact. Such differences in professional responsibilities are even more likely to occur when clients are in the custody of that institution (e.g., prisoners, inpatients) or when the behavior of the clients is under strict authoritarian control (e.g., children, military personnel). For example, the professional may see his or her role as therapist, with rehabilitation as the primary goal. At the same time, the therapist likely has a responsibility to the institution (and frequently to the general public) to follow security regulations, even in situations where such regulations appear to be countertherapeutic. At times the institution may go so far as to interfere with therapeutic contact; for example, in instances where the client's privileges are restricted as a form of punishment for wrongdoing. This type of therapeutic intrusion is particularly a problem in prison settings in which mental health professionals not only function as clinicians but also as overseers and evaluators of the client's level of rehabilitation.[9]

Custodial treatment facilities are also known for influencing admission and discharge decisions, thereby freeing or filling beds in accordance with institutional needs rather than client needs. In other words, the client's therapist may feel pressured to discharge his or her client before the individual is ready or to admit the client even though such an admission is not really necessary or therapeutic.

To whom should the therapist give allegiance when conflicts of this nature arise? On the one hand, the professional has a responsibility to assist the client when necessary; on the other hand, the institution has the expectation that all employees will assist in the maintenance and development of that facility. Regrettably, many professionals enter into this type of relationship without realizing the full implications of their commitment. These conflicting responsibilities become even more complicated by the allegiance to his or her professional body and the standards established by that body for proper service provision. As described by Daniels

> when a member of one of the "free" professions becomes an employee of a bureaucratic organization, the organization often supersedes the ultimate control normally invested in his professional colleagues and the professional thus becomes a "captive." The captivity of employment may then create conflicts for the professional caught between the value system of his profession and those of the organization to which he submits.[10]

Even mental health professionals working solely on an outpatient basis are subject to a number of administrative pressures, most of which are designed to keep the organization operating in a cost-effective and efficient way. Social workers working within a welfare organization, for example, may be pressured to conduct "midnight raids" on their clients; in other words, checking on their clients' behavior at unexpected times.[11] Such "spying" behavior connotes a lack of trust and disrespect for their clients and therefore violates standards established by their professional group regarding the proper way to treat their clientele. In addition, professionals are often pressured to work with more clients than they can realistically help, with management personnel being more concerned with quantity rather than quality care in order to satisfy and maintain funding bodies.

Additionally, mental health personnel may be pressured to release information about a particular client to an "external" party on the basis of an administratively acceptable, but professionally unacceptable, signed release. Most standardized release forms adopted by employers are sufficiently general to "cover" all circumstances and do not typically inform the client regarding the purpose for which the released information could be used, the intended recipients of that information, and so on. Similarly, employers might pressure their professional staff to reveal information to "internal" parties (e.g., medical records department) that is considered personal regarding a particular client (e.g., sexual problems) and irrelevant for administrative purposes. Psychologists, for example, have been adamant about refusing to release psychological test material to their employers. Such resistances have resulted in growing unpopularity for any professional body that does not succumb to such administrative pressures and results in periodic battles regarding the ownership of material that has been gathered by an employee, regardless of his or her professional status. School systems have been quite notorious in initiating and maintaining this type of employer–employee dispute and may be inclined to accuse staff who resist such pressures of being obstructionists and elitists.

Union versus Client. In institutions that are unionized, professionals have the added burden of supporting union regulations and other union members, as well as considering obligations to themselves as employees. Although professionals as employees have the right to consider their own employment needs, "certain union activities, such as the strike, appear to militate against maximum fidelity and service to clients,"[12] thereby interfering with their professional responsibilities.

Employees versus Client. When a professional is working parallel to, or in cooperation with, other professional staff, there is room for professional conflict, particularly when the professional's obligations to a fellow employee are at odds with obligations to a client. For example, in a treatment facility a professional may become aware that another employee's personal problems are intruding into his or her delivery of health care services and having adverse effects on the recipient of these services. This ethical conflict has been reported by consultants within the educational system,[13] industry,[14] prisons,[15] and the police department.[16] For example, for mental health professionals involved therapeutically or otherwise with prison staff, "the responsibility . . . to keep the Warden advised of staff problems which may affect the overall security of the institution must override keeping staff statements confidential."[17] Similar comments have been made regarding therapists working within a police department. Professionals are therefore forced to weigh their obligations to their client, fellow employees, management, their professional body, and the general public.

Payer versus Client. When the professional is self-employed, services provided to the client may be paid directly by the client or by third parties (e.g., spouse, parent, insurance company, lawyers, government agency). The professional obviously owes some responsibility to the party that purchases his or her services, primarily in the area of accountability. In other words, the professional has an obligation to provide the service purchased and may have to substantiate that this has, in fact, been done. When payment is made through an insurance company, for example, the dilemma facing the professional involves maintaining confidentiality with the client and yet providing sufficient statistical information to satisfy the insurance company's investigative requirements.

The professional who is seeing one family member in therapy and getting paid by another family member may also experience conflict if the individual paying for the service insists on obtaining privileged information regarding the content of such contacts. Obviously, the parents' right to information concerning their children is also an issue when they are not paying for the service in question. Adolescents may be particularly sensitive to parental intrusion into their therapy contacts, placing pressure on the therapist not to comply with such demands. If the professional chooses to support a client's request to withhold information with the view that this choice is more therapeutic, the therapist takes the risk that such services will be terminated by the purchasing party which, in turn, is not therapeutic for the client. Trachtman offers the view that it is presumptuous of a professional, for example, a school psychologist, to come between a parent and a child. "The psychologist is there, as is the school, to serve the parent. He should share his knowledge with parents freely and openly, offer advice if he has any, even try to convince the parents if he chooses, but he must keep in mind that he is a consultant and that the parent must reserve the right to ignore his advice. This means that records must be open to parents,"[18] a disputable point among administrators and professionals alike.

Another common dilemma faced by professionals arises from confusion as to who owns their reports. In situations when the professional has conducted an evaluation of a client at the request of a third party, the formal evaluation report is typically sent to the purchasing party with provisions made to provide verbal feedback to the client. A conflict arises if the client pressures the professional for a copy of that same report to be used for personal interests, particularly if the referring party objects to its release. For example, if a referring party (e.g., workers' compensation board) chooses not to follow through on recommendations in a report because it is not to its advantage, does the client have the right to use this same report to the possible disadvantage of the party that paid for it? In other words, what limits are there on the professional's obligations to the client versus the paying client?

Variability in Roles

In many situations a conflict of interest does not simply arise because the professional has responsibilities to more than one party but because he or she has more than one role with a particular party at different times. For example, the mental health professional may initially function as a therapist but because of a change of circumstances that role may evolve into a different one (e.g., evaluator, expert witness, informant). With the physically disabled client, for example, the counselor may be asked to assist the client in dealing with his or her emotional reactions to the disability. If the disability is the result of an accident, litigation is often involved and the therapist may later be called on to make comments about the client's progress or lack of it in court. Another example is that of the therapist who is counseling a couple because of marital problems and is later summoned as a witness to testify against one of the spouses. This change in roles is particularly problematic if the therapist refuses to testify on ethical grounds and risks being held in contempt of court or even imprisoned (*In Re Lifschutz*).[19]

In other situations the professional may have established a dual relationship with the client from the beginning. For example, when a client has been referred for therapy by the court, the professional has already agreed to assume two roles: first, as a therapist for the client; and second, as an evaluator for the court. In assuming such a function professionals may deceive themselves into believing that either service can possibly be adequate. On the one hand, the professional is aware of the importance of trust in forming a therapeutic relationship while at the same time knowing that the client cannot expect his or her comments to be kept in strict confidence. Since most clients would prefer a positive evaluation under such circumstances, the likelihood is high that they would purposefully try to be seen in a favorable way by their therapist. Not only does such deception interfere with therapy but it also reduces the usefulness of any evaluative report provided to the court. While this type of conflict is problematic with voluntary clients, it creates an even greater ethical dilemma when interacting with involuntary clients (e.g., inpatients, prisoners). In a study of psychologists within a prison setting, Clingempeel et al.[20] stated that "the most frequent and ostensibly bothersome role distortions stemmed from the subtle linking of conflicting treatment, punishment, and custody goals," for example, "the linkage of treatment participation . . . with reduction of sentence."

In certain circumstances professionals may also feel pressured to change their role to that of informant (i.e., in situations when the professional fears that the client is in danger of harming someone) and struggle with the effects that this breach of confidentiality could have on their therapeutic relationship with the client. The responsibility to warn potential victims of the possibility of violent attack derived from the landmark ruling in *Tarasoff v. Regents of the University of California.*[21] The mental health professional involved in this court case had warned the police, but not the potential victim, that his client was considered dangerous. When the victim was later killed, the police and the therapist were sued by the victim's family. Despite the therapist's arguments that mental health professionals, first of all, have an obligation to maintain therapeutic confidentiality, and second, that they are not skilled at predicting specific dangerous acts, the judge ruled that the victim should have been warned and that "the protective privilege ends where the public peril begins."[22] This "duty to warn" law, as it was later dubbed, has created much anxiety and confusion for mental health practitioners. First, the professional has to deal with the lack of adequate criteria for determining when a client is "a clear and imminent danger" to others.[23] Second, many professionals are unclear as to what they are required to do if the intended victim is unknown or part of a general class (e.g., all Catholic priests). Should the therapist attempt to contact the Church, for example, and give a general alert or simply advise the police department of the threat? Finally, therapists are also concerned regarding their "duty to warn" in potentially suicidal clients; in other words, should family members be apprised of this risk? The recent ruling from *Bellah v. Greenson*[24] states that the duty to warn does not extend to possibly self-inflicted violence or destruction of property. Adding to this confusion is the lack of consistency across states on the "duty to warn" issue. In *Shaw v. Glickman,*[25] for example, the Maryland court ruled in favor of the defendants. "Unlike California, the privileged communication statute of Maryland does not allow for breaches of confidence when the lives of others are threatened. . . . if interpreted literally, a Maryland court could have found the psychotherapists guilty of breach of confidentiality if they had attempted to warn the intended victim, even if there were a foreseeable threat to a specific person."[26] Such inconsistent and mixed messages from the court system is bound to be anxiety-provoking for the therapist and lead to a state of "learned helplessness" in that he or she may feel "damned if I do and damned if I don't."

Even when a client is in a controlled setting (i.e., institutional custody), the professional is faced with the same dilemma. Consider, for example, the mental health professional working in a prison setting who has been informed by a client/inmate that an escape attempt is imminent. The ethical dilemma confronting the therapist is even worse if the client subsequently regrets his or her admission and begs the therapist not to tell authorities out of fear that any interference with the plan could result in the prisoner's being killed by fellow inmates. In such a situation, there are many allegiances pulling at the therapist, serious implications to consider on all sides, and no definitive answers regarding proper professional conduct under the circumstances. "In other words, if an escape takes place and guards and prisoners are killed, a psychologist with foreknowledge could be charged with failure to warn prison officials and thus with neglect of a compelling ethical and moral duty. On the other hand, if a client is harmed because a therapist warns prison officials, the violation of confidence may have equally grievous consequences."[27] In addition, the professional has to deal with the possible loss of life that could result from making the "wrong" decision.

Professionals have differed significantly in their reactions to such pressures: some adopting a purist and idealistic view, considering only their therapeutic obligations to the client and ignoring their obligations to other parties; and others trying to juggle their various responsibilities while walking the proverbial tightrope. Shah[28] argues that mental health professionals have overreacted to the "duty to warn" regulation, implying a rather grandiose and narrow view on the part of clinicians regarding therapeutic privilege. "Some clinicians are utterly convinced that therapeutic confidentiality must remain an *absolute* and paramount value over all other societal interests. Such ethnocentric zeal seems to demand that the entire society should accept the value and ideologies of psychotherapists. In other words, what is good for psychotherapists is good for society!"

LIMITS TO PROFESSIONAL COMPETENCE

Most professional groups include in their service standards the importance of behaving within the limits of professional competence. The academic and experiential training often provided to prospective mental health professionals, however, is overly traditional in content, that is, client-centered rather than system-centered. The few system-centered courses that are offered are likely to be overly theoretical and broad-based rather than practical or specific. When a professional agrees to be a consultant in a nontraditional setting (e.g., industry, school, court), he or she has the added challenge of recognizing and dealing with limits in knowledge and skill in order to avoid professional misrepresentation. Too often, service providers overestimate the possible contributions they can make in nontraditional settings and enter a new field with an overly narrow and limited perspective. The presence of mental health "blinders" when embarking on a nontraditional task seems destined to result in inadequate service provision and disappointment. For example, mental health professionals who have been employed within the juvenile justice system have been accused of providing "useless 'diagnoses,' behavioral predictions with high error rates, naive theories of prevention and rehabilitation, and ineffective treatments."[29] In other words, premature and naive entry into a nontraditional setting under the assumption of presumed competence can have disastrous results. Areas that should provide the mental health professional with serious concern are described in the following sections.

Lack of External Knowledge

Whenever one profession is required to interface with another profession, there are numerous opportunities for confusion. Suarez and Hunt[30] refer to the "mutual ignorance" that typically occurs in such situations in that neither party has a good understanding of the other party and how it functions. Such ignorance may create a chain of events that culminates in negative feelings and alienation between the two parties. In turn, such professional alienation and arrogance likely interferes with constructive communication in future transactions and therefore serves to perpetuate the problem.

One of the primary sources of ignorance is terminology, that is, a misunderstanding as to the meanings given to different terms. Additional problems can arise because the mental health provider misunderstands the type of service that is being requested. These problems are particularly evident when the professional is interfacing with the legal profession because of the breadth of professional jargon between both groups. When involved in a court situation, the mental health professional is typically in a foreign arena. In court settings, for example, the consultant is frequently confused as to what constitutes a "mental health" opinion versus a legal conclusion. In cases of criminal responsibility the mental health expert may be asked "whether individuals have acted with appreciation of the nature of their acts or with the free will to avoid violations of the law if they so choose."[31] Such legalistic terms have no real meaning to the mental health professional who unsuccessfully struggles with trying to translate these terms into language he or she understands, for example, what does the legal profession mean by the expressions "appreciation," "nature of the act," and "free will." Not only are there no mental health criteria for defining such terms but legal guidelines are either lacking or equally confusing.

Studies that have been conducted on the quality of such evaluations have commonly found that professionals have failed their clients and the third-party system by resorting to irrelevant criteria in formulating legalistic opinions. Serious complaints have been made about the dire consequences of such inadequate opinion making: for example, "many defendants . . . have spent decades in institutions following minor offenses, on the opinion of psychiatrists as to competency."[32] Professionals frequently overstep their bounds when giving opinions on the psychological state of the subject being examined. Instead of limiting their statements to a mental health opinion, they offer a legal opinion as well. The stage for legal opinion making is frequently set by the legal system itself when the referral is first made: for example, "Is the subject criminally responsible?" "Is the defendant fit to stand trial?" Professionals who respond in accordance with the terms used in the referral question (e.g., by stating that they believe the subject to be incompetent) err in that they are giving a legal opinion that, by definition, is obviously beyond their professional training and expertise. Since the referral question has been worded in a legalistic format, however, mental health professionals may be lured into believing that they have the right and therefore the skill to respond accordingly. Such an approach often leads to "hand-slapping" and professional embarrassment when they are confronted with their inappropriate behavior in court. In some situations, however, they may be confronted with judges or attorneys or both who purposefully and inappropriately try to pressure them to go beyond their expertise and to offer conclusory statements on matters of law. Once again, the professional is placed in an awkward situation, especially if he or she is unclear as to what constitutes proper professional conduct under such circumstances.

Although the major emphasis to this point has been on the dilemmas faced by mental health professionals involved with the court system, similar difficulties confront the mental health consultant in other settings, particularly those in which the primary emphasis is not on mental health matters but on achieving other goals (e.g., production, education, rehabilitation). As in the legal setting, professionals frequently lack comprehensive or adequate knowledge about the organization that hires them and the best way to interface their approach and data base with that of the hiring organization.

Lack of Internal Skill and Data

Even when mental health professionals are reasonably aware of gaps in their knowledge regarding external third-party systems, they may fail to recognize or admit to "internal" gaps; in other words, missing skills or data on which to base such skills. Professionals may be too eager to enter a third-party arena and provide services based on theoretical assumptions rather than on "real" knowledge or expertise. Since a particular service has been requested, the mental health professional behaves as though the request gives reality to the presumed skill necessary to provide the service in question.

Unanswerable Questions. A common dilemma for the mental health consultant arises when third-party systems assume that the mental health field can provide scientific answers to questions which are in reality unanswerable at this stage of professional development. For example, mental health consultants to the court are frequently asked to give an opinion on the presence or absence of psychopathology at the time a certain crime was committed. It would seem impossible for a mental health professional who does not see the client until months after the event in question to give an opinion about the client's mental state at that time. How can any mental health professional presume to do this under the guise of scientific analysis? It is quite common for mental health consultants to accept such a role when evaluating such areas as criminal responsibility, testamentary capacity, and competency to contract. In other words, if a court consultant is asked to determine whether a client knew the difference between right and wrong at a certain point in time, he or she may agree to make this judgment without having any data base for doing so just because the question was asked. In personal injury cases, for example, the professional may be asked to determine whether the client has suffered emotional trauma as a result of an accident without knowing the client's level of psychological functioning prior to the trauma in question. Without knowing the client before the trauma the professional has no way of knowing with any certainty whether the emotional problems predated the accident. An accurate diagnosis of traumatic neurosis is made even more difficult by the likelihood of malingering in clients who may have much to gain by presenting their symptoms in the "appropriate" way. Despite these difficulties clinicians may rationalize "who better to answer such questions than the mental health expert?" because they know more about human behavior than the typical layperson. "Knowing" from a professional perspective should ethically necessitate scientific (i.e., empirical) knowledge rather than educated intuition. In agreeing to perform tasks that they are not really capable of doing they help to perpetuate the inappropriate role they have been asked to play and risk becoming "rubber stampers for the process."[33] Regrettably, when mental health professionals choose to answer unanswerable questions and provide retrospective opinions there is the risk that they will mislead the recipients of such opinions (e.g., judges and jury) into viewing them as scientific and therefore real. The risk of a disservice to some or all of the recipients of such a service is highly likely.

Another impossible task that is frequently directed toward the mental health professional is prediction. There are many settings in which a mental health consultant is asked to provide an opinion regarding how a particular client might function in the future: for example, will the client commit acts of violence if released or, as an added example, will the physically injured client always be emotionally traumatized as a result of the injury sustained? Predictive opinions may also be asked in the following settings:

1. Correctional facilities: to estimate the potential for future dangerous behavior when an inmate is eligible for parole
2. Psychiatric units: to determine the likelihood that a psychologically disturbed client may be dangerous to self or others in order to initiate or prolong civil commitment

3. Child welfare organizations: to assess the likelihood of child abuse or neglect on the part of a parental figure
4. Courtrooms: to predict which living environment is in the "best interests" of a child involved in a custody dispute
5. Educational institutions: to determine which students are more likely to experience academic success
6. Industrial settings: to influence hiring and promotion decisions by predicting which job candidates or employees are more likely to be successful workers in a particular field

From the number of settings in which predictions are requested it is apparent that this is an important area of concern for professionals, especially in view of their lack of formal training and therefore expertise in this area. Despite their lack of competence in making predictions, most professionals have allowed themselves to be lured into this type of opinion making with the erroneous view that they add a measure of objectivity to the predictive task. Indeed, in most situations they agree to perform such a grandiose task without any specific criteria or clear guidelines regarding the behavior in question. In the area of child abuse, for example, the practitioner may be asked to estimate the likelihood of harm befalling a child under certain circumstances without knowing the basis for making such a judgment. As an illustration, mental health providers are legally bound to submit the name of a parent to a child welfare agency when they have reasonable grounds for suspecting child abuse or neglect. Professionals are often perplexed as to what constitutes reasonable grounds because of the absence of adequate legal criteria. As a result, they are forced to develop intuitive and possibly idiosyncratic interpretations of such terms.

Although all areas in which predictions are requested have serious implications for an individual's future, those areas of greatest concern involve the potential deprivation of liberty. A person's right to liberty is considered void if he or she is considered seriously disturbed (i.e., sexually or psychologically) as well as potentially dangerous. Studies that have been conducted on the topic of prediction have tried to isolate variables, or combinations of variables, that increase the likelihood of specific future behaviors, for example, violence. These studies typically involve group comparisons rather than repeated measures with individual subjects. In all fairness, group studies should ethically be limited to "group" conclusions because individual differences that do exist among the group members are averaged out as part of the statistical analyses. Prediction of individual behavior is therefore impossible on the basis of such studies. Most research that has been conducted in this area has been extremely pessimistic about the accuracy of professional predictions, with the result that mental health consultants have been frequently cautioned against making such judgments. For example, Morse[34] has concluded that "future specific behavior, especially infrequent behavior, is terribly hard for anyone to predict with accuracy, even with the use of actuarial data." Similarly, Megargee[35] states that "no structured or projective test scale has been derived which, when used alone, will predict violence in the individual case in a satisfactory manner. Indeed, none has been developed which will adequately postdict, let alone predict, violent behavior."

Finkel[36] refers to a classic example (Operation Baxstrom) which demonstrated the lack of competence of the psychiatric profession in making predictive judgments. In 1966, approximately 1000 mentally ill exconvicts were examined by psychiatrists and declared too dangerous to be released to a traditional psychiatric facility. Despite this evaluation, the court chose to transfer them to a regular treatment facility, thereby providing an empirical test of the psychiatric predictions. The behavior of the ex-convicts after their transfer revealed that "out of almost 1000 predictions the psychiatrists were right only 7 times." Other studies have obtained similar results.

Part of the tendency to predict dangerousness in mentally ill offenders derives from the erroneous assumption that dangerous behavior is more frequent in individuals who are psychologically disturbed. Research on this topic does not support this assumption, that is, "the incidence of violent behavior among those labelled mentally ill appears to be no greater than among the general population."[37] Despite this lack of substantiating data, mental health professionals still tend to overpredict dangerousness in emotionally disturbed populations. There appear to be a number of factors that motivate professionals to overpredict violent behavior in their clientele. First of all, the desire to protect potential victims of the client may cause professionals to selectively attend and overreact to any signs of aggressiveness in the clinical picture and to therefore err on the side of caution. They can then "rationalize overcautious prediction resulting in commitment because medical treatment is provided for those in need. There is, in addition, the fear of professional humiliation for failing to confine one who proves to be dangerous."[38] In suspected child abuse cases or in situations when a client is threatening to harm a third party, the risk of legal sanctions that could result from failure to report becomes a serious personal and professional threat in that the clinician may be held legally responsible for harm befalling the client's victim as well as the client. In other words, numerous factors exist that are likely to bias a professional's "objectivity" in a negative direction and thereby interfere with competent service provision. Despite this evidence many professionals continue to accept this role, thereby misleading the public as well as other parties involved regarding their capacity to adequately provide such a service. According to Morse,[39] the issue is "not whether mental health professionals have general prognostic information . . . but whether they can predict better than lay persons future, specific, legally relevant behavior." Unless evidence exists that their success rate of making clairvoyant judgments is significantly higher than that of a layperson, they should not present themselves as "prediction" experts when testifying in a courtroom. Dix[40] refers to a court case in which a judge reversed a previous court decision because it had been inappropriately influenced by a psychiatrist making predictions about a defendant's future behavior. The judge concluded that predictive opinion making does not fall within the realm of a psychiatric expert and therefore is inadmissible because of the prejudicial effects such testimony could have on the jury.

Another dimension to this problem is a philosophical one and relates to the potentially discriminatory way of treating individuals who are psychologically disturbed in comparison with the general public. According to Ennis and Siegel

> we know that 85 percent of all convicted criminals will commit additional crimes after they are discharged from prison. But when their sentences expire, we let them go. On the other hand, if a person . . . is thought to be insane, he can then be deprived of liberty because of what he might do in the future. Why should that be? Why should we prohibit preventive detention of the sane but permit preventive detention of the insane?[41]

The discriminatory treatment of psychologically disturbed individuals should constitute a serious ethical concern for mental health providers in that their professional standards typically warn against prejudicial conduct toward clients.

In summary, the prediction arena is obviously fraught with ethical pitfalls for professionals choosing to engage in such tasks: first, the lack of training and expertise in this area; second, the lack of empirical data to justify one-to-one prediction; third, the greater potential for negative overpredicting because of external and internal pressures; and fourth, the potential for differential and therefore discriminatory treatment of specific target groups.

Inadequate Skills. Not only are many questions unanswerable considering the present state of the art, but questions in many areas that are historically considered within the realm of the mental health practitioner are answered inadequately, for example, diagnostic formulation. Research reviews in this area have typically demonstrated that the reliability and validity of psychiatric diagnoses have been embarrassingly low. Despite these negative findings, psychiatric experts frequently rely on a diagnosis in formulating an opinion about a defendant's mental state at a particular point in time. As expounded by Greenspan it is clear that psychiatrists disagree frequently on broad diagnostic judgments; they disagree more often than not on more specific diagnoses; and important consequences flow from the introduction in a judicial setting of one or another of the possible but unreliable expert categories. When such important issues as the liberty of the subject are involved, the available evidence surely does not justify the abrogation of the traditional safeguards afforded by our legal adversarial system to a well-meaning but disputed belief in the reliability of psychiatric judgment.[42]

Unsubstantiated Assumptions. Even assuming that the diagnosis of a specific psychological condition were accurate, no positive relationship has yet been found between "craziness and any legally relevant behavior."[43] In fact, studies on factors that predispose individuals to criminal behavior have found that poverty is more a factor in contributing to crime than is mental disorder; and yet, the court system would never use poverty as an excuse to exonerate an individual's responsibility for illegal acts.

When professionals are asked to evaluate an individual's ability to work as a result of a psychological problem, they are confronted with a similar dilemma in that research does not support the assumption that a client's illness will necessarily or significantly affect his or her ability to work. Professionals who accept such referrals add to the myth that such a relationship does, in fact, exist. In addition, they risk doing a disservice to their subject if a psychological disorder is found because of the assumptions that will likely follow from this finding.

Inappropriate evaluations are also a problem in nonlegal settings (e.g., industrial, educational), particularly when dealing with "minority" groups. Many diagnostic tools have been developed by studying the performance of overly specific groups, for example, first-year college students, middle-income Americans. When used with individuals outside that particular normative group the assumption has been erroneously made that the assessment provides a fair evaluation of the client's level of functioning in specific areas. Such an assumption has been successfully challenged in court because such evaluative tools may be inadequate or discriminatory when used to make decisions about an individual who is not a member of the group on which the evaluative technique was developed.

Skill Deficits. At times mental health professionals agree to perform a service under conditions that are not conducive to such a service. In agreeing to do so they mislead the recipient of the service, as well as the third-party system, regarding the possibility of doing their job adequately. For example, mental health professionals within the correctional field frequently complain that treatment is destined to fail in such a set-

ting because of the nature of the clientele in combination with the puni-
tiveness of the environment. Despite the lack of treatment success within
such settings, they continue to offer therapeutic assistance even though
such services may go beyond their level of competence. Research studies
on the effectiveness of treatment within these facilities have been pessimistic, regardless of whether the clientele are adult or juvenile offenders.
Not only do many professionals lack the skills necessary to treat such
clients effectively but they may experience significant difficulty in distinguishing real from disguised rehabilitation in clients that do show improvement. Judge Bazelon[44] has been extremely critical of the role that
psychologists, for example, have played in the correctional field and suggests that they are working for the good of themselves rather than for
the good of the individual client or society. According to Brodsky

> Bazelon's charge that psychological explanations for criminal behavior
> lead to the development of programs to employ more psychologists is
> accompanied by his observations that there has been no significant psy-
> chological contribution to knowledge of criminal behavior, that psycho-
> logical treatment programs don't work, and that hopes that psychology
> can resolve the problem of criminality must either arise from profes-
> sional ignorance or be the product of deliberate deception.[45]

Others argue that mental health professionals have failed in another
way, that is, by becoming overly pessimistic about working with certain
populations. In comparison with other diagnostic categories, for example,
little work has been done with sociopathic offenders although it may be
premature to conclude that therapy with such clientele is futile. The ethical demands to develop such expertise is in contrast with the obligation
of any professional to work only within the bounds of competence. When
working within such a custodial setting, the ethical concerns confronting
the mental health professional are even greater than the typical third-
party situation in that the professional has to consider not only the inmate or client and the third-party institution or client but societal welfare
as well.

Another area in which mental health professionals have become involved and yet are lacking in scientifically based skills is in jury selection.
Studies that have been conducted on the role played by psychologists in
"scientific" jury selection have revealed a "paucity of evidence on the
reliability or validity of techniques proposed by the social scientists."[46]
In 1979, a series of experiments with simulated jurists was conducted
conjointly by a psychologist and a lawyer. On the basis of their experiments they concluded that "the personality characteristics of jurors and
their verdicts were almost completely uncorrelated."[47] The lack of any
positive evidence in favor of scientific jury selection raises serious concern regarding the ethics of taking on such a task except within a research framework.

Limited Resources

In some circumstances limits may be placed on the clinician by restricting access to relevant data on a particular client. Such limits may be self- or externally imposed. Some service providers purposefully limit their assessment to the immediate client and situation and make assumptions about past behavior and circumstances on the basis of present behavior. The availability of pertinent assessment tools may also limit the breadth of an assessment. For example, a diagnostician may prefer to make assumptions about a client's intellectual functioning based on a subjective evaluation of the quality and content of that client's speech during an interview rather than to extend the evaluation to formal cognitive tests. Personality evaluations can be similarly limited to clinical impressions derived during direct contact with the client to the exclusion of formal diagnostic testing. Although such abbreviated assessments obviously have a short-term advantage to the professional by freeing up time, the long-term disadvantages are obvious because of the greater risk of inaccurate judgments.

In other situations restrictions are placed on the mental health professional externally, that is, by either the client or third-party client. At times the professional may find it difficult if not impossible to formulate an opinion regarding a client's behavior without access to formal records (e.g., school, hospital) or without consultation with other individuals familiar with the client (e.g., employer, family physician, spouse). Without permission from the client such avenues are closed and the professional is faced with the dilemma of whether to come up with an opinion based on such a narrow data base, or to refuse to give an opinion.

Limitations may also be imposed on the professional by the third party. In a custody battle a lawyer may wish to restrict the professional to contact with only one party in the dispute and therefore only "one side of the story" to increase the likelihood of getting an opinion in favor of his or her client. Professionals who provide a service under such restricting conditions risk doing a disservice to the other parties and being perceived as a "hired gun."

ENTRAPMENTS

Not only do mental health professionals struggle with conflicts in loyalty and gaps in their knowledge but also they are exposed to numerous pitfalls that can entice or coerce them into providing less than adequate professional service. Professionals may or may not be consciously aware of these traps and therefore may perform as if they didn't exist. Some of the more frequent entrapments are outlined in the sections that follow.

Ego Inflation

Many service providers, when they are placed in a position of power, lose their professional modesty and become carried away with the trappings of the situation. Whenever this happens there is the increasing risk that abilities will be overrated and therefore misrepresented. This type of problem is more likely to occur when the professional is suddenly placed into an unfamiliar role, for example, promoted from the role of a frontline service provider to that of an administrator. The prestige attached to the new position may entice the professional into ignoring or forgetting the original goal (i.e., client welfare); instead, the professional may focus attention on maintaining a position of power by streamlining service provision through time- and cost-efficient practices.

The more important the role and its implications the more likely is the professional to be caught in a trap of self-importance and grandiosity. This type of overconfidence is a common failing, for example, in consultants employed by police departments[48] or the court system. In the judicial system, for example, "a strange thing happens to some clinicians in the witness box. Usually modest in his claims and professionally objective, the unwary expert witness sometimes gets carried away with the trappings of expertise and power and makes outrageous claims of certainty."[49] Such exaggerated confidence undoubtedly arises for a number of reasons, not the least of which is the need to appear sufficiently strong in the face of attack. In other words, this portrayal of power may either be a self-protective facade or self-aggrandizement, neither of which is warranted under the circumstances. Individuals who maintain such an inflated posture over a prolonged period of time take the risk of developing a "know-it-all" attitude which can only result in professional stagnation.

Interprofessional Arrogance

Interprofessional arrogance is yet another manifestation of ego inflation and has as its consequence an increasing sense of alienation between different professional groups. Psychologists in the school system, for example, have often been accused of being disdainful toward professionals within the educational system.[50] In the educational environment, psychologists are frequently hired to assist staff in teaching students with special needs, that is, those children who differ from the norm for behavioral, cognitive, or emotional reasons. On some occasions, the psychologist acts as a classroom observer in order to evaluate difficulties that may be characteristic of a certain student or of the student in interaction with the teacher. Operating from a theoretical base, it is often too easy for the consultant-observer to underestimate the multiple roles and many demands imposed on the teacher and to focus only on the educator's "theoretical" shortcomings. Unfortunately, teaching staff may become overly sensitized to the narrow perception of their role by mental health professionals which in itself causes further alienation and communication barriers when an educational issue has to be discussed. Since teachers are inclined to feel misunderstood and unappreciated by the mental health consultant, they are less likely to follow through on suggestions and problems that have been provided to them. The mental health professional needs to take some responsibility for this type of adverse consequence if his or her interprofessional demeanor implies such an air of superiority.

Even within the mental health field there is much evidence of arrogance and alienation between the different professional groups. Psychiatrists and psychologists have long been competitors and have engaged in numerous power struggles, particularly when third parties are involved. In the area of third-party payment there has been ongoing dispute as to "what kind of training—medical or other—qualifies one as a psychotherapist."[51] Since psychiatrists are more likely to be covered by health insurance plans because of their medical background, the animosity and rivalry regarding service provision has increased. Despite the noblest of efforts this degree of competition seems destined to affect client care, especially in situations when clients are exposed to a "team" approach. Interprofessional rivalry has also been evident within the court system. In 1962, psychiatrists attempted to establish a professional monopoly as mental health experts for the court by arguing that mental health matters have a medical basis and therefore nonmedical professionals should not be allowed to give opinions in this area. This outlook was rejected by the presiding judge, who referred to it as "guild mentality" and stated that the American Psychiatric Association "chose to overlook the fact that the problem of criminal responsibility is not the exclusive terrain of psychiatry."[52]

Social workers have also experienced interprofessional discrimination, especially within the court system. More often than not their professional status has been viewed with skepticism by many judges when called on as experts even though they may possess high qualifications and relevant experience in a particular area (e.g., child abuse). This lack of credibility is likely to make social workers overly defensive regarding their position in the mental health "hierarchy" and seems fated to create resentment and strained relationships with other professionals.

Competition can also have adverse effects when it exists within a professional group, that is, when experts are forced to compete against each other within the judicial system. "The spectacle . . . of equally qualified psychiatrists or psychologists testifying in diametrically opposed fashions . . . suggests to the public at large both the inaccuracy of clinical judgments and the misrepresentation that exaggeration fosters."[53]

Service Abuses
Another trap that is set for the unwary professional is in the area of service abuse. Professionals may perform a service in good faith; in other words, with the expectation that the service will have a useful function

and will be implemented in the appropriate way. In some situations, however, the service may have "hidden benefits" to the third party which are in sharp contrast with the client's needs. As an illustration, mental health staff within the military system may be used to get rid of troublemakers in that an evaluation of character disorder is sufficient to justify "something less than an honorable discharge."[54] Diagnostic tests have also been inappropriately used to discriminate against various minorities. Abuses are rampant within the court system as well because of the selective use to which isolated components of an evaluation may be put. Both sides in an adversarial system will inevitably choose to take comments out of context and distort those areas of a report that support their respective positions. The mental health consultant is frequently helpless in preventing this type of misrepresentation from happening.

Service abuses are also found in correctional facilities. In the name of therapy, treatment services may be geared toward "good" intrainstitutional behavior rather than toward behaviors that are personally relevant to a particular inmate and functional outside the prison system. Not only might the professional's services be abused by the system but also by the client or inmate. Discussing the role of psychotropic medication as a form of treatment, Kaufman[55] states that "minor tranquilizers and sedative-hypnotics are grossly abused; they are hoarded, used as currency, misused for acute intoxication or overdose, or lead to dependency." On the other hand, the psychiatrist may feel pressured by the system to use medication to keep the prisoners in a malleable state.

In addition, in many custodial facilities mental health consultants are hired to provide a service that has no useful function to the client from the professional's point of view. Staff working within a psychiatric facility or a correctional institution may feel that they are conducting mental health evaluations and making treatment recommendations, even though no adequate treatment resources exist. Many of these institutions are plagued with staff shortages or unqualified staff and all efforts are devoted to keeping the client population under control and maintaining the status quo. In situations when resources are limited, staff burnout is common and any attempt to get staff more therapeutically involved with the residents is likely to meet with resistance. Even when treatment services are available, they may be inadequately provided when implemented by staff who are unqualified to administer them. A classic example is the behavior modification program that has developed a bad reputation because of the inappropriate ways in which it has been implemented by untrained staff. Since behavior modification programs appear deceptively simple, many novices have presumed to implement or coordinate them without understanding the critical principles underlying the approach or the ethical limits to their use. Without knowledge of these principles naive implementation of a behavior modification program can be disastrous, or at the least ineffective, because of the potential for misuse or abuse or both. Improper program implementation is even more of a dilemma for a professional if he or she was responsible for its initial development. Attempts to train or supervise relevant staff to administer such programs may be thwarted by employees who prefer to operate independently or by administrative personnel who may prefer to rely on less qualified staff because of the cost benefits.

Pressure to Comply

One of the most common entrapments for the mental health professional is the temptation to behave in a way that is expected and desired by one party regardless of professional obligations to other (possibly more silent) parties. A variety of different pressures exists that is likely to confront the mental health professional in different settings.

Social Pressures. When entering or maintaining a position within a third-party system, the professional often has to interface with other service providers who may or may not have a different orientation to client care. Within a "team" approach to treatment a common pressure is to gossip among staff about such things as client intimacies, idiosyncrasies, interpatient relationships, and so on. Attempts to resist such pressures or to point out the inappropriateness of such behavior are likely to lead to rejection by fellow workers. Such rejection, in turn, may affect the professional's ability to work with "team" clients because of the need for cooperative effort. Social pressures are also placed on consultants within other settings. In a school environment, for example, not only may fellow workers wish to gossip about the student body but also about the consultee and other staff. Consultants may also feel pressured to develop a more personal relationship with staff (e.g., sharing information about their family life, participating in after-hours recreational pursuits) in order to be accepted within a system where such familiarity is the norm. Failure to comply with such social expectations may result in superficial cooperation or subtle sabotage when programs need to be implemented.

Social pressures may also be used to lure the professional into tolerating less than adequate programming and lower standards of care than should reasonably be provided. Consultants may feel reluctant to comment on programs established before they entered into the third-party relationship, especially if they were not hired to evaluate such programs. Social pressures and the fear of rejection are likely factors in creating such reluctance.

Administrative Pressures. Administrative pressures are yet another form of entrapment. Many third-party systems operate under the assumption that a professional's job description should be completely defined by them rather than by the professional. In the school system, for example, psychologists may be relegated to the role of testing technician with little, if any, use made of other areas of professional expertise. Similar frustrations may be experienced by nursing staff in a treatment facility. Resident psychiatrists or attending physicians may assume a dictatorial role with nurses, viewing them as "handmaidens" rather than equals. Since nurses have been in this potentially servile role for so long they may believe that the role is appropriate or, if inappropriate, that they can do nothing to change it. If they adopt the attitude that they can only "do as they're told," passive dependence on the psychiatrist becomes inevitable and potentially interferes with nursing staff providing the kind of client care for which they are qualified. Occupational therapists have similar complaints within a medical system. Historically occupational therapists have been used to keep the client population occupied, for example, doing crafts. This role is a limiting one to the occupational therapist and a disservice to the client in that the occupational therapist is capable of helping them in a variety of useful ways. Attempts to change any of these traditional roles have often met administrative resistance and authoritarianism. The consequence for the professional staff is a growing sense of dissatisfaction with the role prescribed for them and frustrations in any kind of client contact. Regardless of how professional the staff, disillusionment and a feeling of helplessness in dealing with a rigid system can potentially lead to a deterioration in the services that are provided. These ethical dilemmas are more prevalent in a third-party system that has definitive views regarding the functions that should be performed by its professional staff, particularly if the goals and orientation of the system vary drastically from those of the service providers (e.g., educational system, industry, corrections).

Self-Serving Enticements. Additionally, mental health professionals may be lured into favoring a particular position because of the subsequent advantages that may result. The bait for the professional may be monetary, status, or the security of additional business with the same third-party client. Although many professionals may insist that they resist such ignoble temptations, much evidence has been found to the contrary. According to Gutheil,

> While the goal of impartial expert testimony is a commendable one and would seem to require only one examination, experienced courtroom observers frequently note that state-employed psychiatrists often give short shrift to defendants' claims of insanity, while private psychiatrists who are being adequately compensated are likely to be more useful in formulating a defense. . . . This is not to say that the former are deliberately undercutting the defendant, although that may occasionally occur, but only to point to the subtle but documented influences that may shape even an expert's opinions.[56]

To win the approval of the court or the third-party agency that hired them, professionals have also been known to engage in "second-guessing," in other words, speculating about the type of decision that would be favored and consciously or subconsciously biasing the evaluation so as to obtain the preferred result. Although there may be many noble court consultants who resist such self-serving enticements, there remains a number of professionals who have been labeled alternatively as "prostitutes" or "hired guns" because of their willingness to sell their opinion. "Some courts have held it permissible to bring out, if such is the fact, that the expert regularly testifies in litigation; or that his testimony is always offered by plaintiffs rather than defendants, or vice versa, indicating a bias."[57]

Monetary gain may not be the only factor predisposing a professional to biased opinions. Professionals, particularly those who are insecure and possibly novices within the third-party system, may feel compelled to agree with their employer's position in order to obtain approval and possibly consensual validation of their viewpoint.

Professionals may also feel obliged to modify the type of service they offer in accordance with funding enticements. Administrative professionals in particular have been accused of "creating problems to promote the existence of the profession."[58]

RECOMMENDATIONS

Obligation to Be Informed

Conflicting Values. Prior to being able to react appropriately in the face of an ethical dilemma, professionals must initially recognize that one exists. Such self-awareness necessitates, first of all, knowing the values that affect their behavior.

To facilitate self-awareness practitioners are encouraged to maintain frequent contact with other service providers. No amount of introspection can eliminate the potentially negative intrusion of values, particularly after prolonged periods of professional isolation. Such isolation is more likely to occur when the practitioner is self-employed or working for a segregated facility in which a professional department is limited to only one or two staff. Professional isolation can also be self-imposed in individuals who choose not to interact with appropriate staff for personal reasons. Ideally the mental health consultant should arrange regular contact with members of the same discipline, for example, through formal meetings with "local" professionals or attendance at conventions and workshops. Under periods of stress (work-related or personal), consultation with other staff and periodic peer review is helpful in examining the possible intrusion of nonprofessional issues on professional behavior. By exposing themselves to scrutiny practitioners are better able to determine the presence of any conflict in their values and those of the individual or third-party client they serve. Once aware of these value differences, mental health professionals are then obliged to establish their priorities and examine any biases that may exist. At this point they then need to examine whether their biases are having an adverse effect on the type of service provided and possibly consider withdrawal from the service if a positive change seems beyond reach.

Conflicting Roles and Accountability. Not only must professionals be aware of the values that influence service provision but also of the roles they are expected to play within the system. Rather than making assumptions that the role will be defined and controlled by the mental health provider, the professional needs to become cognizant of the third-party expectations re (1) services to be provided and (2) the nature of the service delivery. Role clarification and negotiation prior to developing a professional relationship is critical in avoiding the types of conflicts that are bound to arise if employment conditions are solely based on assumptions. In negotiating a specific role, it is important for professionals to avoid accepting a dual relationship within the system as this could affect the quality of their work. Dual roles are particularly a problem when one of those roles is that of therapist. In situations when this type of dual relationship is unavoidable, professionals should be clear in their own minds that their priorities lie with the client. In other words, "the primary responsibility of the [mental health professional] is to the client. The [professional] must resolve conflicts of interest between the employer agency and the client on the basis of this responsibility."[59] The primary area of concern in such dual relationships is the issue of confidentiality, as employers occasionally put pressure on their professional staff to reveal internally, or release externally, private information regarding a client. The Krever Report has recommended that legislation be enacted to protect the employee from such demands and the client from an unfair intrusion into private matters. More specifically, the Krever Commission recommended legislation "to make it clear that the professional employee's duty of confidentiality transcends his or her duty or obedience to the employer's orders."[60]

Once the role has been properly defined, the professional then has the obligation to live up to that role; in other words, fulfilling his or her responsibilities to all pertinent parties within the limits of competence. To do this, professionals need to be accountable for their actions by evaluating their work and periodically subjecting it to review. When discussing the role of psychologists within a police department, for example, Mann recommended periodic reviews of the professional's relationship with relevant parties in order to maintain a positive working environment. "These pre-planned reviews give both the police agency and the psychologist a regularly scheduled opportunity to correct misunderstandings and modify procedures as needed. They also underscore the need for flexibility and openness in the relationship."[61]

Limitations. Professionals also need to become aware of their shortcomings, internal and external, to set limits on their behaviors in accordance with such deficiencies, and to take remedial steps. Before initiating a service, professionals first of all have an "ethical obligation to educate themselves in the concepts and operations of the system in which they work."[62] Because of the risk that self-teaching will be overly narrow and possibly distorted, formal training and supervised experience are obviously the preferred approaches. Prior to accepting the role of expert, professionals must be able to prove to themselves as well as others that they have the appropriate qualifications. When discussing expert testimony, for example, Kaslow[63] states that "experience is the essential legal ingredient of competence to render an expert opinion. It must be shown that any witness, to qualify as an expert, possesses special experience and knowledge in relation to the subject."

Additionally, in the area of diagnostic evaluations professionals should ensure that their judgments are not unduly limited by a narrow approach to assessment. Particularly in situations when human liberty is at risk or there is the possibility of a serious loss, professionals should not offer an opinion without having all the relevant facts; more specifically, "an extensive personal clinical examination of the subject; an exhaustive history, not limited to information obtained from the subject himself; and the results of psychological tests."[64] In a child custody battle the evaluator needs to examine the inevitable and often quoted "three sides to the story: his, hers and the truth." Without examining all relevant parties (and ideally, impartial observers) to the dispute, the professional is more inclined to make an error in judgment based on distorted information. Under certain circumstances professionals may be wiser to avoid participating in one-sided evaluations if the alternative option is not possible, or should qualify and severely limit the extent of their opinions in the formal report.

Obligation to Inform

Mental health professionals are obligated to notify all parties with whom they have a relationship of their rights, the professional's respective obligations to each party, potential and realistic conflicts that might arise, and limitations in knowledge and therefore service. If, on the basis of this discussion, the mental health professional concludes that he or she is not appropriate to provide the requested service, the client or third-party should be referred to a professional or service with the necessary qualifications.

Obligations to the Client. With clients in particular, it is important to inform them prior to initiating a professional relationship of any potential or existing limits in the confidentiality component of their proposed relationship. Some experts also suggest that such notification be done in writing as an added protection for the professional and as a reminder to the client. It is further recommended that the client be given a "full" warning regarding confidential limitations; in other words, that nothing can be considered entirely confidential. To do otherwise is to risk misleading the client about the limits of the relationship and the possible adverse effects it could have on the client.

Such warnings are particularly critical when the mental health professional has an evaluative relationship with the client and can make recommendations that would have adverse effects on the client's life. Particularly in court situations "assessment clients should be informed that they have the right to remain silent, have the right not to participate in the procedure, and have the right to have a lawyer present."[65] Failure to warn the client of the professional's role and possible implications for the client can be considered entrapment. In addition to advising clients of their rights, they should be reminded of the implications of any disclosure if they "seem to be slipping into the 'therapeutic' frame of mind, revealing material that they would probably not reveal if they were aware of the actual nature of the interview."[66] Aside from competency evaluations, the assessment process should be avoided if the client does not appear sufficiently competent due to psychosis or intellectual limitations to understand the purpose of the evaluation and his or her rights in the situation. In situations when an evaluation has taken place professionals have a responsibility to give feedback to the client, regardless of how unpleasant the results might be.

In therapeutic relationships professionals also have a responsibility to advise clients of their "duty to warn" third parties of possible danger from their client. All comments of violent intent should be taken seriously and fully discussed. There is a number of steps professionals can take before deciding to breach confidentiality in such cases. More specifically, after having informed the client of their obligation to warn the potential victim, professionals could additionally attempt any or all of the following interventions: first of all, persuade the client to turn in any lethal weapons; second, increase the frequency of therapy sessions or convince the client to consent to voluntary admission; or if he or she satisfies the criteria for civil commitment, consider involuntary admission. Another possibility is to ask the potential victim to join some of the therapy sessions with the client so that their negative relationship can be treated. As an extra precaution, the professional would be wise to consult with other professionals in order to explore and examine the different possibilities and to assist in making the "right" decision. Under all circumstances involving risk, professionals are encouraged to accurately document all contacts with the client and other consultants, whatever choices are made and the reasons for each choice. Assuming that all avenues have been unsuccessfully pursued, professionals are then obliged to warn the appropriate party as well as public authorities.

Third-Party Obligations. Prior to establishing a relationship with a third party, consultants have an obligation to keep everyone apprised of their professional rights and responsibilities, to themselves, the third party, and the client. This step is necessary in order to examine value differences, clarify expectations and establish ground rules regarding the quality and delivery of service. Having established ground rules at the outset the professional is in a better position to confront or negotiate with the third party if such ground rules are violated.

When a professional's opinion is being sought the mental health consultant should clarify beforehand that what the third party is purchasing is the professional's skills and the time required to formulate an opinion rather than the opinion itself. In other words, the third party should not have the expectation that the professional's opinion will conform to the desired outcome. Fees should never be contingent on the success of a particular legal case so that the professional has nothing to gain from the outcome. In addition, professionals should only agree to formulate an opinion on a particular issue if they are, in fact, experts on the topic, as demonstrated by formal training and relevant experience. Once these preconditions have been met professionals should then attempt to provide as thorough an evaluation as possible and to provide a report that is clear and comprehensive in order to be accountable for statements made. As an illustration, when submitting a psychological report to the legal system

> it should not be necessary for a lawyer or judge to resort to guesswork regarding a psychologist's methods, findings, conclusions or recommendations. A psychological report written for the court should explicitly detail why the assessment was conducted and which methods were used by the examiner. It must specify who was seen, when, and how they were assessed (including a list of all tests administered). The sources and use made of any other information deemed by the clinician to be useful in the assessment should be indicated and set apart from the information arising from the actual assessment procedures themselves. Findings from the latter should be reported in a manner which distinguishes them from any interpretations made. Finally, all recommendations offered must be shown to derive logically from both the assessment findings and the interpretations made of the findings.[67]

Similar recommendations have also been made to those experts who are required to testify. To avoid misleading jury members or the judge or both, expert witnesses need to acknowledge the basis from which they derived their opinions as well as the limitations of their views. Additionally, if professionals are asked questions that are beyond their competence they should inform the court of their lack of knowledge or expertise in the issue under examination.

Self-Imposed Restrictions and Standards

Personal Intrusion and Revelation. When engaging in an evaluative task the practitioner has an obligation to the client to obtain, or disclose, only that information that is relevant to a particular issue. In other words, every effort should be made to avoid invading an individual's privacy unnecessarily. This recommendation should apply to therapy contacts as well as evaluations. Pretrial reports, for example, "should not contain any statements or implications as to whether the accused did or did not commit the alleged offense."[68] Such restrictions are extremely important when a serious offense is involved. If required to testify in court regarding information derived in the course of prior professional contact, particular care should be taken to withhold information that is potentially prejudicial and irrelevant to the issue under examination. When pressure is placed on professionals to make unsuitable disclosures, they have the option to refuse and to request that the reasons for their reluctance be discussed in the judge's chambers. If the judge subsequently rules that the information is pertinent and therefore admissible, the onus is on the professional to cooperate or risk facing legal consequences.

Professional Boundaries. It is also important for different professional groups to recognize and respect the services offered by other disciplines. Although administrative hierarchies exist within most institutions, such hierarchies should not be based on professional lines. Different professions working together on a particular unit or service should avoid behaving as if a "subtle" hierarchy does exist to avoid promoting or encouraging such a viewpoint. The consequence of adopting the appropriate equalitarian stance is that each profession is given the "right to establish and maintain its identity and independence by defining its own function and areas of competence."[69] This recommendation was made by the Board of Trustees of the American Psychiatric Association, who further added that "no profession should attempt to define the functions and responsibilities of any other profession."[70] This professional position has obvious implications in terms of the type of relationship that should exist between psychiatrists and other mental health professionals.

The major exception to this rule occurs when a supervisory relationship has been established between different professional bodies through mutual agreement. For example, the psychologist introducing a behavior modification program into a unit has an obligation to ensure that the program is properly implemented and a benefit to the clients. In order to fulfill this requirement, staff responsible for carrying out the program (e.g., child care workers, nurses) require sufficient training as well as on-going supervision so that the program is not improperly administered and a disservice to the clientele. When staff are paid through medical insurance plans, supervisory lines may also exist between psychiatric and nonmedical professionals if medical supervision is a requirement of the third-party payer. Mental health disciplines that may view this type of supervisory relationship as a violation of their professional rights should either avoid entry into this type of third-party relationship or advocate for change.

Qualified Services. Professionals should only accept a client if they have the expertise and appropriate conditions for working with that client. As an example, if a client does not seem appropriate for a particular type of therapeutic intervention he or she should be notified of that decision, the reasons for refusal, and referral to the appropriate resource.

In the case of diagnosis and evaluation there are numerous areas in which the professional should impose limits. Such restrictions are more obvious when the professional is functioning within a nontraditional setting as he or she is then treading on foreign territory and should be more cautious.

First, professionals need to be aware of the traps that may be set for them in this "new" environment. Because of the nature of the legal system, pitfalls seem more prevalent as the goals are different from the traditional ones. Through careful examination of potential trouble spots the professional is in a better position to "qualify" the service, that is, to limit it in accordance with his or her area of expertise. Most mental health professionals who have acted as court consultants recommend restricting comments to mental health matters and eliminating entirely statements on legal issues. Some suggest that the consultant should only provide "observations and comments about the individual's current functioning, and leave the ultimate decision to the judge."[71] Others argue that the report be limited to a description of psychological symptoms (e.g., auditory hallucinations, suicidal ideation, physically aggressive outbursts); therefore leaving any conclusions about the presence or absence of mental disorder to the judge or jury or both. In part, this suggestion derives from the low validity and reliability of traditional diagnostic judgments which therefore removes them from the realm of scientific reality. In other words, since they are not within the repertoire of "scientific" skills they should not be included in an evaluative report or testimonial comments.

The professional should also be careful regarding the choice of words used to express an opinion, keeping in mind the different meanings that might be attached to certain words within the legal, or other, systems. For example, the use of the word "planning" in a court report could suggest, possibly inappropriately, "premeditation." The word "knowing" could be interpreted to mean that the client understood what he or she was doing and therefore should be held criminally responsible. This interpretation may not have been the intention of the professional when choosing to include such words in an evaluation. It is therefore critical that the professional "avoid expressing an opinion unless he is certain of the meaning the *law* gives to the important parts of the standard."[72] To reduce misunderstandings professionals should also take efforts to distinguish between factual information, self-report data, and clinical impressions. Additionally, they should avoid offering "personal, social and moral judgments in the guise of scientific judgment"[73] and should not "overstate the certainty of the conclusions" offered or "understate the likelihood that alternative interpretations are correct."[74]

Within a court system the most difficult challenge for mental health consultants occurs when they are asked to derive an opinion of a person's behavior remote in time (past or future). One way to minimize this problem is to limit statements to a description of relevant mental health data without actually providing a speculative opinion as to what that data suggests to the professional. Having heard the information that the professional considers relevant in understanding the defendant's behavior, the judge or jury or both can derive their own conclusions.

Within the fuzzy realm of predictions mental health professionals do not have sufficient scientific evidence to justify offering opinions on how a client might behave in the future. They should certainly avoid making predictive commentaries when a client's liberty is at stake. According to Dix,[75] "present skills clearly do not justify a mental health expert's expressing any more precise an opinion than that the subject of the testimony is within a group which, as a whole, poses a comparatively greater risk of dangerous behavior than the general population." Having made this statement, the responsibility to make the ultimate decision is again placed on the judge or jury or both, which is obviously where it belongs.

Refusal to Participate and Advocacy

Rather than simply limiting the role the professional is willing to adopt in a particular setting, the professional may choose to refuse participation in the first place or terminate a commitment that has already been established. In general, a professional is obligated to refuse participation in activities that are not beneficial to a client, regardless of whether that person is a client or a third party. Professionals also should refuse to become involved in activities if they believe their values could negatively affect the quality of the service they provide.

Frequently, the conclusion that a service is not helpful develops after attempts have been made to change the system under which the service is offered. For example, if a professional believes that his or her expertise is being improperly used (e.g., discriminatory testing, evaluation for punitive purposes), the first step is to confront the system with whatever unfair or inadequate practices may exist and then openly advocate for change. In other words, the initial stage of correcting a service would be "precipitating agency reform . . . within the administrative structure of which he himself is a part and . . . using legitimate and sanctioned agency processes."[76] Failure to make necessary improvements after adopting an advocacy role may lead professionals to withdraw their service completely or be compelled to accept lower standards of care. In exiting from a service the professional also has an obligation to consider the service needs that may be affected by withdrawal and to ensure that appropriate measures have been taken to reduce the effects of such a withdrawal on client welfare. This same requirement exists for temporary service withdrawals (e.g., vacation periods, union walkouts).

In court settings professionals have a similar obligation, that is, to refuse to participate in an activity that is beyond their expertise. If pressured to make a legal conclusion, for example, professionals can react by reminding the judge and lawyers involved that their expertise lies in mental health rather than legal matters. Idealistically, professionals should also refuse to offer retrospective or predictive statements despite any pressure to do so although many professionals continue to believe that such opinions can be offered if worded with caution.

REFERENCES

1. Gutheil, T. G., & Appelbaum, P. S. (1982). *Clinical handbook of psychiatry and the law* (p. 350). New York: McGraw-Hill.
2. Monahan, J. (1981). *The clinical prediction of violent behavior* (p. 102). Rockville, MD: National Institute of Mental Health.
3. Hardisty, J. (1973). Mental illness: A legal fiction. *Washington Law Review, 48,* 735.
4. Gutheil, *Clinical handbook,* 307.
5. Ibid., 289.
6. Dix, G. (1977). The death penalty, dangerousness, psychiatric testimony, and professional ethics. *American Journal of Criminal Law, 5*(2), 171.
7. Clingempeel, W. G., Mulvey, E., & Reppucci, N. D. (1980). A national study of ethical dilemmas of psychologists in the criminal justice system. In J. Monahan (Ed.), *Who is the client? The ethics of psychological intervention in the criminal justice system* (p. 150). Washington, DC: American Psychological Association.
8. Vann, C., & Morganroth, F. (1965). The psychiatrist as judge: A second look at the competence to stand trial. *University of Detroit Law Journal, 43,* 3.
9. Clingempeel, A national study, 150.
10. Daniels, A. K. (1969). The captive professional: Bureaucratic limitations in the practice of military psychiatry. *Journal of Health and Social Behavior, 10*(4), 255.

11. Levy, C. S. (1976). *Social work ethics* (p. 172). New York: Human Sciences Press.
12. Ibid., 196.
13. Davis, J. M., & Sandoval, J. (1982). Applied ethics for school-based consultants. *Professional Psychology, 13*(4), 550.
14. Sashkin, M., & Kunin, T. (1979). Psychological consultation in industry. In J. J. Platt & R. J. Wicks (Eds.), *The psychological consultant* (p. 59). New York: Grune & Stratton.
15. Monahan, J. (1980). Report of the task force on the role of psychology in the criminal justice system. In J. Monahan (Ed.), *Who is the client? The ethics of psychological intervention in the criminal justice system* (p. 6). Washington, DC: American Psychological Association.
16. Mann, P. A. (1980). Ethical issues for psychologists in police agencies. In J. Monahan (Ed.), *Who is the client? The ethics of psychological intervention in the criminal justice system* (p. 34). Washington, DC: American Psychological Association.
17. Federal Bureau of Prisons. (1977). *Task force and executive staff report on the role of psychologists in federal prisons* (Note 2). Washington, DC: Federal Bureau of Prisons.
18. Trachtman, G. M. (1972). Pupils, parents, privacy, and the school psychologist. *American Psychologist, 27,* 41.
19. *In Re Lifschutz,* 85 *California Reporter,* 829, 476 P.2d 557 (California Supreme Court, April 15, 1970).
20. Clingempeel, A national study, 149.
21. *Tarasoff v. Regents of the University of California,* Supp. 131 *California Reporter* 14 (1976).
22. Ibid.
23. American Psychological Association (1979). *Ethical standards of psychologists* (Principle 5a, p. 4). Washington, DC: APA.
24. *Bellah v. Greenson,* Cal. App. 3d, 18 141 *California Reporter* 92 (1977).
25. *Shaw v. Glickman,* 415 A.2d 625 (Md. Ct. Spec. App. 1980).
26. Knapp, S., & Vandecreek, L. (1982). Tarasoff: Five years later. *Professional Psychology, 13*(4), 514.
27. Brodsky, S. L. (1980). Ethical issues for psychologists in corrections. In J. Monahan (Ed.), *Who is the client? The ethics of psychological intervention in the criminal justice system* (p. 70). Washington, DC: American Psychological Association.
28. Shah, S. Editorial. *APA Monitor,* 2 (1977).
29. Rappaport, J., Lamiell, J. T., & Seidman, E. (1980). Ethical issues for psychologists in the juvenile justice system: Know and tell. In J. Monahan (Ed.), *Who is the client? The ethics of psychological intervention in the criminal justice system* (p. 95). Washington, DC: American Psychological Association.
30. Suarez, J. M., & Hunt, J. (1973). The scope of legal psychiatry. *Journal of Forensic Sciences, 18,* 63.
31. Gutheil, *Clinical handbook,* 287.
32. Suarez, J. M. (1967). A critique of the psychiatrist's role as expert witness. *Journal of Forensic Sciences, 12*(2), 175.
33. Suarez, The scope of legal psychiatry, 61.

34. Morse, S. J. (1978). Law and mental health professionals: The limits of expertise. *Professional psychology, 9*(3), 395.
35. Megargee, E. J. (1970). The prediction of violence with psychological tests. In C. Spelberger, (Ed.), *Current topics in clinical and community psychology* (p. 145). New York: Academic Press.
36. Finkel, N. J. (1980). *Therapy and ethics: The courtship of law and psychology* (p. 45). New York: Grune & Stratton.
37. Weisstub, D. N. (1980). *Law and psychiatry in the Canadian context* (p. 338). New York: Pergamon Press.
38. Ibid., 339.
39. Morse, Law and mental health, 395.
40. Dix, The death penalty, 163.
41. Ennis, B. J., & Siegel, L. (1973). *The rights of mental patients* (ACLU handbook series) (p. 23). New York: Avon.
42. Greenspan, E. L. (1978). The role of the psychiatrist in the criminal justice system. *Canadian Psychiatric Association Journal, 23*(3), 114.
43. Morse, Law and mental health, 394.
44. Bazelon, D. (1973). Psychologists in corrections—are they doing good for the offender or well for themselves? In S. L. Brodsky (Ed.), *Psychologists in the criminal justice system.* Urbana: University of Illinois Press.
45. Brodsky, Ethical issues, 87–88.
46. Suggs, D., & Sales, B. D. (1978). The art and science of conducting the voir dire. *Professional Psychology, 9*(3), 383.
47. Sealy, A. P. (1979). The contribution of psychology to legal processes: An analysis of jury studies. In D. P. Farrington, K. Hawkins, & S. Lloyd-Bostock (Eds.), *Psychology, law and legal processes* (p. 64). Atlantic Highlands, NJ: Humanities Press.
48. Fenster, C. A., & Schlossberg, H. (1979). The psychologist as police department consultant. In J. J. Platt & R. J. Wicks (Eds.), *The psychological consultant* (p. 138). New York: Grune & Stratton.
49. Awad, G. A., & Chamberlain, C. (1982). The process of psychiatric work with the juvenile courts. In N. Bala, H. Lilles, & G. Thomson (Eds.), *Canadian children's law* (p. 675). Toronto: Butterworths.
50. Dorr, D. (1979). Psychological consulting in the schools. In J. J. Platt & R. J. Wicks (Eds.), *The psychological consultant* (p. 21). New York: Grune & Stratton.
51. Chodoff, P. (1978). Psychiatry and the fiscal third party. *American Journal of Psychiatry, 135*(10), 1143.
52. Bazelon, D. L. (1976). Psychiatrists and the adversary process. In J. M. Humber & R. F. Almeder (Eds.), *Biomedical ethics and the law,* 2nd ed. (p. 191). New York: Plenum Press.
53. Fersch, E. A., Jr. (1980). Ethical issues for psychologists in court settings. In J. Monahan (Ed.), *Who is the client? The ethics of psychological intervention in the criminal justice system* (p. 51). Washington, DC: American Psychological Association.
54. Hussey, H. H. (1974). Psychiatry in medical services. *Journal of the American Medical Association, 228*(2), 203.

55. Kaufman, E. (1980). The violation of psychiatric standards of care in prisons. *American Journal of Psychiatry, 137*(5), 568.
56. Gutheil, *Clinical handbook,* 285.
57. Slovenko, R. (1973). *Psychiatry and law* (p. 300). Boston: Little, Brown.
58. Del Rio, V. B. Y. (1975). Psychiatric ethics. In A. M. Freidman, H. J. Kaplan, & B. J. Sadock (Eds.), *Comprehensive textbook of psychiatry II,* 2nd ed. (p. 2547). Baltimore: Williams & Williams.
59. American Psychological Association (1972). Guidelines for conditions of employment of psychologists. *American Psychologist, 27,* 332.
60. Krever, Honourable Mr. Justice H. (1980). *Report of the Commission of Inquiry into the Confidentiality of Health Information* (p. 168). Toronto: Queen's Printer for Ontario.
61. Mann, Ethical issues, 36.
62. Monahan, A report of the task force, 8.
63. Kaslow, F. W. (1979). The psychologist as consultant to the court. In J. J. Platt, & R. J. Wicks (Eds.), *The psychological consultant* (p. 159). New York: Grune & Stratton.
64. Dix, The death penalty, 177.
65. Brodsky, Ethical issues, 92.
66. Gutheil, *Clinical handbook,* 263.
67. Groves, J. R. (1982). Lawyers, psychologists and psychological evidence in child protection hearings. In N. Bala, H. Lilles & G. Thomson (Eds.), *Canadian children's law* (p. 195). Toronto: Butterworths.
68. Weisstub, *Law and psychiatry,* 122.
69. Guidelines for psychiatrists in consultative, supervisory, or collaborative relationships with nonmedical therapists. *American Journal of Psychiatry, 137*(11), 1489 (1980).
70. Ibid.
71. Suarez, Critique of the psychiatrist's role, 175.
72. Dix, The death penalty, 171.
73. Morse, Law and mental health, 371.
74. Gutheil, *Clinical handbook,* 343.
75. Dix, The death penalty, 198.
76. Levy, *Social work ethics,* 170.

II
Applications

Assessment Issues

5

Problem analysis is the first essential step in providing an adequate service. Besides gathering background information in the course of an interview, each mental health profession has developed its own idiosyncratic ways of assessing a client's needs and developing a working knowledge of existing problems. Social workers, for example, have become experts at examining the client from a historical perspective and at discovering how the client interfaces with other social systems, that is, the family, the work force, and so on. Other fields have similar areas of expertise. Within psychiatry, the mental status examination is the method of choice; with psychology, the use of standardized psychometric tests; in occupational therapy, a measure of the client's life skills as they are observed under a variety of different conditions.

An assessment within the mental health field consists of a collection of information about the client. Information is primarily obtained from the client but also from significant people in the individual's life. Self-report data are only one part of the assessment process because they may be distorted by defensiveness on the client's part or limited by his or her perception of problem areas. Formal tests are introduced to provide a more accurate and comprehensive evaluation of the client and to compare his or her level of functioning to an appropriate normative group.

If tests can be considered as mere samples of behavior, the problem becomes one of deciding which samples to take and how to take them. Because of demands on professional time, practitioners rarely have the luxury of examining a client at their leisure, especially when the client is still an outpatient. The assessor must therefore decide which samples of behavior would be best to take and whether to do a broad-based evaluation or to concentrate on a few narrow areas. There are obviously advantages and disadvantages to both approaches but because the practitioner is obliged to make choices, there is room for bias and errors in judgment. The following sections review potential difficulties that can arise within the assessment arena.

COMPETENCE

Competence is a prerequisite for all professional activities. Many of the broad-based concerns related to competence have been covered in earlier chapters and will not be repeated in this section except as they specifically relate to assessment.

In order to provide an adequate evaluation, two essential conditions must be met:

1. Only assessment tools that have been properly developed should be used.
2. Such tests should be restricted to individuals with the proper training and experience at using and interpreting them.

Individuals who assume a responsibility for assessing clients also need to be knowledgeable about their clients' rights in such an evaluative process. Berndt[1] has concluded that although diagnostic trainees may have received extensive training in testing, they "are likely to have encountered little discussion of ethical and professional standards for test administration and interpretation." Therefore, to prevent potential abuse to the client, competence should extend beyond mere knowledge of how to test and what tests to use to clients' rights in an assessment situation.

Competent Tools

In the early stages of mental health practice assessments were loosely defined and would often be limited to the ongoing therapeutic process. Diagnostic procedures have evolved over the years as practitioners became aware of the limitations of earlier approaches. Within the psychiatric profession, a number of classification systems has developed to assist the psychiatrist in making a diagnostic formulation. To facilitate decision making, the *Diagnostic and Statistical Manual of Mental Disorders,* 3rd ed. *(DSM-III)*[2] has evolved into a flow-chart approach in which symptom areas are operationally defined and choice points established to rule out alternative explanations of the problem.

Since an assessment can only be as good as the tools used to conduct it, additional precautions have been established in the use of standardized, psychometric tests. More specifically, the psychology profession has established a set of standards with which to assess the development, reliability, and validity of specific tests that are available to the assessor (*Standards for Educational and Psychological Tests*[3]). Through familiarity with such standards, the professional has an obligation not to use inadequate tools in order to minimize the risk of making erroneous conclusions about a specific client. Projective tests are notorious for not meeting such test standards and yet professionals continue to rationalize their use. At the least, such tests should only be used as part of a larger assessment battery consisting of tests that have been better developed. Rather than being used in isolation, they should always include direct contact and be used within the context of background information, therefore allowing alternative interpretations of problem areas to be explored.

Competent Professionals

Within most mental health professions, codes of ethics have been developed to protect the public from the misuse of assessment instruments by individuals outside the profession. Even within a particular professional body, there should be limits to the type of assessment strategies and techniques that is used by any one professional. Within the psychology profession, for example, neuropsychology is a highly specialized field requiring years of training and supervised practice. Similar expertise and background are required in the use of projective tests, biofeedback instruments, behavioral assessments, forensic hypnosis, and so on. The licensing or certification body of most professions has the right to investigate, fine, and severely sanction any member of its organization who provides a service without the required expertise. The possibility of negative sanctions provides at least some control over untrained diagnosticians and some measure of protection for the public.

A greater difficulty arises in preventing nonprofessional groups or individuals from acquiring and using these same tools, or lesser ones, and implying competence where none or little exists. Although most companies responsible for selling such tools state in their test catalogues that the sale of their products is restricted to appropriate professionals, it is common for evaluative technology to be sold without examining the credentials of the purchaser.

The consumer is therefore at risk even if valid assessment instruments are used if he or she has no way of knowing whether the evaluation has been conducted or interpreted properly. According to Stagner,[4] "quacks and charlatans are always quick to move in on a new field and replace solid utility with glittery generalizations." He labeled such generalizations "Barnum statements." It would be easy for the consumer to be deceived into accepting a cheaper, but glossier, product rather than the service available through a fully qualified diagnostician. In an experiment which took place within an industrial setting, Stagner[5] demonstrated "the gullibility" of people who are given personality tests. In this study, personnel managers were given fake personality results. Ninety percent of the clients judged the fake analysis to be a good representation of their personality until such time as they discovered that each person received the same analysis. This result was achieved through the use of vague generalities (Barnum statements) that could be applied to almost everyone.

Professional bodies occasionally assume a policing role when they become aware that the public has been deceived into believing that specific evaluative devices are valid or that the individuals administering them are qualified. Scientology is one such organization that has been investigated by professional groups for promising quick personality analyses and IQ results based on questionable procedures.

In recent years, there has been a tendency for large organizations, even at a governmental level, to provide training to interested staff within narrowly defined assessment areas, for example, vocational aptitude and interest tests. Although this may have an economic advantage to the organization involved, the danger in this approach is that such individuals may not be adequately trained in the ethical use of such instruments. As a result, they may be tempted or even expected to venture beyond their data or training and to make interpretative statements about untested areas, for example, their client's intelligence, emotional functioning, and personality. Certainly in some situations a client's level of intelligence and personality style may be easily guessed, especially since most individuals do fall within some normal range. For individuals who have learned to disguise their deficits or who are presenting with subtle problems, however, it is risky to offer unsubstantiated interpretations of the client's functioning, particularly if such statements could have an effect on the client's future, for example, his or her ability to qualify for welfare assistance or to be admitted into a specific program. When an assessment report is to be used in court, it is even more critical that the professional have the appropriate credentials to perform such a function as well as detailed knowledge regarding the tests used and their limitations.

REASONS FOR ASSESSING

Routine Screening

In many inpatient or institutional settings, it is common practice to obtain evaluations by one or more professional groups (i.e., psychiatric consultation, social work history, occupational therapy assessment) out of routine practice rather than for any specific purpose. Although such assessments can sometimes serve a screening purpose and help to highlight problem areas that might have otherwise been missed, more often than not they are part of a mechanical procedure that goes into effect as soon as the client enters the institutional door. For professionals who are paid on a fee-for-service basis, there is the added conflict of interest that arises if the professional obtains a fee for each consultation that is requested.

Over time, there is the increasing risk that mental health staff will become overly dependent on such a broad-based approach to assessment. It can also provide them with a false sense of security that everything that can be done for the client has been done, therefore justifying a move onto the next "needy" candidate. Routine assessments therefore become costly and possibly a waste of time for the staff and client involved. Staff are often so busy conducting routine evaluations that they lack the time or energy to put their suggestions, or those of anyone else involved with the client, into practice. The client may also be frustrated from "telling the same story" repeatedly and seeing no results from his or her efforts. As a result, the client may leave the treatment setting disillusioned with the type of professional contact that was available and be less likely to consider treatment in the future. Professionals need to be careful not to fall into such an administrative trap unless they have reason to believe that the client will experience some benefit from the evaluative process.

Similar pressures have been noted in other institutional settings, for example, prisons and schools. Within an educational system, for example, many boards insist that a student's IQ be reassessed every few years even though such a task consumes most of the professional's time and has no utility for the majority of students tested.

Decision-Making Aid

Routine screening appears justified in situations when different therapeutic strategies are available and a decision must be made as to which client requires which treatment. Prescreening is an important step for many therapists conducting groups, for example. Not all clients can respond to group forms of treatment and it could be a negative experience for them to be placed in such a program if a negative outcome is likely. There is the added risk of psychological harm to the client. Although group leaders' opinions differ on this issue, the American Psychological Association[6] has developed a set of guidelines specifically relating to growth groups in which they advocate pre-group interviews to screen out inappropriate candidates and to advise potential group members regarding the expectations and rules of the group.

Aside from prescreening purposes, mental health professionals should recommend an assessment if they believe such an evaluation will be helpful in understanding or improving the client's level of functioning. Not only should the evaluation try to identify important strengths or difficulties or both but also it could potentially determine the underlying reasons for problems that do exist.

Accountability

Assessment is also a way in which professionals can keep themselves accountable for their actions, particularly within a treatment context. Although it may be more expedient to assume that a client has improved on the basis of self-report information alone, self-statements are notorious for being inaccurate. Comments regarding therapeutic progress may occur because the client is reluctant to be completely honest about his or her lack of improvement. Such deception may arise for a variety of different reasons, for example, anxiety about upsetting the therapist, guilt or embarrassment over failure to change, and denial. Even clients who have changed in significant ways may provide misleading self-statements about progress, for example, if they are overly perfectionist, demanding of themselves, and still see areas requiring improvement.

The use of objective evaluative tools enables the professional to monitor change, or the absence of it, in the course of treatment or after sessions have terminated. Through formal evaluation, the therapist is more likely to become aware of problems in the treatment approach and to modify it as necessary. It also provides the client with useful feedback regarding progress.

ASSESSMENT CHOICES

Choice of Assessment Tools

A decision as to the form of evaluation most appropriate for a particular client should be the responsibility of the professional being asked to perform the evaluation rather than the decision of the referring party. Much interdisciplinary conflict has arisen because one professional body has presumed to advise a different professional what types of tools to use (e.g., electroencephalogram, brain scan, Rorschach test), rather than limiting service requests to the referral question. Nonmedical professionals, for example, may be naive about the most recent assessment tools for diagnosing certain medical problems (e.g., epilepsy, hypoglycemia) based on their limited exposure to this field. Similarly, medical professionals have sometimes alienated psychology staff by insisting on projective testing with their clients, even though other assessment devices appear more appropriate. Although a debatable issue, some counselors feel that they should even let the client choose what tests should be used rather than make such decisions on their own. This type of professional stance could certainly create a dilemma for the diagnostician if he or she considers the client's choice to be inappropriate and possibly a waste of the client's or evaluator's time and resources. The professional has a responsibility to extend or limit the assessment procedures in accordance with the client's needs.

In choosing specific assessment tools, practitioners must also keep in mind what they are trying to assess and which tests are most sensitive at picking up which problems. Professional biases frequently come into play at this point. Understandably, the assessor will choose to give tests with which he or she is familiar. It is important to be cognizant of other tests or assessment approaches that might be more appropriate, however, so that a particular client can be referred to someone trained in applying them. Inpatient nurses play an important role in this decision-making process because they observe the client from many different angles and serve as a reminder to other staff to make use of alternative assessment resources. For example, the client who is admitted to a hospital because of depression may be experiencing difficulty dealing with leisure time and his or her depressive symptoms become exacerbated by this. Referral to a recreational or occupational therapist provides a different outlook on the client by staff trained at evaluating the client's daily living skills. This type of input is extremely valuable in treatment planning and would be missed by the traditional assessment process if such an evaluation were not pursued. In other words, it is important for each profession to recognize the contributions that can be made by other professions within the assessment arena and to take advantage of these resources for the sake of the client.

Appropriate Application of Tests

The use of specific test instruments should additionally be limited to areas for which they were designed. It would be naive to assume that tests developed on high school or college students will necessarily yield similar conclusions when given to individuals outside such a group. For example, a 50-year-old man may have average visual-motor coordination for his age group but score significantly lower than a 16-year-old. Norms therefore need to be used that allow meaningful comparisons and conclusions in order to avoid an inaccurate interpretation of the results. In addition to age differences, test results may also vary between the sexes and among different cultural groups. Such variations have led to cries of discrimination when results have been interpreted without taking these factors into consideration.

Not only should tests reliably and therefore consistently obtain similar results, but also they must be able to demonstrate their validity in measuring what they claim to measure. Improper use of tests has led to blanket criticism of standardized assessment procedures, although even more criticism should be directed against opinions based on interview data alone. According to Bersoff,

> psychological tests are seen as tools of discrimination that deny full realization of the rights of minorities and the handicapped and as devices fostering impermissible intrusion by the government into the private lives of its citizens. As a result, since the mid–1960s, litigation and legislation affecting the administration, interpretation, and use of psychological tests have multiplied.[7]

Professionals who use tests in uncharted territory on the basis of mere intuition and armchair rationalization have created professional embarrassment as well as public scrutiny when legally challenged (e.g., pre-screening managerial talent, picking potential college graduates, and selecting appropriate jurors). In the area of employee screening for job placement, "incomplete analysis of validity is typically found where unsubstantiated inferences are made that some particular verbal and/or quantitative ability (such as a certain IQ score) is required to perform a job."[8] Under the assumption of racial bias, IQ tests have also been legally attacked when used "to determine placement of school children in special programs."[9] The Education of the Handicapped Act demands that materials used to evaluate "handicapped children . . . are not unfairly discriminatory,"[10] although putting this into practice has been more difficult than it would appear.

In court assessments, similar problems exist. When an assessment report is to be used in court, the "test user should be able to relate the history of research and development behind the intended application of the test to justify the choice for the legal issues being considered. Characteristics of the examinee such as age, cultural background, or handicaps should be carefully evaluated in test-selection situations."[11]

From a strictly ethical point of view, assessment experts have an obligation to know and follow test standards whenever test results are used to substantiate professional statements. Prior to using an evaluative device in a situation other than that for which it was designed, the diagnostician has a responsibility, first of all, to obtain or develop appropriate normative data on which to make comparisons, and second, to establish that the test reliably and validly measures what it purports to measure under these novel circumstances. Although tests designed for one purpose may have relevance in different areas, such utility must be empirically demonstrated rather than assumed so that the tests in question are not misrepresented to the public as appropriately standardized instruments.

As a further protection for test takers and to force assessors to be accountable for statements made, a number of legislative proposals demanding "truth-in-testing" have been made. These proposals have recommended that

(a) individual test takers have access to corrected test results within a specified period after test administration;
(b) test sponsors or publishers file information on test development, validity, reliability, and cost with government agencies; and
(c) testing agencies give individual test takers information on the nature and intended use of tests prior to testing and guarantee their right to privacy.[12]

With the above information available to the test taker, he or she has concrete data by which to question professional statements and the underlying assessment process.

Specialized Tools

With the advent of computers professionals are being tempted to try variations in test administration, particularly because of the ease with which clients can be assessed and the resulting information sorted, scored, and interpreted. Glossy advertisements make many promises about the wonders of computerized technology as an assessment device and offer programs designed to obtain social histories, medical background, personality analyses, vocational testing, and so on. Although computerized assessment is a viable technique and certainly serves as an organizer and time saver for the busy practitioner, few studies have been conducted to demonstrate that the information obtained through this modality is valid or even comparable to tests or interviews given under more "personal" conditions. Clients vary significantly in their understanding of the written or spoken word, in their frustration tolerance when working with mechanical devices, in their level of attentiveness, motivation, and so on. These factors may affect the client differentially when tested via the computer and may lead to qualitative reactions on the part of the professional that would be otherwise absent. The possibility of a difference between computerized and noncomputerized testing conditions should contraindicate comparisons being made between the client and the normative group on which the test was developed if the test was standardized under noncomputerized conditions. Therefore, in adapting traditional tests to computerized administration, it would be critical to follow appropriate testing guidelines in establishing equivalent procedures, norms, etc., rather than to assume that standardized procedures and data from one modality can be generalized to a dissimilar format.

Criticism has also been directed against the use of hypnosis and bio-feedback instrumentation as evaluative devices because of "a lack of substantial and rigorous experimentation."[13] More specifically, in the use of hypnosis for forensic evaluation challenges have been made because it has the "potential for distorting memory."[14] To restrict the use and abuse of hypnosis as an assessment technique, the Northern California Society of Clinical Hypnosis has published a set of hypnosis guidelines to be followed in forensic cases. Adherence to appropriate procedures is important when using an approach as controversial as hypnosis, particularly in legal matters. Relinger refers to a case (*People v. Bamberg,* October 1982) in which "charges were dismissed against an alleged rapist even though the victim was hypnotized for therapeutic rather than forensic purposes."[15]

Biofeedback technology as a form of assessment has also been challenged. In the use of biofeedback instrumentation, there are many internal and external conditions that can affect the reliability and validity of biofeedback results besides the behavior being studied. Lie detectors are a classic example of the use of biofeedback information to make assumptions about an individual's private thoughts. "Inasmuch as the device records physiological changes, not 'lies' or 'truths' as such, the accuracy of results depends greatly upon the method of conducting the examination (e.g., what questions are asked in what order) and on the interpretation of the results."[16] Results are also likely to vary in accordance with the sophistication of the equipment being used, the emotional stability of the client, and so on.

PROCEDURAL CONCERNS

Testing Conditions

Certain conditions must be met if test results are to be considered valid. First of all, standardized procedures should be followed to ensure that each person gets a fair and equal chance of getting optimum results. Otherwise, the client's performance may vary according to the mood and clarity of the assessor, whether the instructions are given in a coherent and comprehensive fashion, and so on. Only by following the same procedure across individuals can meaningful comparisons be made between the client's level of functioning and individuals in a similar normative group. Second, environmental conditions should be conducive to good performance so that identified problems cannot be attributed to such factors as poor lighting, visual distraction, inadequate temperature, lack of privacy, or noise. If the test-taking situation is not ideal, specific problems should be indicated in the client's report so that the test results can be given the proper weight.

Content of Report

What to Include. The professional must also grapple with what to put in the report and what to leave out. In the course of an assessment, many topics are covered and the client may volunteer a number of intimacies that do not relate to the referral question. Although the compulsive report writer may feel uncomfortable leaving information out, the client has the right to privacy in areas that do not relate to the question under study. The professional should also avoid asking questions that are irrelevant to the purpose of the assessment. For example, if the assessor is evaluating a client's competency to stand trial, he or she should not question the client regarding the client's state of mind or behavior at the time of the crime.

Labeling. The use of diagnostic labels is another debatable practice and has led to much professional dissension. One argument against the use of diagnoses is that they are notoriously unreliable. Professionals frequently disagree in the labels they attach to specific clients. These differences can be extreme and it is not unusual for a client to be labeled as a schizophrenic by one clinician and a personality disorder by another. Such discrepancies are highly significant and may have serious implications in terms of the client's future, especially when the client's rights are at risk. Regrettably, the general public may accept such labels as absolute and real entities, possibly because of professional trust and the erroneous assumption that diagnostic statements have a scientific basis.

When test results are to be presented in court, "mental health professionals would do well to supplement or, if possible, exchange their psychiatric diagnoses for clear behavioral descriptions."[17] Professionals should also avoid making absolute statements about an individual's state of mind at a time other than the present. Psychiatrists and psychologists are frequently asked to render an opinion regarding a client's mental state at the time a crime was committed. This is a risky function to perform and necessitates reliance on a number of assumptions because the professional does not have direct access to the behavior in question. Alternatively, some professionals in this position may assume the role of a detective and try to reenact the "scene of the crime" and the client's mental state at the time by talking to other witnesses. Obviously, there is much room for error in taking on such a role.

The development of the *DSM-III*[18] appears to be a first step in trying to operationalize various psychological disorders and in improving the decision-making process in this difficult area. Even if the reliability of diagnoses is improving, however, many professionals continue to argue against their use because of the stigmatizing effect such categorization can have on the client. The use of a label to describe a particular client is bound to set up expectations and to place limits on treatment planning.

For example, individuals diagnosed as mentally retarded or brain damaged may have difficulty getting the kind of training they need to help them. Since there are limits on what they can potentially do, such individuals may be placed in non-stimulating environments in which little teaching is provided, even though the individual may be able to learn a number of functional skills if the right materials are used and if given sufficient structure.

As an added problem, people in the client's immediate environment may overreact to a specific label (e.g., schizophrenia, sociopathic personality) and may not be able to behave normally in the client's presence. This problem may be more prevalent among relatives, fellow workers, or anyone who is unsophisticated regarding psychopathology. The consequence for the client is that he or she may feel even more alienated and misunderstood. Biases against certain psychiatric conditions are often made worse by the media. As an example, television dramas frequently revolve around a psychotic killer and often imply that anyone who is psychotic or sociopathic is unpredictable and violent. The client who is unfortunate enough to be laden with such a diagnosis must be justifiably confused and upset by this representation of his or her condition. Since clients may be treated by those around them in accordance with such preconceived notions, there is always the danger of a self-fulfilling prophecy. In other words, clients may begin to behave according to expectations, not because of their mental state but because they are shaped into behaving that way.

Accountability. A report should be written in such a way that the results can be challenged and the professional held accountable for what is said. To do this, the professional must communicate how the results were obtained and how the interpretations were derived. Ideally, formal tests should be listed and results presented separately from self-report and observational data so that the reader is aware of what sources of information influenced the professional and in what ways. In addition, the rationale for making specific interpretations should be outlined, with an indication of any dubious findings that may exist. The test report should not be misleading and the results should never be presented as absolute entities. Even tests that provide concrete scores (e.g., IQ results, aptitude scores) should be presented as estimates of performance that may vary according to the mood of the client, test conditions, and so on. Interpretations should also be presented within an appropriate context. For example, it would not be sufficient to say that a client has a temper and is likely to behave in a violent fashion. The professional should describe the conditions under which this type of reaction is likely to occur so that the report does not imply that the behavior is generalizable to all situations.

By structuring the report in the manner presented, the reader should have sufficient information to challenge any of the findings. Without concrete knowledge regarding the assessment process, the report is shrouded in mystery. The client or any other party that may be surprised or confused by statements made in the report would either have to rely on professional trust and accept the analysis as valid or challenge the assessment findings in a vacuum. It is easy for the practitioner to defend a position when no one really knows what was done. This professional stance smacks of cowardice and is a failure on the professional's part to take responsibility for his or her actions and to acknowledge the client's right to disagree.

CLIENTS' RIGHTS

Informed Consent

Clients need to be apprised of their rights before consenting to an assessment. They need to know what to expect during the evaluation, what the professional's obligations to them are, and what limits there may be to the relationship. Although professionals may agree in theory that the client's rights must be respected, a survey by Berndt[19] suggests that professionals are typically vague regarding "how they describe their role to the patient." Furthermore, "18% of the respondents indicated that they did not attempt to get informed consent for testing, and oral consent was obtained in a 3:1 ratio over written."[20]

Unless clients are provided with sufficient information about a proposed evaluation, they do not have the knowledge with which to question it and risk being misled regarding how the results are to be used. The mental health worker should guard against being defensive if procedures are questioned so that the client is not inhibited into being passive and accommodating because of the professional's demeanor.

The practitioner must also be sensitive to external pressures falling on the client as such pressures may interfere with the client's right to refuse participation. In the employer–employee relationship, for example, testing has been "analogized to the extraction of involuntary confessions and to the demand for self-incrimination."[21] Similar pressures exist for clients asked to participate in a mental status examination when involuntary commitment is a possibility.

As an added complication, the need to inform the client of the purpose of the assessment before he or she agrees to participate is likely to affect the validity of the test results. For example, if the client is told that he or she is being tested to determine the presence of sexual deviance or violence, the client is rightfully placed on guard and, if sufficiently clever or sophisticated, may screen out any responses that could be interpreted in a negative way. Although the assessor may be able to assert that the client responded in a defensive fashion, little can be said about the content of the client's answers and the referral questions cannot be answered. Although the client has a right not to be tricked into revealing incriminating evidence, it seems wasteful to go through the motions of conducting an assessment if it has little chance of being accurate. Even worse, there is unequal protection for psychologically naive clients who do not have the expertise, or possibly the intelligence, to fake the test results in any believable fashion.

Confidentiality

As in other areas of client involvement, clients need to know whether the information they provide to the professional will be kept confidential. The client should be informed whether privileged communication does or does not exist in that locality and which individuals may have a right to the information.

As a further protection for the client, regulations have been established regarding the storage of client records. One expectation is that client files be kept in a secure place so that only appropriate individuals have access. Security is often a problem in institutional settings when files are kept in a central location and are available to most of the staff.

Rules also exist regarding the destruction of obsolete test results. Standards that address themselves to this issue[22,23] recommend that caution be exercised when handling dated material. Test data should be destroyed after a set period of time so that the client is not confronted with a situation in which obsolete test material is used against him or her.

Right to Feedback

Besides having obligations to the client prior to and during an evaluation, the mental health worker has a responsibility to give the client feedback regarding his or her performance and to make recommendations regarding any identified needs. Value judgments may come into play when deciding how much to tell the client, especially if some of the results are negative. This type of screening is sometimes recommended when working with a client who is not "therapeutically ready" to receive certain information and could possibly experience psychological harm if all the test results were revealed. Since the professional is under an obligation not to harm the client, he or she may be torn between protecting the client and respecting his or her rights. The mental health professional needs to decide whether the client can handle the feedback without being seriously harmed, for example, thrown into a severe depression or a psychotic break. Although some clients are psychologically fragile, there is the risk that the practitioner will use the above excuse with everyone in order to avoid communicating any unpleasantries and having to deal with the client's reactions. Even though few individuals appreciate hearing negative feedback and may experience some distress when the results are first communicated to them, they still have a right to know and their immediate reaction to the results is often short-lived.

According to the Berndt survey,[24] the extent to which results are shared with the client varies according to the test instrument that is used and the behavior being measured. More specifically, "the most frequently mentioned feedback was the IQ range, with most respondents emphasizing the range rather than the score and several stating they would not share below normal IQ information." Berndt further found that results from projective tests (i.e., the Rorschach, projective drawings, and the Thematic Apperception Test) were less likely to be shared. The results of Berndt's survey therefore suggests that professionals are highly selective about the results they provide and that they screen out information they prefer not to share, despite the client's right to feedback.

More and more, clients are demanding not only an oral interpretation of their results but also access to the written report. The survey conducted by Berndt[25], however, indicated that although professionals may acknowledge their client's right to oral feedback they are unlikely to give a written report unless specifically requested. Although the practitioner may argue that the report contains too much professional jargon and is likely to confuse the client, there is no reason why this problem couldn't be corrected by writing the report in language that the layperson can understand. Another argument is that the client will have difficulty reading about himself or herself in the third person and that he or she will focus only on those aspects of the report that are unpleasant. To minimize the above risks, the professional should never let the client read the report alone. The professional should be with the client when the report is being read in order to answer questions and to assist the client in attending to the entire report. For example, the professional must ensure that the client is not exclusively focused on whatever negative results exist but should help the client to recognize the positive findings as well. The practitioner must also be receptive to challenges that may be directed against the test findings, with changes made in the report if the professional feels such challenges are valid.

REFERENCES

1. Berndt, D. J. (1983). Ethical and professional considerations in psychological assessment. *Professional Psychology: Research and Practice, 14*(5), 580.
2. American Psychiatric Association (1980). *Diagnostic and statistical manual of mental disorders*, 3rd ed. (*DSM-III*). Washington, DC: American Psychiatric Association.
3. American Psychological Association (1974). *Standards for educational and psychological tests.* Washington, DC: American Psychological Association.
4. Stagner, R. (1967). The gullibility of personnel managers. In D. N. Jackson & S. Messick (Eds.), *Problems in human assessment.* New York: McGraw-Hill.

5. Ibid., 830.
6. American Psychological Association (1973). Guidelines for psychologists conducting growth groups. *American Psychologist, 28,* 933.
7. Bersoff, D. N. (1981). Testing and the law. *American Psychologist, 36*(10), 1047.
8. Schwitzgebel, R. L., & Schwitzgebel, R. K. (1980). *Law and psychological practice* (p. 123). New York: John Wiley & Sons.
9. Martin, R. (1978). Quarterly analysis of legal developments affecting professionals in human services. *Law and Behavior, 3*(1), 1.
10. Schwitzgebel, *Law and psychological practice,* 122.
11. Blau, T. H. (1984). Psychological tests in the courtroom. *Professional Psychology, 15*(2), 183–184.
12. Haney, W. (1981). Validity, vaudeville, and values: A short history of social concerns over standardized testing. *American Psychologist, 36*(10), 1027.
13. Schwitzgebel, *Law and psychological practice,* 133.
14. Relinger, H., Stern, T., & Minsky, P. J. (1983). *Guidelines for forensic hypnosis* (p. 1). Berkeley, CA: Northern California Society of Clinical Hypnosis.
15. Ibid.
16. Schwitzgebel, *Law and psychological practice,* 137.
17. Cohen, R. J. (1979). *Malpractice: A guide for mental health professionals* (p. 268). New York: Free Press.
18. *DSM-III.*
19. Berndt, Ethical and professional considerations, 582.
20. Ibid.
21. Schwitzgebel, *Law and psychological practice,* 124.
22. American Psychological Association, *Standards.*
23. American Psychological Association (1977). *Standards for providers of psychological services.* Washington, DC: American Psychological Association.
24. Berndt, Ethical and professional considerations, 582.
25. Ibid.

Treatment Issues

6

This chapter will attempt to cover legal and ethical concerns relevant to the mental health therapist. More specifically, the chapter will describe, first of all, therapy issues from the client's perspective, how such issues may vary in accordance with the exact nature of the client, professional concerns at different stages of therapy, and finally, problems pertaining to different treatment modalities.

THERAPY ISSUES FROM THE CLIENT'S PERSPECTIVE

The rights of clients involved with mental health providers have been described in earlier chapters. The following issues have specific relevance when examining the obligations of professionals to clients involved in treatment.

Right to Refuse

"The right to autonomy over one's body, that is, the power to decide whether something will be done to or with it, has long been recognized in common law."[1] Despite societal expectations and pressures to fit within a certain mold, individuals have the right to deviate from the norm and to refuse offers to be "modified" to fit the norm as long as they are not considered a risk to themselves or others. In other words, a client now has the opportunity to maintain "craziness" or to indulge in idiosyncrasies as long as such behaviors do not pose a threat to self or others. Historically, the concept of risk was loosely defined with the result that clients who would presently not qualify for involuntary treatment were being forced to tolerate interference with their life style. In the 1970s, attempts were made to define this concept more stringently so that therapists would not overstep their bounds with clients. As a result, the client's right to be different is more respected at the present time and more protected by law.

Right to Treatment

When clients have the right to treatment, that treatment must be considered adequate from a legal perspective. Many court battles have been fought because clients were not given treatment that was considered sufficient for their needs (e.g., *Rouse v. Cameron,*[2] *Wyatt v. Stickney*[3]). Although minimum standards have been legally established regarding treatment requirements, such standards have been difficult to implement because of budgetary problems and the subsequent lack of resources. Interestingly, "there has never been judicial extension of the right to treatment to voluntary patients or to outpatients. It applies only to involuntarily committed patients."[4] For this reason, most hospitals and outpatient programs do not "provide a sufficient array of treatments that patients can decide which to select or refuse."[5]

In order to obtain adequate treatment, the client also has the right to be protected from therapists who are not qualified to act within a treatment role. Many abuses have resulted when individuals have falsely portrayed themselves as fully qualified therapists. Slovenko[6] reports the results of a 6-month investigation of therapists who were unlicensed to practice. Some of the major findings of this study were that such unlicensed therapists frequently misled their clients by displaying "bogus degrees and titles." In addition, "'sexual interplay' is routinely imposed on women clients in the name of therapy by male practitioners." Attempts to protect the public from unqualified therapists have focused on the development of certification acts covering different professional groups. Although such acts limit the use of a certain professional name they do not define what the professional actually does. "Thus, if the certification statute prohibited the use of the title *marriage counselor*, a quack could simply change his title to *family counselor* and continue with the same work he was doing previously."[7] Historically, physicians attempted to exclude other mental health professionals from practicing as therapists under the assumption that psychotherapy is a medical intervention. This extreme viewpoint has not been upheld legally. In fact, "one prominent psychiatrist . . . suggests that any restrictive legislation on psychotherapy be aimed primarily at the general medical practitioner. In many medical schools the only training a student acquires about psychological problems amounts to about forty hours of class lectures over a four-year period."[8]

With the increasing emphasis on self-help groups and the use of paraprofessionals as a more cost-efficient way of offering mental health services, there is the added risk that clients will not receive the quality of service that they deserve. Lower-quality service delivery is also typical in larger institutional settings in which lower-paid staff have been allowed or encouraged to implement certain treatment strategies with various clientele without having sufficient supervision or training as a therapist. The economic advantages to the institution are obvious. Staff may be tempted into accepting such a role as it is often more rewarding than their former role.

Within the community, many social service agencies have learned to rely on minimally trained staff or paraprofessionals to provide necessary service because of budgetary constraints. Through their affiliation with an agency, clients may be misled to believe that they are being serviced by professionals who are legally and ethically accountable to an external body regarding their behavior. A problem arises because "paraprofessionals have not been regulated in the provision of services. . . . Without regulations or professional accountability, there can be little enforcement or protection of client rights other than through lawsuits."[9]

Right to the Least Restrictive Alternative

Not only does the client have the right to adequate treatment by qualified professionals, but also he or she has the right to the least restrictive treatment alternative; in other words, the least intrusive approach that can be potentially helpful to the client. What this means is that voluntary treatment should be considered over involuntary, day care over inpatient, and outpatient over day care. With regard to specific treatment modalities, therapies that produce effects that are potentially reversible are less intrusive than those considered permanent (e.g., psychosurgery). Moreover, those interventions that produce fewer adverse side effects should be chosen over those with more side effects (e.g., counseling vs. medication vs. electroconvulsive therapy [ECT]); and those in which the client has more control over his or her behavior are considered to be less intrusive than those in which the client has less ability to resist its effects (e.g., counseling vs. medication).

Within this same context, clients also have the right to be free from harm; in other words, from procedures that are overly coercive. The use of aversive procedures should only be considered after less intrusive procedures have been tried and failed, and only for behaviors that are considered a danger to the client or others (e.g., severe head banging). To avoid misuse of such procedures, clear guidelines should be established by an external committee regarding the conditions under which such procedures can be considered. Additionally, such a procedure should not be imposed on a particular client without following due process requirements.

Right to Confidentiality

Within the context of treatment, clients have the expectation and the right to expect that information divulged in the course of therapy will be kept confidential. The onus is on the therapist and the system within which a therapist may work to provide adequate environmental safeguards regarding client information. Exceptions to the confidentiality rule have been described in Chapter 3 and include, primarily, legal proceedings in which privileged communication does not exist between the therapist and client, court-ordered treatment in which all parties agree at the outset that the therapist has reporting obligations to a third party, situations where public safety is a factor, and accountability requirements for third-party payment. Additionally, information regarding therapy contacts can be released to third parties at the request of the client. When the client's permission is necessary before releasing information, the client should be informed regarding the type of information that will be released, to whom, how the information is to be used, whether there is a reasonable risk of misuse, and his or her right to withhold permission.

Right to Informed Consent

Prior to engaging in any type of therapeutic intervention, the client has the right to make a decision regarding the type of therapy, if any, that he or she will accept. In order to give a valid consent, the client first of all must be considered legally and mentally competent to make such a decision. Second, the client must be able to consent or withhold consent without coercion or unfair influence. In addition, he or she should have sufficient information on which to base a decision. More specifically, the client should be informed first of all of the right to refuse and should know what qualifications the therapist has for the treatment approach in question.

With regard to the actual treatment procedure that is being recommended, the client should be given a reasonable description of the treatment plan in language he or she can understand. This description should include an outline of the treatment stages, the role that will be played by the client and the therapist throughout treatment, the likely benefits and risks as well as the probability of such results, a *fair* description of alternative treatment approaches, and the reasons for recommending one procedure over another. In addition, the client should know if the procedure is experimental in nature. The only occasion on which a consent may not be required (i.e., for nonexperimental procedures) is in an emergency situation in which the client is considered a threat to himself or herself or others. Under such circumstances the therapist should obtain permission to proceed from the closest relative if he or she appears to be acting in the client's best interests, and subsequently from the client as soon as the emergency has been resolved.

Right to Due Process
When the status of a particular client is likely to change (i.e., transfer from one facility to another, change from voluntary to involuntary status, declaration of incompetency vs. competency, restriction of movement or communication), the client has the right to reasonable notice of the likely change in status, a fair hearing in the presence of an impartial judge or committee, and the right to appeal a particular decision at a later time. For a hearing to be fair, the client should have the right to information available on him or her, particularly information that could be used to justify a change in status. In addition, the client should have access to counsel and the opportunity to defend himself or herself in a legally appropriate manner.

NATURE OF THE CLIENT

In addition to recognizing the rights clients have in the treatment arena, it is important for mental health professionals to recognize what issues are pertinent to certain client groups. More specifically, treatment issues and professional concerns may vary in accordance with the following factors.

Age
Issues affecting intervention with minors and adults have been covered in preceding chapters. Within the treatment area, the issues that are of the greatest concern for the professional and client alike include the right of the client (1) to refuse or obtain treatment, (2) to control the nature of therapeutic involvement, and (3) to maintain confidential communications with the therapist.

Conflicts seem inevitable in many areas of child treatment, particularly when the child is targeted as the problem and coerced into treatment by other members of the family. If the therapist "takes action on behalf of the troubled family, he may put himself in opposition with the family's 'troubled' member; a likely consequence of this is that the therapeutic relationship with the 'troubled' member becomes an *adversary* relationship rather than an *alliance*. A likely consequence of that is reduced effectiveness."[10] Dilemmas also develop, for example, when counseling adolescents who have become sexually active and the client is dealing with such concerns as birth control or the possibility of having an abortion. Attempts on the therapist's part to be supportive and helpful with the client may be misconstrued by the parents if and when they discover the content of the therapy sessions with their child, particularly as the parents may consider the therapist to have professional and legal obligations to them as well.

With younger children, complications can arise if the parents seem to be pressuring a child into treatment and the therapist believes that the child is not the source of the problem but the family's scapegoat. Conversely, the therapist may occasionally encounter situations in which the parents refuse treatment for a child who is obviously in need. Under such circumstances the therapist could potentially notify the local children's aid society that the child's emotional needs are being neglected. In some states failure to satisfy a child's health care needs is considered grounds for abuse.

Regulations regarding the treatment of minors vary from one location to another and often depend on the degree of maturity and emancipation of the minor from parental figures. Even when it is clear that the parents have the legal right to decide for their child, the therapist is confronted with the dilemma of trying to work with an involuntary client whose goals may be different from those of his or her caretakers. The conflict for the therapist is even harder if the goals of the parents and the means by which they prefer to reach those goals are in contrast with what the therapist believes is in the best interests of the child. To minimize these problems, the therapist should be fully informed regarding the rights of children. In addition, parents need to be made aware of their responsibilities to their child. For example, when a child is placed in treatment, the parents should discuss the reasons for taking this step and help the child to understand what to expect in the course of therapy. Despite parental pressures to the contrary, the therapist has the obligation to provide treatment in accordance with the client's right to the least restrictive alternative. Ideally, this would mean treating the child in an outpatient versus day care versus inpatient setting if possible and using "positive" (i.e., nonpunitive) approaches over "negative" ones.

Level of Competence

By definition, minors are not considered to have the legal competence to manage their "therapeutic" affairs. As described in earlier sections, level of competence is also considered an issue with adults who do not appear to have sufficient mental ability to make appropriate judgments regarding certain areas of their life. Competence must be assumed unless proven otherwise by an impartial body satisfying due process requirements. When working with clients who have been declared incompetent to make decisions about therapeutic procedures, the therapist is still obligated to protect and respect the client's rights through interaction with the client's appointed guardian.

One right that is frequently violated when dealing with incompetent clients is the right to adequate treatment. This concern has often been raised in large institutions or when the incompetent client is an elderly adult who is residing in a nursing home. The elderly client is often ignored or overly regimented when residing in an institutional setting. Rather than assisting the nursing home resident to regain or maintain day-to-day coping skills, staff often reinforce helpless and dependent behavior on the part of the residents by doing too much for them. Although the rationale for doing this may be to keep the residents comfortable, it may also be the easier and faster route for staff to follow. Regrettably, the behavior of nursing home residents has been found to deteriorate under such circumstances because the resident acquires a state of learned helplessness. Professionals working within such a facility, or in other facilities in which clients are considered incompetent, should take precautions to avoid developing inappropriate dependency either out of "tender loving care" or for the sake of efficiency. Regardless of the age or level of competency of the client, he or she has the right to rehabilitative rather than custodial care.

Client Status

Most therapists would agree that the ideal therapeutic relationship is a voluntary one. Not only should the client have the right to decide whether he or she wants to change certain thoughts, feelings, or behaviors, but also which changes are to be made and the way in which to go about making them. Clients who are forced to accept treatment may develop feelings of resentment as well as passivity regarding their ability to make choices about their own life. As a result, they are less likely to put forth much effort, if any, in making or maintaining changes. In some cases, the application of mind-altering methods (e.g., medication, ECT) may result in a more receptive or at least less resistive frame of mind, thereby leading to the client's "voluntary" cooperation with treatment. The expectation of "voluntary" cooperation after a period of forced treatment may be inappropriately used as justification for imposing treatment in the first place. In many instances, however, such cooperation is short-term and apparent gains not generalized to the "natural" environment. The pressure of being in an institutionalized setting may additionally encourage the clients to "play the game"; in other words, behave in accordance with staff expectations in order to earn their voluntary status. Conversely, clients have also been known to work at maintaining their involuntary client status because of some secondary gain attached to being in a controlled setting.[11] Regardless of the existence of a real or contrived positive or negative client style, the role of the therapist is complicated by the client's status in that decisions must be made that could potentially violate the client's right to refuse or receive treatment, the right to informed consent, and other rights affecting client movement and activity. Even if the client should eventually consent to treatment and be made a voluntary client, the mental health professional must recognize the possibility that such a consent might be legally unacceptable. First of all, the client's competence to make such a decision could be questioned if, in fact, his or her thinking has been potentially affected by mind-altering treatment techniques. Second, the incentive provided by voluntary status and possible discharge helps to negate the voluntary component involved in giving informed consent. The impossibility of obtaining "true" informed consent has been pointed out by many practitioners involved with institutionalized clients, both in a psychiatric facility and in a prison setting. There is the added risk with institutionalized clients that the goal of therapy will be the goal of the institution (e.g., conformity, passivity) rather than that of the individual client. In addition, confidentiality and inconsistency in treatment may be more of a concern in an institutional setting in that more than one individual is responsible for the client's behavior. To avoid these numerous pitfalls, the therapist must, first of all, be aware of the risks and, second, take steps to overcome them through knowing and following both ethical and legal standards.

Gender

In working with male versus female clients, there is the added risk that therapists may have sexual biases that could intrude into the treatment process. Many of the articles written on this topic primarily focus on the likelihood of bias toward women clients.

Referring to a study conducted by Broverman et al. (1970),[12a] Goldfried and Davidson state that "both male and female clinicians considered the healthy woman to be more submissive, less independent, less adventurous, less aggressive, and less competitive than men."[12b] When specifically referring to assertive or expressive communication, they state that "a particular response by a woman is apt to be viewed as aggressive or 'bitchy' and hence not adaptive, whereas the same response in a man would be viewed as appropriately assertive."[13]

Relevant surveys conducted on the topic of sexism among therapists reveal that clients are often influenced to behave in accordance with such sexual stereotypes. Some of the major issues identified by Nadelson et al.[14] include:

1. Greater emphasis on "interpersonal relationships than career-related issues, regardless of the priority the patient assigns to this area"
2. Different factors suggesting the presence of psychopathology or therapeutic resistance in women vs. men (e.g., aggressiveness vs. dependency)

Based on a Task Force on the Status of Women in Canadian Psychology, the Canadian Psychological Association obtained more specific examples of unsatisfactory therapeutic experiences that suggested biases on the part of therapists toward their female clients:

I consulted a therapist because of depression following my being threatened with dismissal from my teaching position. The therapist disregarded completely the importance of this threat to my self-esteem as a career woman, and insisted on focusing entirely on my relationship with my husband.[15]

I have hard days at home with a somewhat chaotic family. My therapist advised me that my husband needs me to always be pretty and cheerful when he comes home, to listen sympathetically to his troubles at work, and not share my problems because this makes it more difficult for him.[16]

My therapeutic goals for a depressed female client were for her to understand her underlying anger, to become more assertive, and to have options other than suicide for resolving her problems. Her husband's therapist advised me to help her become more passive, dependent and accepting of her husband because her assertiveness and increasing interests outside of the home were upsetting to them both.[17]

I had no money, no self-confidence, nowhere to turn, and had made a halfhearted attempt at suicide. My therapist certainly has no sympathy or practical advice for me. I was told that I precipitated my husband's violent behavior because I enjoyed punishment, otherwise I would not have tolerated it and would have left him. The therapist asked what I was feeling guilty about that I needed to be punished.[18]

Men encounter a different form of sexism which may revolve around the need to be always strong, emotionally controlled, and to assume complete responsibility for all members of their family. Such expectations are certainly unreasonable and, if the therapist reinforces this role, the male client is limited in terms of the therapeutic choices and life style open to him.

Obviously, it is important for mental health counselors, male and fe-

male, to engage in self-exploration and to be honest with themselves regarding, first of all, the mere existence of such stereotypes. D'Augelli
offers an interesting example of a therapeutic interchange for this purpose:

A client is crying, tears pouring out:

Client: "I feel so desperately miserable. I'm the one who's rejected.
I'm the one who's pushed out of the family, excised like a
tumor. I feel so lonely."

Therapist: "Feeling unloved is so awfully painful."

Client: "You're darn right is is."

Therapist: "You're hurting so much."

As you read this brief exchange, there are questions to ask yourself.
What was your assumption about the client's sex? How did you react to
the information that the client was crying? Answers to these questions
provide you with some clues as to your sex-role stereotypes. The client,
in fact, was a male, newly separated from his spouse. A therapist colleague was surprised to realize that he read it as if it were a woman and
did not think that it might be a man. Another male colleague com-
mented, "I didn't think of myself as sexist, but I was and I am."[19]

Having determined whether such sexual stereotypes exist, the second
step is to examine the effect that such viewpoints may be having on therapeutic encounters.

    In addition to the differential way in which men and women may be
treated within a counseling format, there are also differences reflected in
the type of psychiatric intervention that is chosen for men versus women.
Psychosurgery and ECT therapy are disproportionately used with
women. Surveys conducted in the United States indicate a ratio of at
least 2:1 in the use of ECT for women versus men.[20] Although some practitioners have attempted to rationalize such a ratio by claiming that the
incidence of endogenous or psychotic depression is higher in women, this
argument has not been supported by empirical evidence. Breggin[21] ex-
presses the opinion that the reason for discriminatory practice in the use
of ECT "is reflected in the recommendation made so often in the literature that ECT be reserved for individuals who do not require the use of
memory and intellect for their livelihood. . . . Such repeated observations
immediately suggest why more *women* are given ECT: they are judged
to have less need of their brains."

    The discriminatory treatment of men and women is also reflected in
the use of various psychotropic drugs as a form of treatment. Cooperstock refers to several surveys that have been conducted in the United
States and Canada that indicate that psychotropic drugs, particularly
minor tranquilizers and sedatives, are twice as likely to be used with
women than with men. A comprehensive study that took place in Sas-

katchewan between 1976 and 1977 examined all prescriptions that had been handed out in a 19-month period in that province. The study concluded that women received more than "63% of all prescriptions for central nervous system drugs" with the greatest gender differentiation being for the 20- to 29-year age group. "Here it was found that tranquilizers and other sedative-hypnotics were prescribed to four times the number of women as men."[22] Such biases are also reflected in the promotional material that has been developed on the use of different drugs. In a study of advertising literature regarding the use of tranquilizers and antidepressants, Stimson discovered that "there are far more women shown in these advertisements. Indeed, women outnumbered men by 15 to one. So the first message is that women are more likely than men to need tranquilizers or anti-depressants."[23] Within the last decade, the media have attempted to sensitize physicians and the general public to such discriminatory practice with the hope that awareness will help to reduce such treatment biases in the future.

In addition to developing public awareness, mental health practitioners need to establish guidelines regarding appropriate nonsexist practice. Although there have been no specific guidelines developed to reduce sexual bias in the treatment of male clients, the Canadian Psychological Association has published a set of guidelines to assist therapists in minimizing sexual bias in working with female clients. These guidelines were developed on the basis of common problems identified by the Task Force on the Status of Women in their 1977 study.

1. The therapist/counsellor is willing to help the woman client to explore alternative life options in addition to the culturally defined gender role. Besides marriage and motherhood, he or she acknowledges the importance of other activities in both creating and solving women's problems.
2. The therapist/counsellor realizes that women do not bear the total responsibility for the success of marriage and for childrearing.
3. The therapist/counsellor recognizes the existence of social bias against women, and explores with the client the possibility that her problems may be based in society's definition of women's role rather than entirely within herself.
4. While respecting the right of the therapist/counsellor to determine the appropriate therapeutic strategy for a client, he or she is sensitive to and avoids the use of theoretical concepts that serve to reinforce the female stereotype of dependency and passivity, or to limit the woman's personal development.
5. The therapist/counsellor avoids interpreting psychological problems that occur at times of biological change in a woman's life—e.g., childbirth, menopause—solely in terms of her reproductive/biological functioning.
6. The therapist/counsellor avoids the use of language implying sex bias, especially sexist jokes and the use of labels derogatory or demeaning to women.

7. The therapist/counsellor recognizes physical violence and sexual abuse as crimes, and does not encourage the woman client to submit to them, to accept their legitimacy, or to feel guilty about being a victim. The therapist actively acknowledges that there is no "provocation" that justifies resorting to physical or sexual violence.
8. The therapist/counsellor recognizes a woman client's right to have a fully adult role in the therapist–client relationship, without guidance from or deference to a man, and helps her to achieve such a role.
9. The therapist/counsellor considers the sexual activity of the client without employing a "double standard" based on gender.
10. The therapist/counsellor does not treat the woman client as a sex object.[24]

Despite the presence of such guidelines, therapists are still confronted with the problem of working with clients who behave and think according to such stereotypes. In other words, just as therapists should not impose their sexual stereotypes on their clients, they must also be concerned about imposing "liberated" views on clients who perceive the world and their relationships with people in a "nonliberated" fashion. This problem is even more of a dilemma in family or marital therapy if the frustrations and goals of the spouses vary in accordance with such sexual stereotypes. Many therapists have attempted to deal with this potential conflict by working with a co-therapist of the opposite sex. Although this type of arrangement may reduce the possibility that one of the clients may feel misunderstood by having just an opposite-sex therapist, it does not eliminate the possibility that the client with the less "liberated" viewpoint will feel that the therapists have "ganged up" on him or her by reinforcing undesired treatment goals in the presence of the respective spouse.

Even when the therapist and client may agree to work toward a "liberated" goal (e.g., to become an assertive woman), the therapist has an obligation to prepare such a client for "likely negative reactions to her more assertive behavior patterns"[25] in a minimally liberated world.

Culture and Race
Biases similar to those previously mentioned can also exist in working with various cultural or racial groups. To sensitize therapists to this possibility, guidelines have been set up by different professional bodies warning against discriminatory practice toward clientele on the basis of such characteristics as gender, race, religion, and so on. Within the realm of therapy, counselors risk having their own cultural values regarding appropriate versus inappropriate behavior affect the goals established within the therapeutic situation. To minimize this problem, the stance taken at an American Psychological Association (APA) conference (1973) was that "counseling of persons of culturally diverse backgrounds by persons who are not trained to work with such groups should be regarded as unethical."[26]

Substance Abusers and Sexual Deviates

Working with clients who have deviant sexual preferences or a substance abuse habit (e.g., alcohol, drugs) creates a number of special concerns for the mental health professional. First of all, because of the nature of the problem, such clients are more likely to experience occasional conflicts with society and therefore come to the attention of the legal system from time to time. The issue of confidentiality and the need for environmental safeguards for maintaining privacy should be carefully examined before initiating therapy contacts. Most importantly, clientele need to be informed of the difficulties that could arise and the possibility that files or professional testimony could be demanded in court. As the degree of confidentiality privilege extending to a therapist varies according to local and federal statutes, it is critical that mental health professionals be aware of the laws that govern them in their area.

In order to protect substance abuse clients from unauthorized disclosure of potentially damaging information, Sobell and Sobell indicate that

several regulatory mechanisms have evolved for preserving and assuring client rights: (1) federal regulations (Department of Health, Education and Welfare [HEW]) for the confidentiality of alcohol and drug client records; (2) state licensing and review standards for treatment programs; (3) accreditation agencies and third-party payer standards for reviewing and accrediting treatment programs; (4) professional and paraprofessional associations and boards, which can review, censure, or expel an individual from professional practice for violation of client rights, and (5) legislative and judicial action.[27]

They further state that

court orders in and of themselves are not sufficient to release information about clients. In fact, a special hearing apart from the regular court proceedings must be held in order to show that there is good cause for releasing the clinical record. If such an order is granted, it can only require disclosure of objective data (facts and dates of enrollment, discharge, attendance, and medication, and similar objective data) relevant to the court action in question. Other client–therapist communications, even though part of the clinical records, are not subject to release by court order.[28]

Another complication for the mental health professional who works with "antisocial" clients arises if the client has been referred to therapy by the court system rather than voluntarily. In court-ordered therapies or supervisory contacts with a probation or parole officer, clients are likely more motivated to present an unrealistically positive picture than to be honest about their social or psychological difficulties because of the threat of sanctions if they have deviated from the legally acceptable path.

The likelihood of being helpful or therapeutic is rather remote under such circumstances. In being called to answer questions for the court on the basis of therapy contacts, the therapist also risks being put in the untenable position of commenting on whether or not the client has been "cured" or the likelihood that he or she will "misbehave" in the future.

In addition to court-ordered forms of treatment, a client with substance abuse or sexual problems may also be pressured to initiate therapy under the threat of losing a job or his or her family. A number of articles have been written, for example, on the dilemma facing the therapist who attempts to help a client change his or her sexual preference. Even if the client has not initiated therapy because of legal problems or coercion from any specific party, he or she is likely experiencing societal pressures as a result of sexual differences. Davison argues that the presence of societal pressures affects the client's ability to enter therapy voluntarily. He therefore proposes that "we stop offering therapy to help homosexuals change and concentrate instead on improving the quality of their interpersonal relationships."[29] His stance has led to a number of counterarguments[30,31] which only serve to accentuate the dilemma facing the understandably confused therapist, that is, whether to accept and therefore respect the client's expressed desire to change his or her sexual preference or to refuse to work toward such a goal with the client on the assumption that the goal has not been voluntarily derived and therefore the client does not really *want* to change.

With substance abuse clients, an added concern is the level of mental competence of the client in agreeing to treatment, particularly as many such clients may enter treatment under the effects of alcohol or drugs or both. Under such circumstances, should the therapist assume that the clients have the capacity to understand their rights in this situation? Because of the varying length of time a client could potentially be affected by different chemicals in the system, at what point in time would a consent be considered truly informed and voluntary? Additionally, what assistance can be provided to the client during this interim "nontreatment" period?

Another professional issue that is more likely to arise when treating substance abusers or sexual deviates or both is the "duty to warn" potential victims if they are considered to be at physical risk because of the client or the duty to protect the client from possibly hurting himself or herself. In treating an intoxicated client, for example, the therapist is under the obligation to prevent, or attempt to prevent, a client who is legally drunk at the time of the therapy contact from driving while intoxicated. If the therapist is unable to verbally discourage the client from driving under such circumstances, law enforcement officers should be notified of his or her condition. "Allowing the client to drive under these conditions, would be tantamount to, at best, allowing a misdemeanor to be committed and, at worst—if the driver fatally injures someone else— creating conditions conducive to vehicular homicide.''[32]

Unavoidably, approaches to many of these ethical difficulties and di- lemmas are rarely definitive and typically vary with the circumstances. First and foremost, therapists should not accept such individuals as cli- ents unless they have been specifically trained for working with such a specialty client group. In addition to acquiring and maintaining an appro- priate level of competence, the mental health professional also has an obligation to monitor his or her therapeutic performance through estab- lishing appropriate accountability safeguards, for example, ongoing self- evaluation, peer review, or treatment evaluation strategies.

THERAPEUTIC STAGES

In general, the therapeutic process can be divided into three major stages: initiation, treatment, and termination. Within each of these stages, there are specific professional issues with which the mental health practitioner must deal, although these issues may not be exclusive to any particular stage in the treatment process.

Initiation Stage

Nature of Contact. Clients come to the attention of mental health profes- sionals through several different routes. The choices facing the therapist will obviously be less complicated if the client has initiated the contact voluntarily and without going through a third party. In many situations, however, the therapist is first contacted by someone other than the client (e.g., the client's physician, a family member, lawyer, social service agency), who attempts to set up an appointment on behalf of the client either out of goodwill or frustrations with the individual in question. Men- tal health professionals who agree to transact business in this way are more likely than not to be faced with missed appointments or a less than satisfactory first contact that could range from passive resistance to ac- tual belligerence. In other words, the therapist errs in assuming that an individual in fact wants therapy simply because other people have taken the responsibility to arrange it. To avoid operating on such an erroneous assumption, many clinicians will only set up initial appointments if con- tacted by the client directly rather than through third parties. Not only does this type of practice constitute better business from a practical point of view, but also it enables the client to decide to initiate therapy. It there- fore constitutes a more ethical and professional way of establishing a rela- tionship with a client.

In the case of forced treatment (e.g., involuntary commitment, court-ordered treatment), the therapist must decide beforehand whether or not to work with a client under such circumstances. In court-ordered treatment contracts, the problem for the therapist is further complicated by his or her reporting obligations to the party ordering the treatment, and thereby obliges him or her to violate the client's right to confidentiality. Although therapists agreeing to enter such a treatment arrangement may rationalize that society has the right to oblige certain members of society to change, they need to weigh society's rights versus the client's while at the same time taking into consideration the decreased likelihood of being "effective" under such negative therapeutic circumstances.

Complications also arise when the client comes into contact with a mental health professional as a result of an emergency situation. In non-emergency situations, the therapist has a choice as to whether or not to initiate a therapeutic contract with a particular client and therefore to assume therapeutic responsibility for him or her. However,

> when a patient is seen in a treatment setting . . . and it becomes apparent even during the initial assessment that an immediate intervention is required, a therapeutic relationship is assumed to exist despite the absence of a formal contract. Failure to provide for proper care (which may consist merely of referral to another, more appropriate facility) leaves the clinician open to a charge of abandonment. Before a patient is permitted to leave, an assessment ought to be made sufficient to rule out the possibility that further immediate steps are required.[33]

On the other hand, the emergency clinician will occasionally be obliged to discriminate between the "true" emergency and the client who is manipulating the system for some secondary gain; for example, "the destitute patient seeking a roof for the night and the felon wishing to escape detection by the police."[34] If a decision is made to commit a client involuntarily on the basis of an emergency assessment, the therapist should ensure that he or she has complied with relevant legal requirements for admission and has obtained sufficient information about the client's functioning to justify such a decision. In other words, the professional must be prepared to be accountable for his or her decision to admit or not to admit.

If, however, the client approaches a therapist voluntarily and is in a nonemergency state, the pressures on the clinician are lessened. The primary issues facing the mental health professional then become an assessment of the presenting problem(s), his or her ability to be of service to this particular client, and the responsibilities to the client under either circumstance.

Competence. A therapeutic contract with a client should not be established unless the therapist is able to demonstrate that he or she has sufficient competence to deal with the specific problem(s) posed by the client or the ability to work effectively with a particular client group. As described in an earlier section, the nature of the client can vary in accordance with such variables as age, gender, treatment status, cultural background, and so on. Special expertise is often preferred in working with different client populations because of the need to be sensitized to issues specific to a particular group. Additionally, the mental health practitioner should have sufficient expertise to decide what type of therapy might be most helpful to a particular client depending on his or her goals, treatment preferences, and existing level of psychological functioning (e.g., short- versus long-term intervention, insight-oriented versus directive, individual versus group therapy, sexual therapy versus marital). To initiate ethically a specific form of therapy with a client (e.g., behavior therapy), the therapist must be able to demonstrate that his or her therapeutic skills have been acquired through formal training rather than through self-teaching and all its inherent risks and limitations.

Another factor to consider is the therapist's own psychological state, that is, any personal factors that could affect the therapist's ability to work with a particular client effectively. This type of self-evaluation should be conducted whenever the therapist is confronted with a client having characteristics the clinician finds overly objectionable. For example, a therapist may feel he or she cannot work with a client who drinks to excess because he or she has unresolved feelings about alcoholics that derive from unpleasant childhood experiences. As another example, a therapist with strict religious views may be unable to work effectively with a client who is sexually permissive, particularly if the client's sexual behavior is not being identified as the problem. In other words, therapists need to know the limits that they should impose on themselves in view of their own background and values as well as the specific areas of expertise that they may or may not have.

When a therapist does not feel competent to establish a therapeutic contract with a client he or she still has an obligation to offer an opinion regarding the client's therapeutic needs and to inform him or her of the appropriate resources available in the community.

Assessment Responsibilities. In order to determine the client's therapeutic needs, the therapist has an obligation to obtain sufficient information from the client to understand the nature of the presenting problem(s) and circumstances. Prior to eliciting information, practitioners should always advise clients of any limits to confidentiality, for example, under what circumstances information can be disclosed to third parties, and safeguards for preventing "internal" staff from inappropriately obtaining access to private information. Clients should also be asked how they wish to be contacted to control the extent to which other individuals associated with them are aware of their involvement in therapy. In addition, the client should be informed of any established limits to the services available (e.g., age requirements, therapeutic limitations) or office practices that could affect the client's decision to enter treatment (e.g., limited office hours, fees, the possibility of being assigned to a therapist in training). In other words, prior to intruding into the client's time and personal life, the therapist has an obligation to inform the client what to expect in return.

Assuming the client has been informed of the professional's obligations in any potential therapeutic contract and that he or she has agreed to proceed with the intake process, the next logical step is to obtain information from the client about the presenting problem(s). The clinician should avoid delving into irrelevant areas and instead concentrate on the problems with which the client wants help, thereby respecting the client's right to privacy.

If, on the basis of this intake assessment, the therapist believes that the client could be a potential risk to self or others (e.g., drunk driving, assaultive behavior, suicidal acting out), he or she should advise the client of the "duty to warn" rule and commitment policies if this information was not provided earlier.

In obtaining assessment information on which to formulate a diagnosis or treatment plan, the clinician would be wise to review previous treatment records to learn what has already been done and to ascertain areas of risk, if any. "Suits charging negligence have been filed for failure to pursue information that on the face of it seemed useful and then turned out to be vital *(Merchants National Bank v. United States).*"[35]

Treatment Planning. If the therapist concludes from the results of the intake assessment that a therapeutic contract with the client is appropriate, the next step is to develop a treatment plan and subsequently obtain the client's informed consent to proceed with therapy. As a first step, the client should be informed of the therapist's analysis of his or her psychological problems. If in doing so, the mental health professional provides the client with a diagnosis, the client should be given sufficient information about diagnostic procedures to recognize their limits and shortcomings. The client can therefore take such information into account in accepting or rejecting any diagnostic pronouncements.

Second, the therapist should discuss with the client the type of therapy that he or she would recommend to help the client achieve the treatment goals. To do this, the therapist must be at least superficially aware of what the client wants from therapy. Since patients will obviously differ in terms of how aware they are of their own treatment goals, their goals are likely to vary from being extremely general (e.g., to understand myself more, to make life more meaningful) to being concrete and specific (e.g., to stop smoking, to obtain more friends). A common pitfall for therapists is to make premature assumptions about desired outcomes based on their position of authority in relation to the client, their own theoretical background and values as to what the client needs and therefore wants. This type of risk is more likely to occur when the therapist is working with a client having characteristics significantly different from his or her own (e.g., cultural and racial discrepancies, age).

Under the assumption that the client and therapist have established reasonably appropriate treatment goals, the next step is to develop a suitable treatment plan. At all times, the clinician should keep in mind the need for offering the least restrictive alternatives and to obtain his or her informed consent before proceeding. "The situations that most obviously, based on the incidence of suits, call for an informed consent are therapeutic approaches involving physical contact (psychodrama, Gestalt therapy, Rolfing) and drug or electroshock therapy. With traditional verbal therapies, no cases based on the failure to obtain informed consent have been reported."[36] In establishing a treatment contract with the client, however, Schutz specifically recommends providing the following information:

1. Focus of the therapy (behavior and/or feeling states).
2. Procedures to be used (for example, interpretation, confrontation, guided imagery, touching, or meditating).
3. Desired and likely outcomes and, if possible, the methods to be used to assess the outcome.
4. If a separate informed consent form is not being used, an explanation of material foreseeable risks, including limits of confidentiality.
5. Fees for specific services and cancellation policy.
6. A statement that this contract can be renegotiated or terminated at any time without penalty.[37]

The therapist should be prepared to discuss in an objective and nondefensive manner any components of the proposed treatment contract and specifically his or her reasons for preferring or recommending one particular form of therapy over another. In addition, the client should be informed regarding alternative ways of getting assistance with his or her presenting problems, particularly (1) where specialty services may be available for a specific type of problem or client (e.g., alcohol day care program, rape crisis center, group program for assaultive husbands), and (2) where similar services are available elsewhere at a minimal cost or without charge.

On the basis of such discussions, the client is therefore better able to understand what is available in the way of treatment facilities, what to expect from therapy and from the clinician in question, as well as the client's rights and obligations should therapy be initiated at this point.

Treatment Stage
Once a therapeutic relationship has been established, the critical issues confronting the clinician primarily involve his or her role as therapeutic trustee and the responsibilities that follow from such a role. Not only

must the clinician demonstrate appropriate professional demeanor as a result of the fiduciary relationship with clients but also must deliver services appropriately and be prepared to deal effectively with therapeutic obstacles or crises.

Professional Demeanor and Fiduciary Relationship. The importance of maintaining a relationship free of undue influence and characterized by professional integrity and respect is typically emphasized by all mental health professions. For example, the Principles of Medical Ethics published by the American Psychiatric Association stress the importance of not taking advantage of a client because of his or her vulnerability in a therapeutic relationship and the trust that has been placed on the therapist as a function of his or her role. More specifically,

> the patient may place his/her trust in his/her psychiatrist knowing that the psychiatrist's ethics and professional responsibilities preclude him/her gratifying his/her own needs by exploiting the patient. This becomes particularly important because of the essentially private, highly personal, and sometimes intensely emotional nature of the relationship established with the psychiatrist.[38]

The Code of Professional Ethics for Marriage and Family Therapy specifically warns against a therapist using "his or her counseling relationship to further personal, religious, political, or business interests."[39] Additionally, therapists are warned "to avoid relationships with clients which might impair professional judgment or increase the risks of exploiting clients. Examples of such relationships include treatment of family members, close friends, employees, or supervisees."[40]

Despite the difficulties this might cause at times, professionals must always be careful to maintain "personal" distance from their clients. Fostering a personal relationship is often a temptation to the novice in the field who may convince himself or herself that all the clients need is a good friend or someone who really cares. Some clients are extremely good at eliciting nurturing or supportive feelings from their counselors. For some clients, however, such demands can become excessive and may be a reflection of their psychological problems. The boundaries between the clinical versus personal relationship may change gradually at first (i.e., the occasional phone call at home, a shared coffee break) and appear fairly innocent and harmless to the therapist at first. Failure to maintain some professional distance may raise false expectations in the client and a demand for more time outside of the formal counseling sessions. The therapist may eventually be put in a position of having to set limits on the client even though he or she may have tolerated such demands previously. In the past, clients have accused therapists of causing psychological harm by doing this and generally blame their counselors for leading them to expect more from the relationship. They may interpret the therapist's change toward them as yet another rejection and possibly react to this in a suicidal manner. Besides the disservice to the client, this is a no-win situation for the therapist and could potentially result in litigation.

Although the standard ethical code among professional groups warns against sexual intimacies with clients, this type of exploitative relationship is more common than would be expected. Davidson refers to studies that found that "10 percent of the psychiatrists in the sample acknowledged engaging in erotic activities with their patient with five percent acknowledging sexual intercourse."[41] According to Schutz, therapists who have come to the attention of the court system as a result of their sexual involvement with clients have unsuccessfully attempted to defend their behavior in either of two ways: first of all, by stating that sexual involvement was a necessary part of therapy; or alternatively, "that the sexual relationship was a separate one from the therapeutic relationship or process and did not impinge on the therapeutic process; hence, there could be no professional negligence or malpractice."[42] Neither justification has been typically accepted in a courtroom or within the professional body to which the therapist belongs. Instead, the warnings against sexual involvements have become increasingly explicit, for example, "the necessary intensity of the therapeutic relationship may tend to activate sexual and other needs and fantasies on the part of both patient and therapist, while weakening the objectivity necessary for control. Sexual activity with a patient is unethical."[43]

In addition to being accused by clients of taking unfair advantage, Schutz points out the increasing risk of being charged by third parties of exercising undue influence with a client, particularly with the advent of directive forms of therapy.

> This action is more likely to arise (1) when family members protest because a patient bestows a lavish gift on the therapist or leaves his estate to the therapist; (2) when a patient's spouse, following a move for a separation or divorce, accuses the therapist of alienation of affection; or (3) when a parent accuses a therapist of suggesting certain courses of action to a minor, against the parent's wishes.[44]

Acknowledging the potential risk of gaining material advantage from a client relationship, certain professional bodies have restricted professionals from accepting anything but token (i.e., inexpensive) gifts from their clients. Specific guidelines on how to avoid undue influence in relationship areas (e.g., husband–wife, parent–child) seem to be lacking and are subsumed under general guidelines regarding appropriate therapeutic behavior. At a minimum, mental health professionals have an obligation to warn clients at the outset or at critical stages in the therapeutic process regarding the possibility that therapy could adversely affect relationships in their natural environment. The therapist should avoid making choices for the client regarding his or her behavior and should assist the client as objectively as possible to explore and evaluate reasonable alternatives prior to making any decision that could affect the client's life or the lives of other people. Appropriate record keeping is critical to substantiate the therapist's role in relation to the client. Consultation with third-party experts is also imperative if therapists are concerned about their objectivity at any point in the therapeutic process.

Professional Demeanor and Service Delivery. An area of professional demeanor that is often taken for granted and sometimes overlooked is the demonstration of reasonable respect for the client's time and feelings. Medical practitioners in particular are notorious for keeping clients waiting for lengthy periods of time beyond their scheduled appointments. This type of behavior may be inappropriately justified by a busy schedule and the common practice of triple-booking to avoid unfilled therapist time if a particular client does not come. Although this type of scheduling has obvious economic advantages for the therapist who is not on salary to a particular institution, it appears to be a blatant example of the therapist's monetary concerns taking priority over human respect and dignity.

There has been at least one occasion in which a client's dissatisfaction with a therapist came to the attention of the legal system as a result of inappropriate professional demeanor (*Hess v. Frank*[45]); more specifically, the therapist used improper and offensive language when discussing fees with his client. The charge was not upheld in court because the inappropriate behavior did not occur within the context of a treatment session but during a "business" discussion. Schutz comments that "if it had occurred in a session, and if the therapist's behavior had led to a premature termination and emotional damage, it might have been seen as negligence."[46]

Therapists must also guard against doing therapy at a distance. For example, clients may occasionally try to avoid an office visit by talking to their therapist on the phone. Although a brief phone discussion may be appropriate under certain circumstances (i.e., when dealing with fairly superficial matters), it is not the recommended way to deal with serious issues. This is a common ploy for agoraphobics who tend to be housebound because of their fear of open spaces but the counselor only feeds into the client's symptoms if formal office visits are not set up. Most therapists recognize that it is extremely difficult to appraise the seriousness of a client's presenting problems on the phone and that the risk of making an error in judgment is increased. For clients taking psychotropic medication, medical practitioners have also been warned against renewing prescriptions on the phone because it is too difficult to ascertain the true state of the client's emotional state without direct contact.

Therapists who get involved in radio talk shows are also advised to exercise caution when responding to a client's phone request. Comments should be kept on a general level and callers who appear to have more serious difficulties should be advised about the clinical services that exist in the community so they can avail themselves of appropriate help.

In order to provide an adequate service to their clients, therapists also have a responsibility to be accountable for what they do. In *Whitree v. State of New York*,[47] the lack of an adequate record was considered an act of negligence "in that such a record does not provide a direction for adequate care in the absence of the therapist, and essentially contributes nothing useful to the treatment history of a patient—information that could have significant bearing on the kind of subsequent care a patient receives."[48]

In order to be accountable, there must be a comprehensive and accurate record of all therapeutic transactions including, when relevant, such information as who was seen, dates seen, duration of contact, self-report data, information from third parties, observational comments, test results, therapeutic interventions, rationale for any critical decision making, consultative reports, progress evaluation, and individual treatment planning. Within a treatment facility, the client's file should additionally include appropriately signed informed consents for any intrusive forms of treatment and a comprehensive client history and assessment.

For the purpose of accountability, care should also be taken to differentiate between different sources of input so that the therapist can demonstrate what information was derived from what source. Not only does this form of record keeping allow the client to know or challenge what has transpired in therapy but also it serves as a reminder and a monitor for the therapist and as a potential source of information for any subsequent therapeutic involvements. When the practitioner has acted prudently and appropriately in the course of therapy, the record acts as a protection. Specifically, it serves to substantiate whether the therapist utilized reasonable judgment and care in treatment planning and delivery as informally defined by the standards of care expected within his or her professional peer group. Meticulous documentation is particularly critical in situations (e.g., involuntary commitment) where the therapist is at greater risk of displeasing the client or any third party having a significant relationship with the client.

Despite the need for accountability through record keeping, the American Psychiatric Association Task Force on Confidentiality has recommended that "records should not contain subjective or speculative material and only minimum detail of patient fantasies or dynamic hypotheses should be kept in the records. However, this speculative material may be kept in a separate 'personal therapist's notes' file."[49] Schutz adds that the "utter sanctity of these notes has been upheld twice in Illinois court tests."

Therapeutic Obstacles. Clients do not routinely progress through therapy at a steady or regular pace. In fact, a study by Bergin and Lambert[50] revealed that a significant proportion of clients become worse as a result of therapy. In their role as fiduciary with their clients, therapists have an obligation to maintain a therapeutic relationship only as long as they believe that relationship to be of benefit to their client. The dilemma for the therapist is discriminating between obstacles that can be overcome and those that cannot. Such impasses may be overt and therefore obvious (e.g., if the client indicates a desire to terminate treatment prematurely because of lack of progress) or more subtle and indirect (e.g., if the client becomes increasingly sarcastic to the therapist, misses appointments, forgets to follow through on assignments). This problem becomes even more complicated if clients do not leave any clues about lack of progress, possibly because they have become increasingly confused about their psychological state and do not recognize the therapist's responsibility to assist them in resolving such confusion. With clients who are inclined toward self-blame and who tend to accept full responsibility for any lack of progress, there is the added risk that they will actually deteriorate psychologically. According to Schutz,

> while therapists are not guarantors of cure or improvement, extensive treatment without results could legally be considered to have injured the patient; in specific, the injury would be the loss of money and time, and the preclusion of other treatments that might have been more successful. To justify a prolonged holding action at a plateau, the therapist would have to show that this was maintaining a condition against a significant and likely deterioration.[51]

Therapists who do a lot of supportive counseling (e.g., nurses, social workers) have an added difficulty because they are often confronted with two types of clients: those that truly depend on external support in order to maintain a reasonable level of functioning and those that take advantage of the system. With some clients, it is often more therapeutic to make them do things for themselves than to take most of the steps for them. With inpatients, this type of problem is fairly common because hospitalization can often add to their insecurity and lack of self-confidence. As such, they may be overly dependent on mental health staff to arrange things for them, for example, to help them find a new apartment, or start a job search. The supportive counselor frequently has to make a decision as to the best way to help such clients to avoid feeding into unwarranted insecurities.

Gutheil and Appelbaum[52] differentiate between treatment refusals, or impasses, based on factors (1) inherent in the illness (e.g., symptom denial, delusional thinking regarding therapy, projection), (2) inherent in the treatment process itself (e.g., secondary gain, reluctance to endure medication side effects, anxiety over a particular form of treatment), and (3) in the relationship that exists between the client and the therapist (e.g., anxiety over therapeutic intimacy, inconsiderate behavior on the part of the therapist, lack of trust). In order to renew the therapeutic component of the relationship, the clinician must, first of all, explore the basis for any impasse or treatment refusal and attempt to resolve it.

For this purpose, Gutheil and Appelbaum have developed an action guide for therapists to follow when confronted with initial or persistent treatment refusal. When the client has first expressed a preference to refuse treatment intervention, Gutheil and Appelbaum recommend that the therapist

1. *Identify* underlying issues, conflict, medication problem, vacation, delusional percept, milieu stress, family pressure.
2. *Explore* identified issue as legitimate therapeutic material in usual ways (clarification, interpretation, reality testing, ventilation).
3. *Recruit* adult, healthy side of patient into alliance, appealing to realistic perception of long-range benefits of treatment/hospitalization.
4. *Ameliorate* contributory factors (counter medication side effects, work through crisis issues, promote staff discussion, resolve milieu disputes, obtain consultations as needed, intensify or redirect casework with families).[53]

If, despite the above attempts, the client continues to refuse treatment, Gutheil and Appelbaum[54] recommend that the therapist should then

1. *Consider* possibilities of alternative treatment and *decide* if alternatives, though accepted by patient, constitute negligent, suboptimal, or unethical treatment.
2. *Offer* alternative treaters, if feasible, who may accept client's preferred treatment and *transfer* responsibility.
3. *Consider* discharge as possibility if clinical condition warrants this; *arrange* for appropriate aftercare and follow-up.
4. If discharge contraindicated, *obtain* guardianship or judicial rulings or authorization to permit involuntary treatment.[54]

Many of these recommendations operate under the assumption that the therapist has made the appropriate treatment decisions with the client and that the client's reluctance to proceed with therapy is based on factors external to the clinician's therapeutic capabilities. In many instances, however, failure to make therapeutic progress is, at the least, partly the fault of the clinician (e.g., inappropriate use of skills, or lack of expertise. When therapy reaches a serious impasse, other therapists should be consulted and thought given to transferring the client to someone else. Prior to making such a decision, the therapist may initially prefer to obtain ongoing supervision to determine if such assistance would be sufficient to overcome existing therapeutic obstacles. If not, there seems to be no justification for prolonging treatment and the therapist has a responsibility to the client to terminate the relationship and make appropriate aftercare plans.

Therapeutic Crises. Crises arise in therapy whenever clients behave as though they may become dangerous to themselves or others. Criteria for dangerousness typically require that danger to be "imminent" and to "require proof of a threat, attempt or occurrence of harm."[55] The major dilemma for the therapist is distinguishing between "true" dangerousness, therapist manipulation, idle threats, or merely wishful thinking.

Dangerousness to Self. Dangerousness to self is more easily assessed if the client is actively announcing an intent to seriously harm himself or herself. This assessment is more difficult to make, for example, if the person has been manipulative in the past or has a tendency toward suicidal ideation, even if he or she has never acted upon such thinking in any serious fashion. A client may also be considered dangerous to self if he or she does not attend to the basic essentials of life (e.g., food, shelter) or takes unnecessary physical risks (e.g., mixing alcohol with prescription drugs against medical advice). The problem facing the therapist is even more complicated if the client is seen on an emergency basis and is therefore unfamiliar to the therapist rather than a client who has been involved with the therapist on an ongoing basis. In an emergency situation, for example, the therapist may be forced to make a relatively rapid decision regarding the need to impose external controls (e.g., hospitalization) on an unwilling but potentially dangerous client versus one who may be malingering. Professionals who are more likely to be confronted with such crises (e.g., psychiatric staff in an emergency department) owe it to themselves, society and, most importantly, their clients to be thoroughly familiar with commitment criteria and suicidal risk factors. In addition, they have a responsibility to be sufficiently trained to deal with individuals in crisis and to be able to make as thorough an assessment as possible under the circumstances in order to formulate a reasonable decision.
According to Schutz,

> liability generally ensues in the management of the suicidal patient in two ways: (1) The therapist failed to act in a way to prevent the suicide; in specific, the causes of action are typically a *negligent diagnosis*, and concomitant failure to hospitalize, or *abandonment* by an inadequate response to an "emergency" situation. (2) A therapist's act directly contributed to the suicide. Examples include a breach of confidence so damaging as to lead to the suicide; negligent prescription of medication in lethal quantities to a suicidal or depressed patient; clear directives for action that lead to a suicide; and, far more subtly, the fostering of dependence in a patient to the extent that a suicidal crisis is precipitated when therapy is, or is about to be, terminated. The key questions

in the assessment of liability are foreseeability and control. Did the therapist know or should he have known of the foreseeable risk? Were adequate attempts made to control the patient?[56]

Despite these potential risk areas for the therapist, he or she must additionally resist the temptation to engage in "defensive" psychotherapy for his or her own protection. The clinician is therefore obliged to balance, albeit precariously, the uncertain need to commit the patient with his or her right to the least restrictive alternative or the right to refuse treatment altogether.

Dangerousness to Others. As with the suicidal client, the clinician needs special expertise to know how to react to a client who appears immediately dangerous to a third party. Basically, the clinician is placed in the tenuous position of trying to predict the likelihood of a violent act being committed by the client in the immediate future, even though empirical studies have demonstrated that such predictions are notoriously poor. As a result of the Tarasoff decision, however, the therapist has an obligation to warn a potential victim, or the police authorities if the person cannot be contacted, assuming the client has openly threatened the person in question. "In the emergency setting, the obligation to notify will most commonly arise when a patient under evaluation leaves or escapes before hospitalization can be accomplished. Other occasions on which a duty to notify will ensue include the receipt of phone calls from threatening patients and face-to-face sessions with patients who have made threats but who do not meet the criteria for involuntary commitment."[57]

From the therapist's perspective, the obligation to violate confidentiality and warn a third party can have adverse, and possibly terminal, effects on the therapeutic process.

(1) It will deter patients from therapy.
(2) It will inhibit their trust of the therapist.
(3) It will inhibit frank discussion of violent impulses and, by keeping them out of the therapy situation, actually increase their risk.
(4) It violates the rights to privacy of the patient.[58]

In other words, the therapist is on the horns of a dilemma whenever a client talks in a violent fashion regarding another person. In most situations, the client's threats are merely fantasy and not to be acted on. The utterance of such a threat, however, may either force the therapist to err in favor of caution and therefore risk a deterioration in the therapeutic relationship, or take a chance for the sake of the client's therapeutic progress and risk a life as well as liability. As in other problematic areas, peer consultation is a useful and advisable step to assist the therapist in evaluating the risks and developing the most appropriate management plan under the circumstances.

Termination Stage

The ideal basis for ending a therapeutic relationship is mutual or collaborative in nature, that is, the therapist and client are satisfied that the client's goals have been reached and presenting complaints resolved. Alternatively, even if the client's problems have not been resolved, both parties may agree that there is nothing to be gained by maintaining this particular relationship. Even when the two parties agree on the need to end the relationship, arrangements for follow-up or alternative services are advisable in order to provide the client with an opportunity for additional support, if necessary, and to monitor the maintenance of treatment gains from an accountability point of view.

Termination issues are more likely to arise whenever the therapist and client fail to recognize the need to terminate their relationship or whenever the therapist and client differ regarding the necessity of treatment discharge or transfer.

Failure to Recognize. An inability to recognize the appropriate end to a therapeutic relationship is more likely to be a problem when the relationship is long-term or when the treatment goals are overly vague and general. Many therapeutic relationships seem destined to become long-term, for example, if neither the client nor the therapist is sure what insights or changes the client is working toward and therefore whether he or she has actually reached initial goals or allowed the goal to evolve into a different one. Therapeutic approaches that deal with more observable and therefore quantifiable behaviors are less at risk in this area, particularly if they have taken pre-post measures of relevant behaviors.

Failure to terminate may also be a function of "inappropriate" reluctance on the part of the client or the therapist to terminate the relationship. Assuming the client is actually ready for discharge, this reluctance often derives from unnecessary insecurity on the part of the client, occasionally coupled by a tendency to foster such dependency on the therapist's side. Lengthy therapeutic relationships have a greater likelihood of developing this type of pathologic "hanging on" and it is therefore imperative for the therapist to recognize such dynamics, if they exist, and help the client to ease into termination several sessions before it actually occurs in order to wean him or her from inappropriate dependency on the therapeutic state.

In order to make a decision to terminate or to transfer a particular client, the therapist must be sensitized to signs that indicate the client's readiness, or need, for such an adjustment in the therapeutic relationship. Progress discussions with the client as well as periodic internal or external review or both are critical in recognizing the client's therapeutic movement, or lack of it, over time.

Differing Viewpoints. Clients may choose to terminate therapy prematurely, or against professional advice, for a number of reasons: for example, dissatisfaction with the treatment approach or lack of therapeutic progress, unsatisfactory relationship with the mental health practitioner or treatment team, reluctance to resolve certain symptoms, family pressures to terminate, lack of motivation to change, delusional thinking, shortage of money, and so on. Clients may also decide to terminate for more positive reasons, that is, after they have experienced initial gains, even though the therapist might view such gains as still tenuous or superficial. At a minimum, the therapist owes a responsibility to explore with clients their reasons for wanting to leave and the therapist's reasons for considering that decision premature. Assuming the client is not an involuntary client and does not pose a danger to self or others, the therapist has an obligation to respect the client's right to refuse treatment. Subsequently, the therapist should take the time to document the termination process and to communicate to the client alternative avenues for assistance and the opportunity to renew the therapeutic contract at a later date.

On other occasions, it may not be the client who wishes to end a particular form of treatment but the therapist or treatment facility. For example, the clinician may believe that the client needs to disengage from therapeutic contacts entirely or to transfer from one therapeutic arrangement to another. The proposed transfer could be to a different therapist, an alternative form of intervention (e.g., family vs. individual), or a different treatment setting (e.g., outpatient vs. inpatient). With outpatients, the most common reason for making a decision to adjust or end a therapeutic relationship derives from lack of progress or preferably goal achievement. The most likely reasons for clients resisting a modification in the therapeutic arrangement include dependency and a resistance to change the status quo. Not only is this risk higher in long-term relationships but also in inpatient settings where the client has experienced a sense of support that has not been available in the community.

Occasionally clients may be discharged from a treatment facility against their will for administrative, rather than clinical, reasons: "(1) expiration of insurance, (2) treatment refusal, (3) infraction of rules (e.g., assaultiveness, theft, sexual acting out)."[59] Clients may also be discharged for refusing to cooperate in whatever forms of treatment have been offered to them, assuming they have been offered a reasonable choice of alternatives.

Regardless of the specific reasons for terminating the relationship, the therapist or treatment facility has a responsibility to give adequate notice to the client regarding any proposed changes and to provide the client with an opportunity to challenge the new treatment plan. If the decision is reached to proceed with the treatment change, the onus is on the therapist to arrange, or assist the client in arranging, appropriate aftercare alternatives so that the client continues to have whatever therapeutic supports appear necessary; for example, transfer to a free facility, or referral to a more appropriate therapist.

In terms of legal responsibility, the critical issue for the therapist is to ensure that he or she does not abandon the client. In general, therapists can be charged with abandonment if they do not make arrangements to provide adequate therapeutic coverage when they are unavailable (e.g., out of town, after office hours, on vacation). In addition, abandonment may be charged if the therapist fails to make satisfactory arrangements for transferring the care of the client to another therapist if termination of that relationship is planned.

Despite a client's objections, public policy gives "the therapist . . . an absolute right to terminate a relationship unilaterally. The relationship is based on mutual trust and rapport; if for any reason the therapist loses rapport with his patient, the basis of the relationship is gone, and the parties must be allowed to separate and seek the requisite relationship elsewhere."[60] The clinical responsibility of the therapist is to take whatever steps are necessary to make this transition as constructive a process as possible under the circumstances.

THERAPEUTIC MODALITIES

The salient issues confronting the mental health professional often vary in accordance with the particular therapeutic orientation or modality he or she chooses to follow, for example, whether the client is treated through psychoanalytic versus behavior therapy techniques, or whether the client is seen individually or within the context of a group. The following section attempts to highlight the issues specific to different therapy formats.

Behavior Therapy

Since its ascent into popularity, behavior therapy has been characterized by a history of misuse and abuse. One of the strengths of behavior therapy has been its need to operationalize goals and therefore be specific regarding changes being sought. Another strength is the typical delineation of treatment steps so that it is clear to anyone interested what techniques and methods are being used. Pre-post measures also allow the therapist and other involved individuals to evaluate progress or lack of it. Not only do these features oblige practitioners to be accountable for what they do, but also they allow the availability of detailed treatment information that could assist a client in giving an informed consent. Regrettably, because of misuse of the techniques many of the advantages of behavior therapy have been turned into disadvantages for a number of reasons. First of all, because of the specificity of some of the procedures and the apparent ease with which they can be administered, many untrained individuals (from physicians to ward staff) have jumped on the behavioral bandwagon and presumed to know what they were doing. This problem has been heightened by the ready availability of packaged programs and the economic advantage quickly recognized by administrators, that is, the ability to use lesser paid, and insufficiently trained, ward staff (e.g., child care workers, mental retardation counselors) as "behavioral" therapists rather than hiring more expensive, but fully qualified, behavioral experts.

Despite the illusory simplicity of behavior therapy, to do it properly requires, at a minimum, a number of prerequisite skills: specialized background in learning principles as well as behavior therapy and behavior modification techniques, a broader-based understanding of psychopathology and a knowledge of which clinical problems and clients seem to respond to behavioral approaches, and equally important, supervised experience in the application of a variety of behavioral approaches through the assistance and guidance of a qualified practitioner. Behavior therapy is obviously not appropriate for all clients and all types of problems and yet it has been indiscriminately used in many settings. The application of packaged procedures and so-called behavioral recipes has rarely been sufficient or effective in producing change and generally requires, at the least, individualization in order to succeed with a particular client. Without a working knowledge of underlying principles, proper program tailoring is impossible and the result is improper modification or the blind application of rote procedures. As a consequence, the client is short-changed and has the likely disadvantage of feeling a therapeutic failure or being changed for the worse. Not only may this likelihood affect the client's faith in other treatment endeavors but also it may unfairly tarnish the reputation of an approach that has been improperly applied. Such disillusionment has been quite prevalent among many professionals. In institutional settings where behavior therapy has been prematurely and incompetently applied, mental health staff have preferred to discredit the techniques rather than their improper use of them.

Another abuse of behavior therapy has derived from a disregard for clients' rights. Although it is unclear why clients' rights were so blatantly ignored in this area, it seems reasonable to assume that several factors could have contributed to this eventuality: (1) the nature of the client (i.e., long-term, institutionalized clients, often ignored by the community); (2) initial awe at behavior therapy's apparent power; and (3) failure to exercise control over who could and should use it. As a result, in the name of treatment many clients were illegally deprived of basic human rights and forced to earn them through "proper" behavior. To a certain extent, this abuse evolved from a rather paternalistic and academic power base in which therapists assumed that they knew best what their clients needed (e.g., more social contact, more physical activity) and suddenly had the behavioral power by which to obtain their goals (e.g., food tokens earned through appropriately spent time). In addition to misusing clients' rights as reinforcers, punitive methods of behavioral control were also introduced to "improve" more effectively the clients' lot in life. Frequently, the professional even lost sight of the individual's needs and began working toward the better management of the ward itself. "For example, a token economy program on a closed ward of a state hospital that shapes up and reinforces correct eating habits, toileting, hygiene, the grounds being kept clean, and quiet time being observed may seem commendable, even innocuous; yet who is the chief beneficiary? It can be argued that the hospital staff or ward personnel benefit as much if not more than the patients."[61] On the other hand, behavior modifiers have argued that the development of such basic behaviors are important for the more chronic client who has been institutionalized to such an extent that he or she has been overcome by generalized apathy and dependency. In any event the excitement, if not power, of being able to shape other people's behavior has likely contributed to earlier violations of basic human rights and a disregard for ethical and legal responsibilities. Such unprofessional behavior has, in turn, led to justifiable public outcry and litigation *(Wyatt v. Stickney, Morales v. Turman)*.[62,63]

As a result, the use of contingent reinforcers has been legally restricted to privileges rather than rights (e.g., a special treat, going to the movies), unless the client willingly and knowledgeably consents to have his or her rights used in the former way. With an institutional clientele, however, it appears impossible to assume that consent can ever be truly voluntary. When dealing with an institutionalized client, there is the added risk that the client may not be competent to consent. The behavioral therapist has to be sensitive to this possibility and must ensure that a consent has been competently given, either by the client or his or her guardian.

In the area of punishment, "most aversive conditioning procedures can be legally constrained by use of one of three constitutional amendments or interpretations: cruel and unusual punishment, due process, or least restrictive alternative. A few administration regulations now exist that relate specifically to the rehabilitative use of time-out and electric shock."[64] Cruel and unusual punishment is considered to apply to a procedure "if it violates minimal standards of decency, is wholly disproportionate to the alleged offense, or goes beyond what is necessary."[65] For example, in *Knecht v. Gillman*,[66] staff were charged with cruel and unusual punishment because they were using apomorphine, a drug that forces an individual to vomit for several minutes, for such behaviors as "not getting up, for giving cigarettes against orders, for talking, for swearing, or for lying."[67]

Under clearly defined circumstances, the controlled use of aversive treatment procedures has been permitted if properly designed and administered. Reliance on in-house and external review boards has been strongly recommended to ensure that the standards have been properly met. Because of the need for close monitoring of such programs, Matson and Kazdin[68] stress the need for adequate staffing; that is, not only properly trained staff but sufficient numbers to follow consistently and appropriately all of the treatment requirements.

Time-out, which is typically restricted to 1 hour, has been legally distinguished from "'isolation' which would require due process procedures (e.g., notice and hearing) if longer than three days."[69] Even for brief periods of seclusion, the courts have ruled that "the client must have access to food, lighting, sanitation, and other basic amenities."[70]

In the use of electroshock, the typical recommendation has been to restrict its use to the control of extreme self-destructive behaviors (e.g., head-banging), assuming all other reasonable alternatives have been tried and failed. Electroshock may be considered justified in these instances in that the pain created by the aversive stimulus is less than the pain and physical damage caused by the client's atavistic behaviors.

Aside from major issues of abuse and incompetent usage, ethical behavior therapists should also exercise caution in their choice of clientele; in other words, screening out individuals who do not seem to benefit from this type of therapeutic orientation. Since behavior therapy is a highly goal-oriented approach, it is not the treatment of choice for clients who are unsure what they want from therapy. Unless the therapist in question is additionally trained in exploratory types of counseling, he or she should ethically refer the client to a more appropriate form of therapy with the option that behavior therapy can be reconsidered at a later stage in treatment. The appropriate stage for initiating a behavior therapy contract is ideally when the client has a reasonably clear idea what goals he or she wants but is unsure how to reach them. Therapists should resist assuming what is in the best interests of each and every client that approaches them for help and allow the client to assume the major responsibility for choosing behavioral goals.

Other clients who do not seem appropriate or ready for behavior therapy are those who have a number of unresolved issues from their past that seem to affect their ability to change at this time. For certain clients, the readiness to change may not occur until they have a better understanding of why they behave the way they do. Although unmotivated or resistive clients are rarely preferred in any type of therapy, they are completely inappropriate for behavioral forms of treatment unless institutionalized and valid permission has been granted for coercive treatment. A critical component of most behavioral programs with outpatients or voluntary inpatients is active participation (e.g., behavioral assignments), particularly as one of the common goals in behavior therapy is to enable the client to develop self-control. Active participation does not seem likely with unmotivated clients and would be superficial at best. Therefore, before being considered a good candidate for a behavioral program, the "resistive" client should ideally work through his or her obstacles to change through a more appropriate therapeutic modality (e.g., insight-oriented therapy). In summary, since the behavior therapist cannot be all things to all people, he or she has a responsibility to screen clientele adequately, to be aware of the type of client and clinical problem that responds to a behavioral approach, and to act as a referral source to more appropriate forms of therapy when required.

Computer Therapy

As in the case of self-help types of therapy, therapy can also be conducted at a distance through computer technology. Within the mental health field, computers have served a number of administrative as well as clinical functions since their inception. Within the clinical area, they have been used for "data collection; identification of symptom clusters; formal assignment of diagnoses, treatments, and prognoses; evaluation of patient progress and treatment outcome; and, treatment per se."[71] Although the role played by the computer in the area of therapy is still limited at this time, concerns have already been expressed about confidentiality (i.e., the problem of maintaining control over private information that has been entered into the computer).

At this stage of application, the use of the computer as a therapeutic tool is obviously experimental and limited in terms of its application to clinical groups. Because of its experimental nature, professionals must take care not to use it prematurely, that is, before it is beyond its experimental stage and before acceptable standards regarding its use have been established. If introduced to clients as a research procedure, care should be taken to adhere to the ethical standards established for such experimental procedures. At a minimum, clients should be informed regarding their right to refuse and the availability of more traditional forms of therapy if they do choose to decline participation.

Even if computers could eventually be programmed to respond to the entire range of clinical problems and possibilities, one of their limitations at this point in time is their dependence on external input. In other words, in terms of interacting with clients, it can only deal with information that the client chooses, or is able, to give to it. More specifically, clues provided by such characteristics as body language and paralinguistics, either by themselves or in interaction with verbal comments, are sorely lacking. For many clients, the qualitative aspects of their behavior, or lack of it, yields more clinically useful information than the content of their speech. As in the use of self-help material, computers might best serve an educative and therefore preventative function in the field of mental health. As a therapeutic tool, human supervision would be advisable in order to protect the consumer from technological limitations.

Group Therapy

Treating more than one client at a time (e.g., through family, marital, or group therapy) has implications for the client and therapist. One of the most problematic issues is in the area of confidentiality. More specifically, members have little protection from gossip by other members when they are outside the group. Specific statutes regarding privileged communication have not generally been extended to include disclosures made by one group member in the presence of another.

In the case of marital or family therapy, the therapist may try to avoid a conflict of interest at the outset by getting a signed agreement from the participants not to call the therapist as a witness in court. The very least the therapist should do is to inform all parties before treatment begins of the limits on confidentiality and privileged communication so the clients have an opportunity to choose for or against group treatment with this knowledge in mind.

The need to maintain confidentiality is an added pressure for the therapist if he or she has had private communications with the client in addition to the group experience and has been informed not to divulge this private information within the context of the group. This type of situation happens when a client initially sees a therapist on an individual basis, with therapy eventually evolving into a group process (e.g., marital therapy) because of a change in treatment needs. If the client wishes certain information withheld, the therapist is therefore placed in the awkward, if not impossible, position of remembering which information was given individually and which in the group and then responding as if he or she did not have access to the "privileged" information.

Another major problem in group forms of therapy is the multiple responsibilities carried by the therapist at any one time. "The dilemma with multiple clients is that in some situations an intervention that serves one person's best interests may be countertherapeutic to another."[72] This predicament is inevitable when treating families in particular in that "the very reason that families tend to seek therapy is because they have conflicting goals and interests."[73] Another problem in family therapy is the issue of consent. Children are frequently given little, if any, choice in entering a therapeutic relationship. This arrangement may place the therapist in an adversarial rather than a helping role with the client and interfere with the therapist's ability to be of much assistance to that individual and therefore to the family per se.

To provide some direction for therapists conducting growth or encounter groups, the APA[74] published a set of guidelines that would seem applicable for other varieties of group contact. They recommend, first of all, that participation in any group process be voluntary and without coercion. Prior to making a decision to enter the group, participants must be informed of the cost of the service, if any, as well as the leader's training background and therefore his or her competence to lead the group. In addition, the potential group members should know specifically what the group leader's responsibilities are as well as what would be expected of the individual group members (e.g., confidentiality, active participation). They should be aware of the overall purpose of the group (e.g., to improve communication, to develop stress management skills), the nature of the group process (e.g., open-ended vs. closed; ongoing vs. fixed number of sessions), what specific goals the group will be working toward (e.g., to be able to give positive feedback to Johnny, to stop swearing, to reduce temper outbursts), and what procedures or techniques will be used to facilitate goal achievement (e.g., roleplaying, interpretation, reinforcement, videotape recordings). The APA further suggests that entry into a group be preceded by a screening interview so that potential clients can be given sufficient information on which to make an informed decision, and also to assess the client's appropriateness for this type of therapeutic experience. For groups that are therapeutic rather than primarily educational in focus (e.g., assertiveness training), the APA indicates that "the leader assumes the same professional and ethical responsibilities he or she would assume in individual or group psychotherapy, including before and after consultation with any other therapist who may be professionally involved with the participant."[75]

Hypnotherapy

On a basic level, hypnosis is "a technique by which therapeutic suggestions may be induced in the patient"[76] to facilitate change. Within the treatment arena, it has been used for a wide variety of different problems, for example, habit control, pain suppression, stress management, and resolution of traumatic memories.

Lee compares the relationship that develops between the therapist and client through hypnosis to the transference relationship that develops within the context of psychotherapy. He identifies a number of risks that can develop from this type of close relationship. First of all, "the hypnotist may become so personally involved, and reap such ego gratification, that he attempts to treat the patient in problems outside his field of competence. On the other hand, the patient may become dependent on this emotional support so that recovery, and independence from the practitioner, is delayed."[77] This risk is likely greater if hypnosis is used within the context of long-term therapy and if the therapist is not properly qualified. The problem of competence is a serious one in that, "as a general rule, hypnotism is not prohibited unless a statute specifies that such practice constitute the unauthorized practice of medicine or psychology."[78] Although hypnosis is an excellent approach when used properly, it historically carries a mystique about it and runs the risk of attracting people for the wrong reasons. Because of its presumed "magical" powers, it may attract, first, therapists who enjoy wielding power over others, and second, clients who are overly passive and therefore prefer relinquishing control to an external party. Passive clients are not as inclined to question the qualifications of their therapists and may be easily influenced by whatever facade may exist. Even if the practitioner has the best of intentions, if not suitably qualified, he or she may periodically have to deal with problems and dynamics too difficult to handle alone, with the result that the client is therapeutically short-changed. Regrettably, the ready availability of unqualified hypnotists only serves to tarnish the reputation of hypnotism per se as well as the individuals who are properly trained to use it.

When competence is not an issue (i.e., if the practitioner is fully qualified), another concern that must be resolved is client expectations. Because of the mystique attached to it, clients may overestimate its ability to change their lives for the better. Prior to initiating a therapeutic contract with a client, the potential client should be given a realistic understanding of what hypnosis is and what it can and cannot do so that he or she does not enter into a contractual arrangement under false pretenses. With this specific need in mind, the Society for Clinical and Experimental Hypnosis has included in its ethical code the statement that "guarantees of easy solutions or favorable outcomes must not be made nor may one claim to have secret techniques."[79]

Milieu Therapy

Milieu therapy primarily incorporates the beneficial effects that are likely to result from being in a therapeutic environment (e.g., an inpatient unit) in which the client is away from community or family pressures and has access to therapeutic activities and various professional staff for assistance with problems. A milieu is more likely to be therapeutic if it can offer more than just the bare essentials of nourishment, shelter, and protection. Kreigh and Perko propose that "there are three major components that contribute to the formation and maintenance of a therapeutic environment. These are *privacy, safety and protection,* and *comfort.*"[80] Added to this is the opportunity for "healthy interactions and learning situations which enable the patient to formulate adequate adjustments."[81]

Traditionally, nursing staff typically bear most of the responsibility for maintaining a therapeutic milieu, partly because they are the individuals who are with the clients the most as well as the caretakers on the ward. In most institutions, however, nursing staff may be hampered in their efforts by administrative regulations. Figure 1[82] serves to highlight some of the possible nontherapeutic aspects of an inpatient milieu and illustrates the dehumanizing effect a setting can have on its clients.

Administrative standards can obviously affect the inpatient milieu in a variety of ways. First of all, there are regulations about the type of belongings clients can bring with them onto a unit, not only for the safety of the client but to protect the institution from liability that could result

Figure 1. Example of dehumanizing elements in a therapeutic milieu. *(From Kreigh, H. Z., & Perko, J. E. (1979). Psychiatric and mental health nursing: Commitment to care and concern (p. 115). Reston, VA: Reston Publishing Company, with permission.)*

if a client hurts himself or herself or others while on the unit. Since clients have been known to hurt themselves in a variety of different ways, there is a wide range of personal belongings that is considered potentially dangerous. Belongings are also held in trust for the client if there is some concern that they could be stolen. Therefore, the kinds of possessions that might be taken from a client at the time of admission include such items as jewelry, belts, shampoo, makeup, and ties. For most individuals, personal possessions are an important part of one's identity. Removal of such possessions could potentially have a depressing and dehumanizing effect on individual clients. The nurse has a responsibility to act as an advocate for the client in such a setting and to challenge existing hospital policies that are unfair and overly restricting.

Administrative regulations can also have a dehumanizing effect in other ways. Because of the practical needs of running a ward and using staff time efficiently, clients are often extremely regimented and forced to fit into a routine that is extremely alien to them, for example, standing in line to get pills, or meals. In addition, clients may be put in the unpleasant position of asking permission to go for a walk, or even for such matters as personal hygiene in that items such as shampoo, shaving equipment, makeup, and so on may have been taken away at the time of admission. In other words, ward staff should be sensitized to any dehumanizing or depressing aspects of the milieu and help the client deal with them constructively.

Privacy is also a privilege that is sorely lacking. From an economic perspective, most facilities are not affluent enough to allow private rooms for their clients. Not only does the client often have to share dressing and sleeping arrangements with strangers but also, in most wards, clients are obliged to get washed in the same room. Aside from a lack of resources, some administrative bodies frown on private rooms because they allow more opportunity for the client to hurt himself or herself or to withdraw from people completely. From the client's point of view, however, he or she may feel deprived of personal space and the therapeutic benefits that sometimes come from solitude. A loss of personal space may also be experienced if staff are inclined to barge into a client's room without knocking or if the client has no place to keep his or her possessions from the handling and examination of other clients. Some clients may also have to deal with the affront of having their personal belongings searched by staff for administrative reasons, for example, if illegal drugs are suspected on the ward or if another client has had something stolen. Often the client is not even given the luxury of talking to his or her doctor in privacy in that many doctors make their rounds on the ward, and clients are asked to give feedback on their condition within the hearing of other clients or staff.

As discussed in Chapter 3, similar abuses on treatment wards have led to court action and a rigid delineation of standards that must be met to qualify as a therapeutic environment. On the basis of *Wyatt v. Stickney*, for example,

> day rooms are to be adequately furnished with reading lamps, tables, chairs, television, and other recreational facilities. Comfortable chairs and tables with hard, washable surfaces are to be provided in dining facilities. . . . No patients can be made to share a resident unit with more than five other persons. Curtains or screens are to be provided for

privacy, and a comfortable bed, closet or locker, chair, and bedside table are to be furnished. One toilet (in a separate stall to insure privacy) may be required for eight persons; one tub or shower for 15 persons. Minimal floor areas per patient have also been specified.[83]

Since nurses are often in the front line of service, they are frequently forced to deal with client demands and tolerate administrative constraints in terms of staffing and environmental conditions. In other words, they are typically forced to be in the middle between the client's demands and those of the institution. A frequent consequence of such a precarious and unsatisfying position is professional burnout. A likely risk of burnout is a deterioration in service to the consumer in that staff who feel that their own needs are not being met are less able to meet the needs of others. The sudden emergence of reading material and workshops on the topic of burnout, particularly in the mental health field, attests to this danger and the need, first of all, to assist nursing staff in filling their difficult role and, second, to monitor staff effectiveness in order to ensure that clients do not bear the brunt of this problem.

Organic Therapy

Organic therapy refers to interventions that alter the physical functioning of the individual under the assumption that such physical alteration will have a positive effect on psychological functioning. There are three major varieties of organic therapy:

1. Psychosurgery—in which specific areas of the brain are permanently destroyed and therefore disconnected from other areas of the brain (e.g., prefrontal lobotomy)
2. ECT—in which a brief electrical current is passed through the brain in order to produce a convulsion
3. Psychotropic medication—in which the chemical balance of an individual is altered through the ingestion of one or more chemical agents

Compared to verbal therapies, organic approaches are considered to be more intrusive because of the permanence of certain changes, the greater likelihood of unwanted side effects, the client's inability to resist the effects once treatment has been initiated, and so on. Since clients have the right to the least restrictive of treatment alternatives, it follows that nonorganic forms of intervention should be attempted first.

The responsibility to offer clients the least restrictive alternative may be complicated by a number of factors, however. First, more training would be needed to be *competent* at psychotherapy than is presently available in the typical medical school and it seems unlikely that most medical practitioners would want to take time away from a lucrative practice in order to get that training. In addition, in psychotherapy, more time is needed with the individual client than is typically required to prescribe or monitor drug usage, for example, or to administer a series of shock treatments. As a result, psychotherapy may be less remunerative than other forms of therapy that allow a quicker turnover of clients because of the efficiency with which the clients can be processed. In addition, on an inpatient unit, much of the monitoring is delegated to nursing staff, thereby freeing the physician's time for even more clients and therefore more financial reinforcement. Although financial gain may not make the world go round for all professionals, it is undoubtedly a temptation to some, with the result that clinical and ethical issues may be relegated to a lesser role.

The medical professional may also be forced to deal with external pressures to use medication versus less intrusive procedures. "Pharmaceutical salesmen, representing a billion-dollar industry, bombard psychiatrists and doctors with ads, sales pitches, free samples, and desk calendars, all in the hope that their brand will be tried. If unpleasant side effects arise, the company is likely to have a second pill, side-effect medication, to offer the physician to offer to his patient."[84] Finally, the client may also play a role in the overuse of organic forms of treatment, particularly in his or her acceptance of psychoactive drugs. Reliance on physical intervention may allow the client to obtain a chemical pacifier, for example, or to play a passive role in the area of treatment, thereby relinquishing responsibility for change to outside agents. For individuals whose problems have derived from their unwillingness or apparent inability to take responsibility for their actions, medication or ECT or both may further reinforce this type of pathology and exacerbate the client's inability to function appropriately instead of assuming a more responsible and active role in society.

The issue of consent is another serious concern when utilizing physical means to improve an individual's psychological state. Aside from the contradictory results regarding the presumed beneficial effects of organic therapies, practitioners may fail to inform clients of the shortcomings and dangers that could follow from treatment. Partial disclosure is typically justified under the paternalistic, if somewhat patronizing, notion that the therapist knows best what the client needs and if the client is told too much, he or she just might refuse. In other words, it is likely that many clients make decisions about an organic procedure without access to sufficient information on which to make an informed choice. Despite their medical background, Culver et al. openly admit that psychiatric intervention is "inherently paternalistic" in that it involves "minimum reliance on the patient's expressed wishes regarding treatment and primary reliance on the treatment team's (or family's) judgment concerning what is in the patient's best interests."[85]

Placebos have also been justified from a paternalistic viewpoint, that is, that the clients' best interests are served by deceiving them into believing that they are receiving chemical assistance. Slovenko states that "physicians have been prescribing placebos for hundreds of years, but curiously their use has increased in the age of technology. A physician who directs a famous medical center says, 'There is nothing organically wrong with 70 percent of the patients who come to us . . . but if a sugar pill helps them to feel better, isn't it really medicine?' "[86]

Since somatic forms of treatment are more available than other forms of therapy on the typical psychiatric unit, the client may be subjected to, at the least, subtle pressure to comply with treatment by staff and other clients. The "hidden" restrictions on free choice are even stronger for the involuntary client. Aside from believing that cooperation will eventually have long-term benefits (i.e., discharge), day-to-day compliance is more likely to lead to ongoing staff approval or at least an avoidance of disapproval. The client is also less likely to feel singled out from other clients and possibly shunned by them for bucking the system. In other words, institutional clients by virtue of their milieu may find treatment refusal an unpopular and therefore uncomfortable stance to take. Occasionally the client may even be coerced into "voluntary" consent by being unfairly presented with a forced choice of treatment alternatives, for example, a choice of ECT versus commitment to a mental hospital.

The problem of mental competence is another issue when using the more intrusive forms of physical intervention (i.e., ECT or psychosurgery) in that these forms of therapy are more likely to be used on clients who are psychologically debilitated and have not responded to psychopharmacologic approaches, among others. It would be expected that reduced competence to make treatment decisions would be more common in this client population than others and therefore safeguards must be followed to ensure that an appropriate guardian is available to protect the client's rights. Clients should not necessarily be viewed as incompetent even though their decision to refuse such interventions as ECT may be considered irrational. In other words, the client's wishes should be respected in most instances.

Schutz[87] delineates a number of risk areas for the professional in the use of drug therapy as well as ECT. In addition to the lawsuits that could result from the failure to obtain a proper consent, he outlines a number of other potential liability areas:

1. The application of drugs or ECT for aversive or punitive reasons
2. Failure to obtain a proper history and evaluation of the client to determine the presence of factors (e.g., heart problems, allergies) that would contraindicate a certain procedure
3. Failure to adequately monitor the client during and after treatment (e.g., cardiac failure, suicidal predisposition, confusion and disorientation)

4. Negligent delivery of services (e.g., improper dosage, faulty equipment)

Because of the many critical issues centering around the use of somatic treatment interventions for psychological problems, a number of states as well as professional bodies have developed legal and ethical standards regarding the application of such procedures (e.g., Recommendations Regarding the Use of Electroconvulsive Therapy prepared by the American Psychiatric Association Task Force on ECT). For example, the task force attempted to define the conditions under which a practitioner might consider using ECT and the relative likelihood of its being effective with different types of clinical problems. Most importantly, they attempted to delineate the steps that should be followed in obtaining an informed consent in order to respect the client's rights.[88] Minimal consent requirements that should be met in using ECT have also been summarized by Schwitzgebel and Schwitzgebel:

1. The person must be specifically informed by the treating physician about the right to refuse shock therapy. If an individual agrees to shock therapy:
   a. S/he must sign an informed consent; such a consent form should include
      (1) description of procedure (i.e., how it will be done, duration of treatments, what physical and emotional phenomena the individual may experience).
      (2) an explanation of the risks and an indication of the anticipated benefits (previously explained in more detail).
      (3) statement of rationale for the use of this treatment as opposed to other modalities or no treatment at all (previously explained orally).
      (4) statement that the individual, guardian, or conservator has read the consent and has had an opportunity to discuss its meaning with the physician.
      (5) patient's and/or relative's dated and witnessed signature.
   b. S/he has the right to refuse further treatment at any time.
2. If the person agrees to shock therapy but is not competent to give consent, the consent is not valid.
3. If the person refuses shock treatment, treatment may be given only if the following conditions are met:
   a. The individual's condition is life-threatening and the intervention is the last-resource treatment of choice. Treatments are limited in number or duration and are adequately documented in writing in the individual's chart, by urgent circumstances.
   b. The parent, responsible family member, guardian, or conservator has signed an informed consent form on behalf of the individual in those cases where the person is a minor or legal ward.
   c. At least two physicians also sign the consent form agreeing with the prescribed treatment.
4. Consent should be obtained at the time treatment is indicated, not at admission.[89]

Psychosurgery has even more stringent requirements because of the irreversibility of its effects and is therefore rarely used at this time. More latitude has been allowed in the use of drug therapy, on the other hand. Although psychopharmacologic agents commonly result in a number of unpleasant and unwanted side effects (e.g., sexual dysfunction, drowsiness, blurred vision, dry mouth, bowel and urinary problems, tardive dyskinesia), clients may not be informed of such possibilities if disclosure is likely to result in undue anxiety and "cause the patient to reject, in the physician's opinion, a minimally risky medication."[90] Ironically, justification to withhold information may also be allowed for the more serious side effects such as dyskinesia on the grounds that full disclosure regarding this possibility "would so disturb the patient's psychological balance as to create an added risk in the use of medication."[91] On the basis of a review by Slovenko, the following recommendations have been made regarding the disclosure of information on tardive dyskinesia in particular, because of the severity and occasional irreversibility of these particular symptoms:

    (1) Information about tardive dyskinesia ought to be disclosed to the patient within three months of the administration of the medication, since the syndrome usually begins to appear after that period of time on medication.

    (2) The patient and family should be informed of early signs of the disorder, to aid in the detection process.

    (3) The therapist should administer the lowest doses possible to achieve acceptable levels of improvement.

    (4) Frequent drug-free holidays should be used, to attempt to unmask latent tardive dyskinesia—although, if such holidays last too long, a psychotic decompensation may be precipitated by the absence of the medication.[92]

As in other forms of therapy, staff that are involved in administering or monitoring treatment have a responsibility to be competent in the use of these techniques and to be fully aware of contraindications and risks. Since unwanted side effects are an added risk with somatic approaches to treatment, professional staff involved in service delivery (e.g., physicians, nurses) have an added responsibility to be knowledgeable about possible adverse effects, how to recognize their onset, and ways to counter them. Rather than making the client bear the full responsibility for informing staff of the onset of side effects, the professional has an obligation to review routinely with the client the existence of symptoms that he or she may not realize are unnecessary or inappropriate, for example, drowsiness.

Psychotherapy

A wide variety of different therapeutic orientations is subsumed under the general title of psychotherapy, most of which focus on the development of psychological insights regarding the ways in which present behaviors are influenced and controlled by past events and relationships. Insight-oriented therapies (e.g., psychoanalysis, Rogerian counseling) frequently evolve into a relatively long-term therapeutic relationship compared to other forms of therapy.

Within the psychoanalytic arena in particular, much therapeutic value has been placed on the development of transference and countertransference between client and therapist and the need to work through the complications produced by this type of relationship problem. Countertransference conflicts may revolve around such common themes as attraction, aggression, authoritarianism, dependency, or nurturance. Gutheil and Appelbaum[93] point out the dangers that could result, for example, when the therapist engages in "rescue fantasies" regarding his or her client. One obvious risk is that the therapist may take on too much responsibility for obtaining change, thereby minimizing the client's role and responsibility in getting "better." This type of therapeutic stance is more likely to have a negative, rather than a positive, effect on treatment and it therefore constitutes a countertherapeutic manifestation of countertransference.

Kermani[94] refers to legal suits that have resulted when therapists were unable to rise above transference or countertransference conflicts. The examples cited by Kermani involve the development of intimate relationships between therapist and client. More subtle but equally devastating consequences can arise for the client if the therapist mismanages a professional relationship. Comparing the therapist–client relationship to that between a parent and child, Finkel states that "if the transference and countertransference go on unrecognized and unchecked, we may wind up not rearing and transforming the child into an adult, but fostering and infantilizing the child."[95] He further points out the difficulty of terminating such a relationship at the appropriate time because of the development of overly strong ties on both sides and the failure to recognize the existence of a mutual dependency. "When therapy goes on for 5, 10, or 20 years, one begins to wonder whether the partners desire to stop the dance."[96]

Many professionals have also argued that psychotherapists, particularly those who present themselves as nondirective, are not completely honest with themselves or their clients regarding the way in which they shape or influence their clients' insights or choice of treatment goals.[97] Simply by virtue of having a theoretical base regarding what constitutes healthy versus unhealthy psychological behavior, the client is expected to eventually fit the definition of "healthy" in order to graduate from treatment. Since nondirective therapists typically deny the imposition of their value systems on therapeutic outcome, it is unlikely that the client will be informed of expected treatment goals. Therefore he or she is denied the opportunity to make a truly informed consent.

Psychotherapists who are more directive in orientation may run the opposite risk, that is, of being paternalistic in their interactions with clients, especially if they operate from a power base and believe their clients are psychologically incapable of making an informed decision because of their role as client. The following quote exemplifies this type of paternalistic shortcoming:

> When I asked an analyst acquaintance of mine whether she and her patients have some explicit agreement about what they are working on together in therapy, she gave me an incredulous look. This highly trained, intelligent, and kind friend tolerantly pointed out to me that "neurotics don't know what they want! How do you expect them to work on goals in their analysis? Instead, I point out to them through my interventions what it is they are working toward."[98]

Another criticism regarding the use of traditional forms of psychotherapy has been advanced by Schwitzgebel who points out the lack of evidence regarding its benefits. Since clients have been legislatively given the right to treatment, he argues that "*effective* treatment needs to be guaranteed to prevent further abuses of patient rights."[99] Since traditional forms of psychotherapy have not been proven to be effective, Schwitzgebel is of the opinion that clients should be advised of their "unproven efficacy" so that they can make an informed choice for or against psychotherapy.

Self-Help Therapy

There are two major categories of self-help therapy:

1. Self-help groups—in which clients are expected to provide, as well as receive, assistance and support from other individuals experiencing similar problems (e.g., Alcoholics Anonymous, Parents Anonymous, Recovery Incorporated, Widows and Widowers).
2. Self-help material (e.g., books, audio- or videotapes)—in which clients are given an opportunity to develop awareness regarding specific problems (e.g., overeating, shyness, depression, sexual dysfunction) and presented techniques that have been found useful in overcoming such problems (e.g., relaxation exercises, assertiveness skills, the squeeze technique).

Self-Help Groups. In the case of self-help groups, the greatest risk for the client is that problems will surface that are beyond the capability of the group members to deal with. In other words, there is a problem of *competence.* For example, the members of a bereaved parents group may not realize that a new member is manifesting behaviors that suggest he or she is a serious suicide risk at this time. If the group member acts out on this urge, there are negative repercussions, not only for the client and his or her family but also for the other members of the self-help group who may feel partly responsible for the suicide and therefore carry a burden of guilt for not treating the individual differently. In less extreme cases, there is the risk that the group would reinforce excessive dependency or nonproductive decision making that coincides with existing pathology in the group. For example, a group of battered wives may reinforce the attitude that all men are cads rather than encouraging members to discriminate on the basis of personality characteristics rather than gender. Although groups of this nature may maintain a formal or informal consultative relationship with a mental health professional or agency, such a liaison typically involves consultation at a distance and therefore is ethically lacking on the part of any professional involved in the program. Since self-help groups are not typically controlled by licensing provisions or monitored by any external professional body, there is little recourse for the client if he or she feels mistreated by the group, which in turn constitutes a problem in the area of *responsibility*.

Although many self-help groups have been shown to serve a useful purpose with a variety of clients, the professional wishing to refer a client to a self-help program would be wise to examine the history of success of any program being considered and the presence of any external monitoring body. With clients who are not committable but potentially pose a risk to themselves or others, the therapist would be additionally advised to combine any referral to a self-help program with ongoing monitoring or therapy until such time as the client no longer appears to need therapeutic contact and has made a "good" adjustment to the new program.

Self-Help Material. Many therapists utilize self-help material as an additional tool for teaching a client to have a better understanding and control of his or her behaviors. Such material can obviously serve a useful adjunct to treatment when used within a therapeutic context. The risk is that the client may use this form of therapy in isolation, that is, as an alternative to face-to-face therapy. Therapists have also been known to rely excessively on teaching aids to save them the time and effort of assisting the client with problems within the context of individual sessions. Without the opportunity to discuss what he or she has read, the client is unable to clarify or challenge viewpoints expounded by the authors in question. Clients are bound to vary in terms of their level of psychological sophistication and personal insight into their problems. In addition, they differ in their ability to learn from written material versus oral communication. This factor may not be taken into account by the therapist who may be relying on bibliotherapy techniques as a time-saver or as a way of disguising his or her areas of incompetence or insecurity. Although this is an extreme example, some therapists have been known to give written material to their clients without realizing that their client is illiterate. Another example derived from actual comments of staff on an outpatient unit is of a client threatening to kill his wife who was then assigned a book by his therapist on how to control his anger. Obviously, not only must the therapist take into account the client's ability to learn from this type of medium but also the appropriateness of this form of therapy under different circumstances.

Looking at the self-help epidemic from another perspective, professionals who serve as authors for such material have the additional responsibility of ensuring that the public is not misled by false promises. To do this, the professional needs to establish preconditions with the publishing company regarding the need to maintain professional standards in the promotional literature or packaging that is to accompany the self-help material or tape. Although no specific standards have been created regarding the development or use of self-help approaches, a Task Force on Self-Help Therapies established by the APA paraphrased existing ethical principles in order to accommodate the special problems inherent in this form of therapy.[100] Although the task force acknowledged the potential advantage of developing self-help material from an instructional and preventative point of view, it stressed the importance

1. Of having such material meet acceptable developmental standards (e.g., similar to the standards established in the development of psychological tests)
2. Of prohibiting sensationalism in the promotion of such material

More specifically, Barrera et al. recommend that instructional material should "contain a face sheet explaining the extent to which and conditions under which the program had been evaluated, recommended uses of the program, reading level of the instructions, and realistic expectations regarding outcome."[101] Such material should also include a statement of potential risk areas and limitations. In addition, the professional author should be encouraged to specify the conditions under which the self-help material is more likely to be effective, for example, accompanied by ongoing therapeutic support and direction.

Sex Therapy

Because of the emphasis society places on sexual characteristics, individuals experiencing problems with sexual functioning often feel excessively vulnerable and inadequate when approaching a therapist for assistance. For most people, sexual capability is strongly tied to self-esteem and feelings of worth. To admit to a professional the existence of a sexual problem is often highly embarrassing to the client and may therefore interfere with his or her ability to exercise appropriate caution in choosing a therapist. "At present the title 'sex therapist' does not belong to any one profession; nor is it regulated by any state licensing laws, as for example are the titles 'psychologist,' 'physician,' or 'social worker.'"[102] The result is "increased possibilities of abuse of the therapeutic relationship and out-right quackery,"[103] particularly as the client's sense of embarrassment and occasional desperation may blind him or her to improper credentials and possibly outrageous charges. To meet competence requirements, Liss-Levinson and Nowinski recommend that therapists do not attempt to treat clients with sexual problems unless they have, first of all, acquired special knowledge on such topics as "sexual anatomy and physiology, developmental sexuality (through the life span), sex roles and sexuality, sociocultural factors in sexual values and behaviors, diverse sexual lifestyles, medical factors interfacing with sexuality (including effects of illness, disability, drugs, pregnancy, contraception, and fertility) and ethical issues in sex therapy."[104] Second, they should have *formal* training in sexual and marital therapy.

Although confidentiality is a concern in all forms of therapy, it is an extremely sensitive issue for clients admitting to sexual problems because they are discussing highly intimate areas frequently surrounded by cultural taboos. Professionals or auxiliary staff who have access to such information, either through a client's file or from staff conferences, may be more inclined to gossip or joke about sexual revelations, possibly be-cause of their own discomfort or as a form of vicarious or voyeuristic entertainment. Since this possibility seems greater when dealing with sexual material, therapists who have access to such information should carefully screen what they say in the context of a treatment conference or what they place in a client's file unless the client's identity can be adequately disguised. Clients should be fully informed of whatever safeguards do exist with regard to confidentiality and what limitations there might be. When dealing with sexual offenders, therapists should additionally warn their clients at the onset of therapy of their obligation to warn a third party if they consider the client to pose a risk to another person.

Embarrassment and feelings of inadequacy may also interfere with clients' making a truly informed consent regarding the therapeutic contract. Voluntariness is considered an issue whenever a client wishes to change his or her sexual preference in that the client's decision to change may be a result of societal or family pressures or both. In areas of sexual dysfunction, on the other hand, the client may be more than willing to change but the desperation to do so may prevent him or her from obtaining such necessary information as the qualifications of the therapist and the acceptability and efficacy of the treatment techniques being proposed. Even if the client fails to obtain these data, the therapist still has a responsibility to provide the client with sufficient information on which to base a decision. Since the client may not adequately attend to information that might discourage false expectations, the therapist would be advised to encourage discussion about critical areas to increase the client's attentiveness to relevant risks and shortcomings. For example, clients should be advised that

> it is not uncommon for persons in sex therapy to change their value system, at least with respect to sexuality. Religious values may also be affected. Equally important is the potential for changes in the client's relationship with his or her partner. Extant areas of conflict may be considerably exacerbated by sex therapy, often with accompanying negative affect. Should clients decide to dissolve their relationship during the course of sex therapy, they should be fully informed regarding alternatives to continuing treatment, especially marital counseling with a different therapist.[105]

Within the realm of sex therapy, legal problems have confronted the sex therapist in the past as a result of providing single clients with surrogate sexual partners in the name of treatment. This practice was utilized in the sex clinic developed by Masters and Johnson and resulted in a lawsuit in 1971 when the clinic was charged with alienation-of-affections by the husband of one of the surrogate wives. The notoriety created by this action discouraged the use of sexual surrogates, despite their assistance in helping single clients deal with their sexual problems. To avoid having such surrogates perceived as prostitutes, Schutz[106] recommends that their role not be limited to sexual interaction with the client but that they be involved in administrative aspects of the treatment program as well.

In general, professional bodies prohibit sexual contact with clients. Because of the nature of the material being discussed, this temptation would seem greater in the course of sex therapy than in other forms of therapy in which the focus may not be on sexual matters. In any event, to deny the possibility of such temptations, "e.g., to argue that the 'mature' therapist is beyond the lure of transference or countertransference—is not merely a fantasy, but a potentially dangerous one from the consumer's perspective."[107] In other words, the ethical therapist is wise to be aware of these risks in order to guard against them.

REFERENCES

1. Gutheil, T. G., and Appelbaum, P. S. (1982). *Clinical handbook of psychiatry and the law* (p. 91). New York: McGraw-Hill.
2. *Rouse v. Cameron*, 373 F.2d 451 (D.C. Cir 1966).
3. *Wyatt v. Stickney*, 325 F. Supp. 781 (Ala. 1971), 344 F. Supp. 373 (M.D. Ala. 1972), *Wyatt v. Aderholt*, 503 F. 2d 1305 (5th Cir. 1974).
4. Gutheil, *Clinical handbook*, 83.
5. Ibid., 84.
6. Slovenko, R. (1973). *Psychiatry and law* (pp. 484). Boston: Little, Brown.
7. Ibid., 463.
8. Ibid., 460.
9. Sobell, L. C., & Sobell, M. B. (1981). Client rights in alcohol treatment pro-

grams. In G. T. Hannah, W. P. Christian, & H. B. Clark (Eds.), *Preservation of client rights* (pp. 157–158). New York: Free Press.

10. Finkel, N. J. (1980). *Therapy and ethics: The courtship of law and psychology* (p. 4). New York: Grune & Stratton.

11. Braginsky, B. M., Braginsky, D. D., & Ring, K. (1969). *Methods of madness: The mental hospital as a last resort.* New York: Holt, Rinehart and Winston.

12a. Broverman, I. K., Broverman, D. M., Clarkson, F. E., et al. (1970). Sex-role stereotypes and clinical judgments of mental health. *Journal of Consulting and Clinical Psychology, 34,* 1.

12b. Goldfried, M. R., & Davison, G. C. (1976). *Clinical behavior therapy* (pp. 269–270). New York: Holt, Rinehart and Winston.

13. Ibid., 269.

14. Nadelson, C. C., Notman, M. T., & Bennett, M. B. (1978). Success or failure: Psychotherapeutic considerations for women in conflict. *American Journal of Psychiatry, 135*(9), 1095.

15. Canadian Psychological Association (1981). Guidelines of therapy and counselling with women. *Ontario Psychologist, 13*(2), 21.

16. Ibid., 21–22.

17. Ibid., 22.

18. Ibid., 23.

19. D'Augelli, J. F. (1982). Some of my best friends are sexist: Therapist self exploration. In P. A. Keller & L. G. Ritt (Eds.), *Innovations in clinical practice: A source book* (p. 363). Sarasota, FL: Professional Resource Exchange, Inc.

20. Breggin, P. R. (1979). *Electro-shock: Its brain-disabling effects.* New York: Springer.

21. Ibid., 188.

22. Cooperstock, R. (1980). Special problems of psychotropic drug use among women. *Canada's Mental Health, 28*(2), 3.

23. Stimson, G. (1975). Women in a doctored world. *New Society, 1,* 266.

24. Canadian Psychological Association, Guidelines of therapy, 21.

25. Goldfried, *Clinical behavior therapy,* 270.

26. Pederson, P. B., & Marsella, A. J. (1982). The ethical crisis for cross-cultural counseling and therapy. *Professional Psychology, 13*(4), 492.

27. Sobell, Client rights, 160–161.

28. Ibid., 165–166.

29. Davison, G. C. (1976). Homosexuality: The ethical challenge. *Journal of Consulting and Clinical Psychology, 44*(2), 157.

30. Halleck, S. L. (1976). Another response to "Homosexuality: The ethical challenge." *Journal of Consulting and Clinical Psychology, 44*(2), 167.

31. Bieber, I. (1976). A discussion of "Homosexuality: The ethical challenge." *Journal of Consulting and Clinical Psychology, 44*(2), 163.

32. Sobell, Client rights, 166.

33. Gutheil, *Clinical handbook,* 34.

34. Ibid., 58.

35. Schutz, B. M. (1982). *Legal liability in psychotherapy* (p. 25). San Francisco: Jossey-Bass.

36. Ibid., 22.

37. Ibid., 40–41.

38. American Psychiatric Association (1981). *Principles of medical ethics, with annotations especially applicable to psychiatry* (Section 1.1). Washington, DC: American Psychiatric Association.
39. American Association for Marriage and Family Therapy (n.d.). *Code of professional ethics* (Section 1.2). Claremont, CA: AAMFT.
40. Ibid., Section 1.8.
41. Kermani, E. J. (1977). Psychotherapy: Legal aspects. *Psychiatry Digest, 38*(9), 35.
42. Schutz, *Legal liability,* 35.
43. American Psychiatric Association, *Principles,* Section 2.1.
44. Schutz, *Legal Liability,* 44–45.
45. *Hess v. Frank,* 367 N.Y.S. 2d 30 (1975).
46. Schutz, *Legal liability,* 44.
47. *Whitree v. State of New York,* 290 N.Y.S. 2d 486 (1968).
48. Schutz, *Legal liability,* 51.
49. Ibid., 52.
50. Bergin, A. E., & Lambert, M. J. (1978). The evaluation of therapeutic outcome. In A. E. Bergin & S. L. Garfield (Eds.), *Handbook of psychotherapy and behavior change: An empirical analysis,* (p. 154), 2nd ed. New York: John Wiley & Sons.
51. Schutz, *Legal liability,* 47.
52. Gutheil, *Clinical handbook.*
53. Ibid., 135.
54. Ibid., 135–136.
55. Ibid., 42.
56. Ibid., 67.
57. Gutheil, *Clinical handbook,* 38.
58. Schutz, *Legal liability,* 62.
59. Gutheil, *Clinical handbook,* 67.
60. Schutz, *Legal liability,* 50–51.
61. Finkel, *Therapy and ethics,* 100.
62. *Wyatt v. Stickney,* 325 F. Supp. 781 (Ala. 1971).
63. *Morales v. Turman,* 383 F. Supp. 53 (E.D. Tex. 1974), *rev'd* 535 F. 2d 864 (5th Cir. 1976), *reinstated* 430 U.S. 322 (1977).
64. Schwitzgebel, R. L., & Schwitzgebel, R. K. (1980). *Law and psychological practice* (p. 83). New York: John Wiley & Sons.
65. Ibid., 84.
66. *Knecht v. Gillman,* 488 F. 2d 1136 (8th Cir. 1973).
67. Friedman, P. R. (1975). Legal regulation of applied behavior analysis in mental institutions and prisons. *Arizona Law Review, 17,* 63.
68. Matson, J. L., & Kazdin, A. E. (1981). Punishment in behavior modification: Pragmatic, ethical and legal issues. *Clinical Psychology Review, 1*(2), 197.
69. Schwitzgebel, *Law and psychological practice,* 86.
70. Matson, *Punishment in behavior modification,* 205.
71. McLemore, C. W., & Fantuzzo, J. W. (1982). CARE: Bridging the gap between clinicians and computers. *Professional Psychology, 13*(4), 502.
72. Margolin, G. (1982). Ethical and legal considerations in marital and family therapy. *American Psychologist, 37*(7), 789.
73. Ibid., 789.

74. American Psychological Association (1973). Guidelines for psychologists conducting growth groups. *American Psychologist, 28,* 933.
75. Ibid., 933.
76. Lee, J. A. (1970). *Sectarian healers and hypnotherapy* (p. 19). Toronto: The Queen's Printer.
77. Ibid., 21.
78. Schwitzgebel, *Law and psychological practice,* 134.
79. Ibid., 137.
80. Kreigh, H. Z., & Perko, J. E. (1979). *Psychiatric and mental health nursing: Commitment to care and concern* (p. 104). Reston, VA: Reston Publishing Co.
81. Ibid., 104.
82. Ibid., 115.
83. Schwitzgebel, *Law and psychological practice,* 46.
84. Finkel, *Therapy and ethics,* 16.
85. Culver, C. M., Ferrell, R. B., & Green, R. M. (1980). ECT and special problems of informed consent. *American Journal of Psychiatry, 137*(5), 586.
86. Slovenko, *Psychiatry and law,* 461.
87. Schutz, *Legal liability,* 79.
88. American Psychiatric Association (1978). Recommendations regarding the use of electroconvulsive therapy. In *Report of the task force on electroconvulsive therapy* (p. 1). Washington, DC: American Psychiatric Association.
89. Schwitzgebel, *Law and psychological practice,* 101.
90. Schutz, *Legal liability,* 80.
91. Ibid., 80.
92. Ibid., 81.
93. Gutheil, *Clinical handbook,* 129.
94. Kermani, *Psychotherapy,* 34.
95. Finkel, *Therapy and ethics,* 71.
96. Ibid., 76.
97. Bandura, A. (1969). *Principles of behavior modification.* New York: Holt, Rinehart and Winston.
98. Goldberg, C. (1977). *Therapeutic partnership* (pp. 3–4). New York: Springer.
99. Schwitzgebel, R. (1974). The right to effective mental treatment, 62 *California Law Review* 936.
100. Barrera, M., Jr., Rosen, G. M., & Glasgow, R. E. (1981). Rights, risks and responsibilities in the use of self-help psychotherapy. In G. T. Hannah, W. P. Christian & H. B. Clark (Eds.), *Preservation of client rights* (p. 215). New York: Free Press.
101. Ibid., 216.
102. Liss-Levinson, N., & Nowinski, J. (1981). Client rights in sex therapy. In G. T. Hannah, W. P. Christian, & H. B. Clark (Eds.), *Preservation of client rights* (p. 125). New York: Free Press.
103. Ibid., 125.
104. Ibid., 127.
105. Liss-Levinson, Client rights, 131.
106. Schutz, *Legal liability,* 38.
107. Liss-Levinson, Client rights, 134.

Research Issues

7

In the past 40 years, the quality of human life has improved greatly. At least partially, these changes have been brought about by the application of research findings to human problems. As an example, consider the advances that have been made in the treatment of major health problems such as heart disease, pain, and strokes. Within the mental health area, many improvements have been made in the manner in which mental illness is treated. Psychotropic intervention has mushroomed as a result of research on different drugs and is used to assist the emotionally disturbed client to lead a more fulfilling and symptom-free existence. In addition to medical research, knowledge about human functioning and nonmedical forms of treatment has also increased dramatically. As an illustration, there is the specialized treatment programs established for sexual dysfunctions that were initiated by Masters and Johnson.[1] As a result of the research by Dr. Kubler-Ross,[2] improvements have also been made in the way in which individuals deal with the needs of the dying and the loss of a loved one. The increase in the knowledge base on which treatments and attitudes are based helps to ensure improved mental health care and a higher quality of life.

The current attitude of cautious support toward "human" research has not always existed. One of the most notorious examples of the way in which humans were exploited for the sake of research was seen in the Second World War. News of inhuman medical experiments on the inhabitants of concentration camps sparked a wave of concern in legislative circles. Until that time, research practices had been regulated, if at all, only by domestic policies. Thus, research practices and constraints varied according to local governmental attitudes. Testimony given during the Nuremberg Trials emphasized the dangers inherent in the lack of systematic controls. On the basis of these trials, ten rules regarding human research were developed and are referred to as the Nuremberg Code.[3] This code differed from existing research policies in two important ways. First, it is extremely specific in describing how research with humans should be conducted in comparison with earlier standards of practice and is extremely sensitive to the rights of prospective participants. Second, the Nuremburg Code is an international code and therefore took precedence over all local codes. As a result, researchers could no longer try to justify their actions on the basis of locally accepted practices if such practices deviated from the international standard.

Although the Nuremberg Code regulates the research activities of the medical profession, it was not meant to cover research carried out by nonmedical professionals or experimentation on mental health matters. Although experiments of this sort did not endanger the physical health of the participants, subjects were still being exposed to such risks as short- or long-term emotional reactions, inadequate treatment of problems, and so on. A classic example is the study by Watson and Rayner[4] in which they taught an 11-month-old child to develop a phobic response to neutral stimuli in order to show how fear could be learned through the use of conditioning techniques. Starting with a rat, the child was eventually taught to fear a fur neckpiece and finally a Santa Claus mask. In the name of science, little concern was given to the negative consequences for this young child even though attempts were later made to rid him of his generalized phobic reaction.

The use of deception in mental health research has also been common and concern was eventually raised regarding the appropriateness of withholding information from individuals that might affect their willingness to be part of the study. The need to regulate mental health research arose partly because of controversial studies in which subjects experienced substantial stress because critical information was concealed from them. One example is the study by Milgram[5] on obedience in which subjects believed they were giving increasingly higher levels of shock to other subjects. Most of the subjects suffered serious emotional distress because of what they were required to do and 15 apparently experienced uncontrollable seizures. Experiments of this nature made it obvious that standards for nonmedical research had to be developed. With this goal in mind, the American Psychological Association[6] published an elaborate set of standards governing research with human subjects. Although the availability of such standards does not prevent research abuses, the standards act as a guideline for investigators in the field. Failure to adhere to such rules can also result in professional sanctions.

GENERAL CONCERNS

Similar to other areas of practice, the ability to do research is a skill and must be acquired through the proper training methods. At the least, such expertise necessitates supervised research experience as well as formal training in such areas as experimental design, data analysis and interpretation, the ethics of doing research, and so on. Despite the need for competence before functioning as a researcher, a survey by Barber[7] indicated that "of the more than 300 investigators who responded to questions in this area, only 13 percent reported they had been exposed in medical school to part of a course, a seminar or even a single lecture devoted to the ethical issues involved in experimentation with human subjects." Understandably, an individual should not take on a research role without the acquisition of such basic skills because of the implications of using improper procedures, mistreating clients, or getting false results.

For those individuals unskilled in research methodology, there is an obligation to know at least enough about this topic to be able to read a research article intelligently. Since many of the advances in the mental health field derive from such material, it is critical for the health care worker to be able to differentiate good from bad studies in order to keep current in the field. Professionals can only do this if they know the basics regarding research and understand experimental terminology.

For those individuals who do feel competent to take on the researcher's role, they have an obligation to use their skills "to extend knowledge for the sake of ultimate human betterment."[8] In addition, they must be prepared to accept full responsibility for their work and whatever assistants they may employ. More specifically, research assistants must be properly trained to follow experimental procedures exactly, to treat subjects properly, to safeguard the information collected so that confidentiality is maintained, and so on. When more than one professional is involved in the research, all of them must share the responsibility of what they do. In other words, "responsibility can only be multiplied, never divided, by such collaboration."[9] To facilitate an examination of these different responsibilities, the rest of the chapter examines ethical issues related to three separate phases of an experimental study: planning, implementation, and postexperimental.

RESEARCH STAGES

Planning Phase

Sponsorship. Research can be a costly process and is often funded by external sources. A conflict of interest can arise when the organization funding a project has a vested interest in the results going a particular way. For example, a pharmaceutical company that is interested in promoting a certain product has a lot to gain if the studies on that product demonstrate that it has a positive result. Despite the presence of federal controls, it is not uncommon to hear of products being introduced into the market before they are properly tested, thereby causing serious problems for the unwary consumer.

Investigators who must depend on external funding for support must be ever-cognizant of the dangers of having a biased sponsor and ideally search for funding elsewhere. A conflict of interest is more likely to arise if the sponsor insists on having veto power over the researcher's right to publish. If this is the case, investigators may find themselves in an ethically awkward position where they obtain results worthy of publication but are forbidden from publishing because they are contrary to the sponsor's interests.

Research Design. The planning stage of a research project is in some ways the most critical. Altman[10] observed that flaws in an experimental design "are nearly always irremediable" because they lead to uninterpretable results. MacKay and Soule[11] further proposed that it is in the planning stages of research that the majority of problems and risks can be eliminated. Having a good research design is ethically critical because, without it, the results may be worthless and the imposition on the subjects inexcusable. A study with serious design flaws wastes the time and resources of the researcher and subject and could lead to incorrect information being disseminated to the public.

Not only should the design be methodologically correct, but also it should be constructed in a way that does not violate ethical principles. The responsibility for carrying out the planning rests entirely with the principal investigators, that is, those individuals who have developed and are heading up the research project. Even if such individuals are well seasoned researchers, they may have a personal interest in doing the research and deny the presence of serious shortcomings. This kind of rationalization may be common in academic settings where staff are forced to be part of the "publish or perish" race.

Not only might methodological flaws be ignored, but also eager researchers may ignore potential risks to the clients and try to minimize their seriousness if the research project is important to them. Researchers must give a lot of thought to the degree of risk to which they are exposing the subjects. At the least, the risks should not outweigh the potential benefits and should be minimally intrusive. If negative effects are anticipated, they should be rectifiable and short-term. In other words, the degree of discomfort and risk to the subjects should be kept to a minimum and removed as soon as possible. Steps should be in place to assist the subjects to deal with whatever effects do occur as soon as this is feasible. Alternatively, if it is possible to achieve similar results using a less risky design, researchers are obligated to do so despite the extra inconvenience this might cause. Pilot studies may be of assistance in identifying potential problem areas or methodologic difficulties. Experimentation on nonhuman animals may also be warranted if there is some concern about the effect the study may have on the subjects. Understandably, detailed ethical codes also exist when doing research with animals so that unjustifiable treatment does not occur.

As another way to counter the above risks, investigators are strongly advised to consult with colleagues to obtain an objective opinion regarding the appropriateness of the research project. External input of this sort may also be of assistance in considering alternative ways of proceeding.

Depending on the nature of the study, consultation with a different professional group might also be important. For example, a study that involves potential risk to the physical well-being of a subject may require consultation with a physician or registered nurse so that such risks are kept to a minimum. As an added safeguard for human participants, many organizations require that all research be approved by a review committee. Such committees should consist of at least one member who is not affiliated with the sponsoring organization so that the committee does not serve as just a "rubber stamp." When the research project involves experimentation on a specialty group (e.g., homosexuals, drug addicts, prisoners), it would be wise to include in the review committee a member of that group since he or she may be sensitive to ethical issues that are ignored by the other members of the committee.

The need to use deception with subjects is another situation in which advisory committees should be established since concealment obviously prevents the subject from making a truly informed decision about participation. The degree of deception is usually a consideration in approving such a study. As an illustration, the use of a placebo in place of medication is a fairly common and benign experimental practice, assuming it does not compromise the physical or mental well-being of the subjects. Where deception results in stress or discomfort, however, increased safeguards and consideration must be instituted. The American Psychological Association[12] charged investigators with a "special responsibility to (1) determine whether the use of such techniques is justified by the study's prospective scientific, educational, or applied value; (2) determine whether alternative procedures are available that do not use concealment or deception; and (3) ensure that the participants are provided with sufficient explanation as soon as possible."

Despite the utilization of review committees, abuses still occur. A study conducted by Adair et al[13] actually found that the use of deception, for example, "has not only increased in frequency and intensity—it has become the accepted model for social psychological research." Another survey conducted by Barber[14] discovered that review committees are far from effective in controlling the quality of research. The responses to Barber's questionnaire indicated that "in 34 percent of the institutions the committees had never required any revisions, rejected any proposals or had any proposals withdrawn in anticipation of rejection for ethical reasons." In addition, the inclusion of committee members from outside the organization was infrequent (i.e., only 22 percent) and the committees rarely monitored the studies while they were in progress to ensure that the proper steps were being followed. In other words, although review committees of this sort can potentially act as a quality control mechanism, they can only work if they do their job properly.

Preliminary Organization. In addition to planning the actual research design, researchers need to give thought to more practical issues. First, the study should be conducted in the most appropriate physical facilities. Variables that are not under study should be kept as constant as possible (e.g., lighting, heating, noise level) so that results are not confounded by adventitious factors. Second, research assistants should be thoroughly trained so that the same instructions and procedures are used with the first few subjects as with the last. Verbatim scripts should be prepared and learned by whatever individuals are running the study so that the steps run smoothly and convincingly. Assistants also need to learn the proper way of treating the participants so that they are given proper respect and are not pressured into continuing with the study if they wish to withdraw at any point. Pressure of this sort may not be uncommon if the assistant is worried about "losing a subject" and being blamed for not maintaining this individual's cooperation. If the assistant has been advised that such withdrawals are the subject's right and that the assistant should not assume the responsibility for making the subject continue, the assistant is less likely to overreact to such occurrences. At the most, the assistant should encourage the subject to talk about his or her concerns with the researcher before leaving in the event that the subject requires clarification on certain issues or simply wants to leave. Aside from their treatment of subjects, assistants should also be instructed to make note of any unusual occurrences and to bring these to the attention of their immediate supervisor. Often it may be necessary to train assistants to make objective observations so that they do not ignore data that might be important to the investigator. For example, if subjects are being studied regarding their manner of drawing the body of a person, assistants might be asked to note such characteristics as whether the subject starts by drawing the person's head or some other part of the body, whether he or she makes a lot of erasures, the amount of time to do the entire drawing, whether the subject tries to elicit a lot of guidance from the assistant, and so on. If such observations are important to the investigator, assistants should be sensitized to critical areas and possibly provided with specific recording forms that facilitate such record keeping. They should also be trained to record unexpected changes in the environment (e.g., interruptions) or accidental deviations in the research steps.

Prior to hiring a particular assistant, the experimenter must also explore the assistant's feelings or attitudes regarding certain procedures. If an assistant, for example, finds a particular procedure to be objectionable, the researcher should not force him or her to do it. As with subjects, researchers have an obligation to inform their assistants of critical requirements prior to the study so that this problem does not surface at a critical stage of the research.

In addition to providing a proper setting and training assistants, researchers need to take whatever preliminary steps are necessary to protect the subjects' rights. More specifically, prior to the study, beginning researchers should make arrangements for securing the data in a safe place so that inappropriate people cannot have access to private information. When the research is of a sensitive nature (e.g., a subject's sexual habits), investigators should decide how to code the data in a nonpersonal way and make arrangements to keep the "key" to the code in a separate secure location. A list should be kept of those individuals who are authorized to see the data so that entry into a file does not easily or accidentally occur. When information is stored on a computer, extra safeguards must be in place so that the data are "hidden" in the computer and only available to individuals who know the secret access code.

In addition to protecting the subject's right to confidentiality, investigators need to respect the subject's right to refuse or to make an informed consent. More detail on this issue is provided in the section on Subject Recruitment. At the least, researchers need to decide ahead of time what information is critical for the subjects to know in order to obtain an informed consent. Consent forms should be prepared in advance and designed in a way that subjects know exactly what they are consenting to do and the uses to which the data may be put. Many consent forms also sensitize subjects to their right to know the risks of what they are doing and their right to withdraw at any moment.

Subject Recruitment

Solicitation. Researchers may try to solicit clients in a variety of different ways, for example, newspaper advertisements, telephone contact, school announcements, magazine surveys, or circulars to relevant agencies. When subjects must be derived from a captive pool (e.g., inpatients on a psychiatric unit), requests to join the study should ideally be done by a group announcement so that individuals do not feel pressured by personal requests. Additionally, attempts to lure individuals into the study through the use of attractive rewards should be discouraged.

Prospective clients should also be solicited in a way that does not violate critical aspects of the experimental design. For example, if the experimental groups are to be representative of a statistically "normal" population, appropriate sampling techniques must be used. Otherwise the sample groups may be biased in a particular direction and their results may not be analyzed as originally planned.

Consent. For those individuals showing a preliminary interest in being a participant, the primary obligation of the researcher is to provide enough information about the study so that the individual can make an "informed consent." The criteria that must be met in obtaining proper consent have been covered in detail earlier in the book. In relation to research, subjects must be informed about all features of the research that might influence their willingness to participate and whatever other aspects about which the individual might inquire. Some of the topics that must be covered are described in the following paragraphs.

Prior to giving consent, participants should be fully informed of the procedures that will be used to safeguard their anonymity and the uses to which the data will probably be put. The *risks to confidentiality* should also be explained. For example, if the research is taking place in a setting that specifically deals with certain problems, subjects risk being identified as a member of a particular group (e.g., homosexual, spouse abuser) if seen entering such premises. Where research is conducted in a small setting with a select clientele, the chances of recognizing a particular subject in the published report is also a danger even though the subject's name has been withheld. The risks incurred in storing data should also be discussed, including a description of those individuals who will have access to the information. *Plans to publish* personal data in the form of a case history or to use the data for *purposes other than research* (e.g., teaching) must be presented to the subject prior to getting consent.

As previously described, subjects should always be informed of their *right to refuse* in order to minimize the demand characteristics of being asked to participate. This requirement is often ignored in telephone surveys. Most individuals have probably had some experience with surveyors calling their home and asking questions of a personal nature without even asking whether the individual is willing to be part of the survey.

Additionally, research candidates must be informed that they have the *right to withdraw* from the study at any time so that they do not feel pressured into continuing as subjects if they reconsider their involvement. Most importantly, participants must be informed of any *potential risks* which they may incur as a result of their involvement and whatever features of the study that might be considered intrusive or objectionable. When *deception* is unavoidable because of the variables under study, participants should at least be aware that they have not been told everything and given the reason for the concealment. Regardless of the need to conceal procedural matters, the possibility of specific risks should never be withheld since such knowledge might affect the subject's willingness to participate. For example, subjects should be told that they may experience some negative feelings (e.g., anger, anxiety, confusion) as a result of the experiment even though they may not be told what conditions will be used to elicit such feelings.

Since a consent can only be valid if the individual is legally or mentally competent to give it, there are several different populations from whom consent is not possible. Minors constitute one such group, as do the retarded and mentally incompetent. When these populations are used in a study, the informed consent of their parents or guardians is required. Despite limitations in their ability to satisfy legal consent requirements, it may be advisable to obtain consent from such individuals if at all possible. If a particular person is opposed to being included in a study despite authorization from his or her guardian, consideration should be given to excluding that person.

In addition, there are other populations from whom it would be difficult to get free and informed consent. Institutionalized clients, such as psychiatric inpatients and prisoners, may feel that they have no real choice when asked to take part in a study. They may also feel that their future (e.g., the opportunity for an early discharge, parole) may depend on their cooperation. Recommendations pertaining to this issue were made by the National Commission for the Protection of Human Subjects of Biomedical and Behavioral Research in the late 1970s. On the basis of their work, for example, "it is now illegal to use prisoners as subjects in research that is not relevant to prisoners. This means that behavioral and medical researchers may design experiments to answer questions like 'What are the effects of incarceration?' but they may not use a population of prisoners to answer questions like 'What is the effect of this new drug in humans?'"[15]

It might also be difficult for individuals with little education to comprehend fully all that is involved when agreeing to take part in a study. Even though the procedures and possible risks might be explained to them, some people may be embarrassed to ask questions because of anxiety about appearing ignorant. This possibility places them at greater risk of being taken advantage of by an investigator who is keen on getting subjects. The use of monetary rewards for participation also raises ethical concerns in that individuals who need such money may have difficulty saying "no" despite reservations regarding specific aspects of the study. Not only is this a concern with impoverished candidates but also with students who often need to earn extra money to support themselves in school. Students at a first-year university level are often faced with the added pressure of earning a specified number of research credits during the year as part of a course requirement. Although many departments may have approved of such a requirement because of their need for research subjects, there is certainly a coercive aspect to this type of recruitment that violates the "voluntary" component of informed consent.

Similar consent difficulties arise when trying to recruit individuals experiencing emotional or physical stress in order to study different treatment techniques. Individuals who feel desperate for therapy and do not believe they can afford treatment through more traditional routes may be more willing to put up with potential risks than would a less desperate individual. These conditions negate the possibility of voluntary consent because there is a coercive element present. Such problems create a serious dilemma for the researcher who is specifically interested in studying those particular problem areas or populations in that no easy answer is available. Research advisory committees are always critical under such circumstances so that ethical practices are followed as much as possible. The committee can also make a decision as to whether the potential gains from the study significantly outweigh any risks.

Mixed views exist regarding whether a formal consent is necessary when conducting certain types of research, for example, when collecting survey information from unidentified clients. MacKay and Soule[16] propose that in situations in which the subjects' identities are not recorded and cannot be ascertained, a formal consent may not be necessary, for example, when using anonymous questionnaires in which no attempt is made to identify the respondent. Even when information is derived from "anonymous" questionnaires, however, researchers could include in the questionnaire information about the purpose of the research and how the data are to be used so that anyone wishing to partake in the study has at least some information about the area under study prior to sending in the self-report material.

Implementation Phase

At this stage, the most important role played by researchers is that of overseeing the project and supervising the assistants. They must ensure that the previously developed procedures are followed closely by their staff and that test results are properly collected and stored. As well, they must be available to give direction regarding any unexpected situations that might occur. The use of assistants to actually conduct the study is highly recommended because researchers themselves may consciously or subconsciously try to bias the results to their advantage. If possible, assistants should be kept ignorant of the underlying hypotheses of the study so they are free from biases of their own that could unduly influence the results in a certain direction.

One important responsibility for the principal researchers is to discontinue a particular subject if his or her health or well-being appears to be seriously affected or if nonexperimental conditions affect performance (e.g., a death in the family). To perform this role, investigators need to maintain sufficient contact with the subjects or assistants or both to know exactly what is happening. The chief investigators also need to advise their assistants of other "discontinue" criteria. Depending on the design of the study, the cutoff point may be a fixed number of trials, a particular reading on an instrument, lack of control over confounding variables, and so on.

In studies in which there is a need to demonstrate objectivity or reliability in following procedures or collecting data, "blind" raters should be used, that is, individuals who are trained to record specifically defined events or behaviors without knowledge of the purpose of the study. Such reliability checks should be done periodically throughout the study to ensure that inappropriate variations do not occur at different phases of the study and therefore bias the results. Ideally, assistants should not be aware of the specific occasions on which they will be watched so that they do not experience subtle changes in their behavior as a result of being observed.

Postexperimental Phase

Behavior toward Participants. As a first step, subjects should be debriefed regarding their involvement in the study so that if deception did occur they now become aware of what was done to them and why. Such debriefing should therefore include a complete explanation of any aspects of the study previously withheld. Subjects also have a right to know the final results of the study. As a professional courtesy, experimental findings should also be disseminated to those individuals or agencies who volunteered their services or settings for the purpose of the study.

In addition, every effort should be made to evaluate and correct any adverse effects the subject may be experiencing as a result of the study. If any harm has occurred, the researcher has an obligation to arrange for appropriate assistance for the subject. If the participant was involved in an experiment that offered treatment as a part of the research, this service should be offered after the study if the subject was not in a treatment group during the time the research was being conducted.

Data Analysis and Interpretation. Much has been written about the misuses and abuses of statistical analyses. At a mechanical level, researchers have an obligation to ensure that test results have been properly recorded and that statistical calculations are computed correctly. On a more abstract level, it is the responsibility of the experimenter to ensure that the statistical procedures used to analyze the data are properly chosen. Before a particular statistical analysis can be conducted, certain preconditions must be met. If the experiment has not been designed or conducted properly, the researcher acts unethically if he or she applies inappropriate statistical techniques to the data. For example, many statistical tests should only be used if the sample group falls within the "normal" curve for that particular population. To ensure that this is the case, one requirement is that subjects be randomly obtained from the population in question so that the sample group is not skewed in one direction or the other. If the sample group is skewed, different types of statistical tests (i.e., nonparametric tests) must be used to analyze the results and mention of this fact must be made in the write-up.

Researchers are similarly warned against manipulating the data to get the results they want. To accomplish this goal, individuals have been known to extract whatever data support their hypotheses and to eliminate information that detracts from their results with the possible rationalization that such results were spurious. Researchers may also subject their results to so many statistical analyses that they are bound to get some significant results simply because of the quantity of tests conducted.

Researchers also have a responsibility to interpret their results objectively. To do this, they must explore alternative ways of explaining their findings by taking into consideration other variables that may not have been under sufficient experimental control because of design problems. In addition, insignificant as well as significant findings should be included in the report and a description given of any problems that could have affected the results, for example, methodologic difficulties, unexpected occurrences, or a high attrition rate.

Reporting. In order to communicate their findings to others, researchers need to protect their subjects' anonymity while at the same time describing the study with sufficient detail so that others could potentially replicate the experiment from what is written in the report. To accomplish this goal, most researchers include in their write-up (1) the rationale for doing the research and the variables under study, (2) critical information on the characteristics of the subject pool, how they were solicited, and how they were assigned to different groups, (3) procedural steps followed when conducting the study, (4) a detailed summary of the results together with an exact description of the analyses applied to them, and (5) a discussion of the research findings together with implications, weaknesses, and so on. Care should also be taken to keep comments on the report value-free and to avoid making slanderous statements about specific groups. It is also important to include in the write-up a description of whatever ethical procedures were followed. Studies have shown, however, that this is rarely done.[17,18] McNamara and Woods speculate that "underreporting of ethical procedures is related to the factors of: poor acceptance of the current ethical standards, a lack of their operational clarity, inadequate training, professional indolence, and ineffective editorial policies."[19]

Publication. The temptation to publish poor research may be strong for those individuals whose list of publications affects their sense of ego or professional status. The implications of this type of unethical practice are many. According to Altman,[20] the time and energy that may be lost by unsuspecting researchers attempting to replicate such findings may be enormous. Even worse, results that remain unchallenged potentially affect such characteristics as client care, societal attitudes, and so on. Altman[21] further recommends that journals "make strenuous efforts to detect substandard research" since research that qualifies for publication "achieves both respectability and credibility."

Another ethical issue related to the publication of results is the type of credit given to the different investigators in the study. In academic settings, it is not uncommon for research supervisors to insist that their students list them as the first author of a research study even though they may have only played a token role. Students may feel they have little choice in this matter because of their subservient position and the need to please those individuals in control of their academic fate. Ethically, publication credit should be ordered from first to last in proportion to the contribution made by the various individuals involved in the research.

Data Storage. As previously described, information on subjects together with test results must be stored in a way that maximally protects the subjects' right to privacy. The period of time for which research data must be kept is another important consideration. Rules vary from one part of the country to the next regarding how long records must be kept, and are generally based on the length of time in which a subject can start legal proceedings for personal damages. When material is to be destroyed, the chief researchers must take proper steps to ensure that it is done in an acceptable manner. Placing it in a refuse container is not sufficient because of the risk to confidentiality. Instead, investigators have to utilize as much care in destroying the data as they used in storing the data. "Safe" procedures include such actions as shredding or incinerating under the supervision of trustworthy staff.

REFERENCES

1. Masters, W. H., & Johnson, V. E. (1970). *Human sexual inadequacy.* Boston: Little, Brown.
2. Kubler-Ross, E. (1969). *On death and dying.* New York: Macmillan.

3. Trials of war criminals before the Nuremberg military tribunals, *United States v. Karl Brandt, vol. 2* (pp. 181 ff.). Washington, DC: U.S. Government Printing Office (1949).

4. Watson, J. B., & Rayner, R. (1920). Conditional emotional reactions. *Journal of Experimental Psychology, 3*(1), 1.

5. Milgram, S. (1963). Behavioral study of obedience. *Journal of Abnormal and Social Psychology, 67,* 371.

6. American Psychological Association (1973). *Ethical principles in the conduct of research with human participants.* Washington, DC: American Psychological Association.

7. Barber, B. (1976). The ethics of experimentation with human subjects. *Scientific American, 234*(2), 29.

8. American Psychological Association, Ethical principles, 7.

9. Ibid., 26.

10. Altman, D. G. (1980). Medicine and mathematics. *British Medical Journal, 281,* 1183.

11. MacKay, R. C., & Soule, J. A. (1975). Nurses as investigators: Some ethical and legal issues. *Canadian Nurse,* 26.

12. American Psychological Association (1982). *Ethical principles in the conduct of research with human participants* (p. 6). Washington, DC: American Psychological Association.

13. Adair, J. G., Dushenko, T. W., & Lindsay, R. C. L. (1985). Ethical regulations and their impact on research practice. *American Psychologist, 40*(1), 70.

14. Barber, Ethics of experimentation, 29.

15. Cohen, R. J. (1979). *Malpractice: A guide for mental health professionals* (p. 72). New York: Free Press.

16. MacKay, Nurses as investigators.

17. Adair, Ethical regulations.

18. McNamara, J. R., & Woods, K. M. (1977). Ethical considerations in psychological research: A comparative review. *Behavior Therapy, 8,* 703.

19. Ibid.

20. Altman, Medicine and mathematics, 1183.

21. Ibid.

Index

	DATE DUE		